STREETWISE®

COMPLETE
PUBLICITY PLANS

Create Publicity That Will Spark
Media Exposure and Excitement

SANDRA BECKWITH
President, Beckwith Communications

adams
media

To my parents, Stephen and Elizabeth Beckwith

A Streetwise® Publication.
Streetwise® is a registered trademark of F+W Publications, Inc.

Published by Adams Media, an F+W Publications Company
57 Littlefield Street, Avon, MA 02322 U.S.A.
www.adamsmedia.com

ISBN: 1-58062-771-4

Printed in the United States of America.

J I H G F E D

Library of Congress Cataloging-in-Publication Data
Beckwith, Sandra L.
Streetwise complete publicity plans / Sandra Beckwith.
p.   cm.
ISBN 1-58062-771-4
1. Publicity. 2. Press releases. I. Title.
HM1226 .B43 2003
659.2—dc21
2002153892

Cover illustration by Eric Mueller.

This book is available at quantity discounts for bulk purchases. For information, call 1-800-289-0963.

Contents

Contents

Acknowledgments

Thanks go to the many people who contributed sample materials to this book, but especially to those who were particularly generous: Doug Buemi, Bob DeRosa, Cindy McVey, and Marcia Layton Turner. More thanks go to Libby Fischer Hellmann and Jill Stewart for introducing me to Jacky Sach at BookEnds.

Introduction

Securing the free media exposure known as "publicity" doesn't require fairy dust. It requires having a good story to tell, packaging that story appropriately, and getting it to the right journalists at media outlets. It's not hard to do—that's why so many business owners do it so well. But it does require knowledge of the tactics and tools, along with a publicity plan.

This book guides you to publicity success by helping you identify the news in your organization, determine the right packaging for each opportunity, and understand which journalists to deliver your news to. It contains useful how-to information for a wide range of small businesses—from a sole proprietor consultant seeking local exposure to a manufacturer desiring increased trade media or national consumer publicity.

Streetwise® Complete Publicity Plans differs from other how-to publicity books in that it includes information on trade media publicity opportunities and tells you how to take advantage of them. From the basics—determining your audience and setting goals—to figuring out your message and knowing who needs to hear it, this book gets you started with a top-notch publicity plan. You find out that the publicity tools you use, and how you use them, will be determined by whether you are targeting trade, consumer, or Internet media outlets and what category within each medium you are targeting. It is, for example, much easier to secure a placement with a trade magazine than it is with a consumer magazine. And most businesses won't have a shot at national television talk show exposure, simply because their products don't lend themselves to the programming needs of these shows. Have you ever seen a manufacturer of backhoes plugging his products on

The Today Show? You won't, unless he has an extremely clever publicist. (But it can be done—see Chapter 2.)

After showing you the basics, this book brings you along to the next level, where you begin to create press releases and pitch letters, write bylined articles or columns, deliver a public service announcement, prepare a press kit, get interviewed, called a press conference, become a public speaker, plan and manage a special event, sponsor an event or group. You also find out how to seek out publicity opportunities in places you may never have dreamed up. Finally, you discover tips for deciding whether to execute your plan in-house or hire an agency, and you also find ways to evaluate your publicity plan to determine what is working— and what is not.

It's worth noting that each communication situation is unique, and there is no "one way" to do things. Much of what is written in business publications and online about communicating with the press stresses using e-mail exclusively. But read more closely—you'll discover that the comments are often made by companies dealing with high-technology media outlets—which operate differently from your local TV station, weekly newspaper, and other media outlets. Use what you learn in this book, and what you then learn from the media outlets you communicate with, to create an approach that is successful for your company without worrying about what works for others.

Good luck—and have fun!

> **Chapter 1**

Understanding What Publicity Is

Part One

Part Two

Part Three

Part Four

Part Five

The Difference Between Advertising and Publicity

For the more than twenty years that I've been a publicist, my oldest brother has been asking me, "So, how's the advertising business?" I used to respond with great indignation, "I'm not an advertiser, I'm a publicist!" "What's the difference?" he'd ask. Fresh out of college with a public relations degree, I would launch into an explanation with great enthusiasm, oblivious to the fact that he wasn't really looking for an answer. Eventually, I caught on. When he asked me about "the advertising business," I skipped the marketing lesson. Even so, I still twitch a little when I hear his question after all these years, because like so many other people, my brother doesn't realize there's a big difference between advertising and publicity. And that difference can have a significant impact on a small company's marketing budget and overall success.

Publicity

Publicity is a subcategory of public relations while advertising is a subcategory of marketing. The Public Relations Society of America (PRSA) defines public relations as the management function that uses communications in a way that "helps an organization and its publics adapt mutually to each other."

Advertising

Marketing, on the other hand, is the function specifically involving the sale of a company's products and services. Publicity is the media relations arm of public relations—the function that gets a company's name in the news. Advertising, under the "marketing" umbrella, is a paid form of communicating a message through the various media. Like publicity, it is designed to be persuasive, informative, and to influence purchasing behavior or thought patterns.

The Difference

So what *is* the difference between advertising and publicity? The simplest explanation is that you buy advertising, but publicity is "free." And because you buy advertising, you can control it. You know what will appear in the media, when it will appear, and what it will look like. Unless somebody has screwed up, there are no surprises.

Not so with publicity. Nobody can control it, no matter what they tell you. You never know *for sure* when an article or interview will be used by the media; you can't even control in what context the information you provide will be used. That's one reason why publicity work is so frustrating—you just have to cross your fingers and hope that your information will be used, that it will be used in the proper context, and that it will be used when you want it to be. Even when the TV cameras show up at your special events, don't relax, because it's possible that a bigger news story will keep yours from making it on the air that night. But the job of a publicist is only to get the cameras there and to influence what they record—we can't do anything about the video once it leaves our event.

On the other hand, publicity is more powerful and more influential than advertising. That's because publicity is usually linked to newsworthy events or information that make it useful or interesting. Studies at the Harvard Business School estimate that a news item that refers to your product, company, or service is worth ten times more than the advertising cost of that space or air time. That extra value—that additional credibility—is because of the implied editorial endorsement of the press.

Let's say you own a landscaping business, and you're quoted in the local newspaper in an article about how to breathe new life into heat-damaged lawns. This article has ten times the value of an advertisement of the same size because readers believe that if a reporter thinks you're knowledgeable enough to be interviewed for an article, then you must really know your stuff.

The following chart helps highlight the key differences between advertising and publicity in terms of where and

Publicist or Press Agent?

Publicists are often confused with press agents. While both publicists and press agents work to generate media exposure, press agents are usually associated with the entertainment industry and often design outrageous stunts to get attention rather than to communicate a message. Basketball star Dennis Rodman was the reigning king of publicity stunts during the 1990s—one of his most visible endeavors involved promoting his autobiography by announcing he was getting married at Times Square. He arrived dressed in a wedding gown to "marry" himself. Rodman was carrying on a tradition begun in the mid-1880s by P.T. Barnum, who promoted his circus museum by harnessing an elephant to a plow and putting him to work in a field alongside the train tracks carrying curious commuters to New York City, home of the museum.

when your information appears, the end result of the information, and which information has the most credibility.

Technique	You control where	You control when	You control the end result	It has the most credibility
Advertising	Yes	Yes	Yes	No
Publicity	No	No	No	Yes

In spite of the drawbacks of publicity, smart small-business owners put their promotional dollars into publicity before spending anything on advertising. Print publicity, in particular, has greater leverage with current and potential customers than advertising does. Mailing a customer or prospect a reprint of an article that positions you as an expert has far greater impact that mailing an ad slick.

Damian Bazadona of Situation Marketing, a small New York City–based firm that provides Internet strategy and consulting services for business-to-business and retail companies, credits publicity for part of his company's first year of solid growth. "Good publicity builds credibility, increases exposure of your brand, gives an 'unbiased' approval of your offerings, and recognizes your organization as a trendsetter or thought-leader, which is extremely important for many businesses," Bazadona says.

Is It Really "Free" Publicity?

People often use the word "free" when they talk about publicity, but is it really *free*? Not really—there's always a cost involved. The time you or a staffer spend on generating publicity has a value. There are always expenses, too. Special events, for example, can be particularly costly, but can also be quite effective publicity generators for small businesses. And mailing a press release announcing a new product to the top 100 newspapers in the country requires spending money for copying and postage.

Using an outside public relations firm isn't free, either (see Chapter 23 for more on working with agencies). But the word "free" refers to the fact that you don't pay the media to use your news and information (while you *do* pay them to run your ads or commercials). In most cases, though, the rewards of a carefully crafted publicity campaign outweigh the costs, and the costs of the campaign are usually far less than what you might spend on an advertising program.

The Impact of Publicity

The implied editorial endorsement of publicity gives it greater weight in the eyes of the consumer. Use yourself as an example. If you have decided you need to hire a market research consultant, what will influence you more: An ad in the back of a trade magazine, or a bylined article in that same magazine, written by a market researcher who talks about some of the unique problems or issues facing your industry? If you're like most consumers, you're more likely to call the author of the article than respond to the ad (which, by the way, you might not even notice).

Bazadona of Situation Marketing uses the publicity he generates for his consulting firm in business and trade magazines to impress clients and prospects. "It's one thing for me to say that I'm a creative force," he explains, "but it means so much more when an editor at a top trade journal says it."

Some forms of publicity allow you to showcase your expertise in a way that advertising can't. The article written by you, as the expert, or written by someone else who *quotes* you as the expert allows you to tell prospects and customers that you know what you're doing and that you can help them solve their problems. When you're publicizing a product, an article that highlights the product's best features is far more believable than an ad that does the same. Most of us know enough about advertising to take what we see in an ad with a grain of salt. We're not so savvy about what we see and hear on TV or radio talk shows, or in newspapers and magazine articles.

What effect will publicity have on you or your business? Take a look at the following sections.

Award-Winning Publicity

If you or your public relations consultant do a great job executing an exceptional publicity plan, your results might win a publicity award. But what does this really mean, and do you really care? What impact will a publicity award have on your business? Unless you're a publicist, not much, and even then the effect is subtle. The publicity success that led to the award will certainly be good for your business, but the award for the effort is primarily fodder for another press release and a self-congratulatory (but necessary) item in your employee or marketing newsletter. How can you make it more meaningful to your business? Use the occasion to celebrate with employees and boost morale. Speak to local business or national trade groups about the steps your company took to generate that level of media exposure. You will have to use it to make a difference.

Is Bad Publicity Better Than None?

A restaurant reviewer wrote a bad article about Chef Monica's cooking on the TV comedy series *Friends*, but her pal Rachel assured Monica that "there is no such thing as bad press!" Is that true? A lot of people believe it. They say that getting your name out there in any form is better than never having any media exposure at all. These folks theorize that people won't remember the context surrounding the exposure—they'll just remember that they've "heard of you before." Those who are more cautious disagree, believing that negative publicity hurts the company's image. Which camp are you in? Give it thought if you're planning an aggressive publicity campaign, because at some point, you might encounter a situation where your work is attacked.

Publicity Can Establish You as an Expert

Michael Webb used publicity generated by his newsletter, *The RoMANtic*, to secure a book contract for *The RoMANtic's Guide: Hundreds of Creative Tips for a Lifetime of Love*. His Web site notes that Webb "is widely regarded in the media as one of the nation's top experts on romantic matters."

Publicity Can Sell Products and Services

When the owners of Children on the Go used a two-page press release to link their Secure View Mirror, which allows a driver to keep an eye on a child strapped into a car seat in the back, to a current national trend, the resulting publicity in seventy-five daily newspapers generated 3,000 orders.

Publicity Can Educate

Aging with Dignity, a small nonprofit organization in Florida, has used publicity for its unique Five Wishes Living Will to educate the public about the importance of advance directives.

Publicity Can Shape Public Opinion

The Seneca Park Zoo in Rochester, New York, used publicity to lobby for public funds for an expansion project.

Publicity Provides Credibility That Opens Doors

Tim Fargo, president of Omega Insurance Services, Inc., a private investigation firm specializing in workers' compensation claims suspected of fraud, uses the exposure from his bylined articles in trade magazines as leverage to secure high-profile speaking engagements at trade shows.

Why Your Competition Is Always in the News

Businesses that emphasize publicity in their public relations mix will be featured in the media more than those that don't. Because they use publicity tools wisely and consistently, they get more exposure, plain and simple. Your competition gets the press for several reasons:

1. The company does something newsworthy or offers information that is useful.
2. It shares this news with the media.
3. The company packages its news in the proper format.
4. The company delivers its news to the right editors, reporters, and producers.
5. The company spokesperson is available for interviews.
6. The company does all of the above better than its competitors.

What most people outside the field of public relations don't realize is that you don't really *have* to be an "expert" to provide reporters with accurate, timely, and interesting information. You just have to know enough about the subject to answer questions with credibility—and you have to make sure that reporters know that you know. You can be the

Report Your Expertise

The business section of a local newspaper frequently publishes articles about retail trends or new retail businesses. Probably 75 percent of these articles quote the same local university professor as a retailing expert, not because he is nationally known for his expertise in this area, but because he doesn't have any competition. "We can't find anyone else who will talk to us on this subject," the section editor laments. This is a wonderful opportunity for another retail expert in that community to get some free media exposure. Sometimes, all it takes to get publicity is to let key reporters know the topics you can discuss with expertise—and returning their calls promptly when they request an interview.

National Publicity Helps

Publicity generates more publicity, especially when your company is featured in a high-profile publication. When I used a press release to announce the first issue of *The Do(o)little Report*, my subscription newsletter, *USA Today* ran one paragraph about it in the left column of the "Life" section. That small, but powerful, news item generated interview requests from more than fifty radio stations by 8:00 that morning. By the end of the day, I had heard from more than twice that number, as well as a handful of national magazines. Six weeks later, when *USA Today* published a major feature on the newsletter, I received invitations to appear on national television talk shows, and calls from book publishers and literary agents who encouraged me to turn the newsletter into a book.

smallest company in your field and get more publicity than your largest competitor. And you don't have to be the best in your industry to get more publicity than anyone else. All you have to do is share what you know using the proper channels and tools.

Publicity Begets Publicity

Surprisingly, one media placement will probably generate others. This has always been the case, but it happens even more so now as articles and transcripts have become available on the Internet. A national reporter searching for information on widgets, for example, might uncover a local newspaper story profiling your new widget design, and call you for an interview. A media placement elevates your company in the eyes of the press looking for information—it's as if you have been "prescreened" by other reporters.

This book is another example of that mushrooming effect. Many of the examples presented in these pages come from articles in the news. These case studies wouldn't be getting additional exposure in this book if the companies hadn't generated the initial publicity.

Good publicists make sure that targeted reporters see those articles, too. They include reprints of published articles in press kits (see Chapter 12 for more information on press kits), to reinforce the company or expert's credibility. Showcasing reprints is one way you can reassure a reporter that you have something of value to say in an interview. It's another way of saying, "I'm low risk." It works the same way with TV interviews. Typically, high-profile national talk shows will ask to see a videotape of your media interviews before they invite you to be a guest on their show. They need to be reassured that you won't react to a TV camera like a deer caught in the headlights.

Publicity as a Component of a Larger Public Relations Plan

Publicity is a subspecialty or subcategory of public relations. Other subspecialties in your public relations plan can include government affairs, corporate communications, employee communications, community relations, marketing communications, or investor relations, among others. It's the publicity element that gets your company's name, product, services, or expertise in the news, so small businesses often build their entire public relations plan around publicity. (They are often too small to need the other public relations components, too.) Whether you incorporate the other elements depends on your communications needs, marketing goals, and other factors. This book addresses only the role of publicity.

Having Realistic Expectations

When you read or hear about publicity success stories, it's hard not to expect the same results for your own publicity campaign. That's why it's important to understand why some companies have achieved success. In some cases, they have truly unique products that are extremely newsworthy. Sometimes they get media exposure because they used an event or a stunt to create news. Still other times, they just did a really good job of working hard over a long period of time to get their messages to the press.

Your Company Must Be Newsworthy

Rarely does a company get an impressive amount of media exposure by not being newsworthy. Similarly, it's not very often that you read an article quoting a business owner, or see her interviewed on a news broadcast, if she doesn't say something interesting or newsworthy. (One of the best ways to stay out of the news, of course, is to be dull and boring during an interview.) Most likely, the publicity-generated stories you see and hear are the result of hard work that can take place over the course of a few months or an entire year. See Chapter 4 for tips on finding something newsworthy about your company.

Your Company Must Have a Publicity Plan

As you'll discover in this book, publicity-generating activities include defining your audience, determining how they get their news and information, uncovering the newsworthy topics in your organization, determining the best ways to package that news, and targeting the appropriate media. It can be a time-consuming process, but it's not rocket science. And once you're hooked on the power of publicity—and appreciate what it can do for your business that advertising *can't*—you will always make it an important part of your marketing mix.

> **Chapter 2**

Trade, Consumer, and Internet Media— Which Is Right for You?

Part One

Part Two

Part Three

Part Four

Part Five

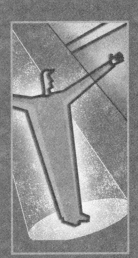

PART ONE   WHAT PUBLICITY CAN DO FOR YOU
■ CHAPTER 1 Understanding What Publicity Is ■ CHAPTER 2 Trade, Consumer, and Internet Media—Which Is Right for You? ■ CHAPTER 3 Defining Your Audience, Setting Goals, and Establishing Objectives

Classifying the Media

There are three broad categories of media: trade and consumer are the two major categories, but a new category—Internet media—has emerged, too. Internet media is a subcategory of both trade and consumer media because Internet Web sites and electronic newsletters (e-zines) are either trade or consumer media outlets.

Trade Media

Trade media refers to publications serving an industry. Does your firm design product packaging? Then you probably read *Packaging Digest*. If you're a wholesale supplier of beads to craft stores, you might subscribe to *Crafttrends*. If you're in the pest control business, your trade magazine of choice could be *Pest Control Technology*.

Then there are trade magazines you read because of your job description rather than your industry. There are trade magazines for plumbers, accountants, physicians, secretaries, CEOs—you name it. A pediatrician in partnership with others in a large private practice might read *Medical Group Management Journal* along with *Pediatric News* and *Physicians Financial News*.

Most business owners probably read more than one trade magazine. An advertising agency owner might subscribe to *Advertising Age* and *Adweek* along with the trade magazines serving the firm's clients' industries. A bed and breakfast owner probably reads *Innsights* along with *Country Inns Bed & Breakfast* and perhaps *Entrepreneur*.

When you start contacting trade magazines, you'll get calls from their advertising space reps. Tell them that you will use your editorial exposure as a test. If the article you write, the article that quotes you, or the product announcement in the news section generates a favorable response from the right audience, then you'll consider advertising with them.

Consumer Media

Consumer media includes newspapers and consumer magazines (think in terms of those sold on newsstands), radio news and talk shows, and television news and talk shows. This is what your targeted customers read, watch, and listen to when they're not working. They range from *Good Housekeeping* to *Field & Stream* to *Jerry Springer*, *Regis & Kelly*, and your favorite syndicated radio talk show. They include local drive-time radio programs, radio public affairs programs and TV news, talk, and public affairs programs.

And while business publications such as *BusinessWeek*, *Entrepreneur,* and *The Wall Street Journal* can be viewed as trade media because most people read them for professional, rather than personal reasons, we are placing them in the "consumer media" category because from a publicity standpoint they are more like consumer magazines than trade publications.

These are the outlets you target when you're selling a consumer product or service. The bed and breakfast owner, for example, will want to promote her business in the travel sections of daily newspapers, on radio talk shows in her own and other communities, and in regional hospitality and city magazines. These are all consumer media outlets.

Depending on what you're promoting, your media mailing list might include both consumer and trade media. While the packaging designer won't make consumer publicity a top priority because he doesn't provide a consumer service, exposure in the local newspaper business page (consumer media) might be on his list of publicity goals.

Internet Media

Internet media refers to content-heavy Web sites, e-mailed newsletters called "e-zines," and to the Web sites of traditional media outlets that have content that differs from what appears in print or on the air. Many of these traditional media outlet Web sites, including *USA Today*'s, feature unique content available only online. How valuable they are from a publicity standpoint depends on your target market. If you

Does Advertising Influence Editorial?

Sometimes, whether or how much you spend on trade magazine advertising influences the magazine's decision about giving you that unpaid editorial exposure called publicity. In other words, while most publications claim that the advertising department does not influence the editorial department, the fact is that it often does with trade magazines. This means that if you advertise in a trade magazine, you can try to use your ad as leverage for editorial coverage. Consumer magazine editors will tell you that advertising departments have no leverage in their publications, and that is true more often than not, but with shrinking ad pages in many newsstand publications, there are more and more reports of large companies leveraging their advertising budgets to influence editorial coverage of their products or category.

know your target customer relies on the Internet for information, or is particularly techno-savvy, you'll probably want to add Internet media sites to your publicity list. E-zines are very targeted and can often do more to boost your business than traditional mass market outlets with wide reach.

"When my books have been mentioned in some of these online newsletters, I've actually had quantifiably better results than I've had with the larger, more mainstream publications that have featured me," notes Shel Horowitz, author of *Grassroots Marketing: Getting Noticed in a Noisy World* and four other books.

Trade Media Exposure Possibilities

Trade publicity opportunities, then, come in the form of printed magazines, their Web-based counterparts, and specialized e-zines such as *Small Business Bytes* and *SpeakerNet News*.

Trade magazine opportunities include:

- General news and information
- New product and personnel announcements
- Staff-written articles
- "Bylined" articles—those written by you
- Case histories

General News and Information

General news and information opportunities include announcements of acquisitions, restructurings, survey or research results, contests, record sales volumes, awards the company or employees have received, and so on. Submit this news in the form of a press release (see Chapter 7 for press release writing tips).

New Product and Personnel Announcements

New product and personnel announcements are short and limited to regular sections of the magazine that run these items. New product announcements, especially when linked to the "bingo" inquiry cards included with many trade magazines ("circle number 15 for more information on this product"), are good lead and inquiry generators. Personnel announcements are an easy and inexpensive way to get additional exposure, particularly if your personnel release includes a sentence about what your company does—and the publication includes this sentence. In both cases, provide the magazines on your media mailing list with a press release (not sales literature) outlining the news and color product photos and personnel head shots photographed by a professional photographer. Good product photography can land on a magazine cover and can be used in sales literature, so it's a worthwhile investment. Staff photos have other uses, too, including capabilities brochures and employee publications.

> Good product photography can land on a magazine cover and can be used in sales literature, so it's a worthwhile investment.

Staff-Written Articles

Staff-written articles, produced by a staff writer or a freelancer, typically include these article types:

- Product category round-ups ("Category Report: Blended and Single-Malt Scotch Whiskies" for *Beverage Dynamics* or "Building Products Review" for *Metal Home Digest*),
- General news and information ("D&PL Offers New Varieties for 2002" from *Mississippi Farmer*),
- Industry trends ("Government Sites Show Improvement, Study Concludes" in *Government Computer News*),
- How-to information ("Placing Insurance for Nursing Homes" in *American Agent & Broker*),
- Case histories ("Data Mining Application Helps BB&T Increase Cross-Sell Ratio" from *Bank Systems & Technology*),
- Leadership profiles ("Management Profile: Skeptic in Chief," about Secretary of the Navy Richard Danzig, in *Government Executive*),
- Business profiles ("Profiles in E-Learning: Media 1st's 'Video with a Purpose'" in *E-Learning*),
- Q&A with an industry leader ("Q&A with Michael Miller" in *PC Magazine*), and
- Topic-driven articles (*Stores* runs articles in each issue on topics ranging from Internet retailing to loss prevention).

Much of a trade magazine's editorial content is identified in an "editorial calendar," a tool that helps advertisers link their ads to relevant themes or magazine content while it helps publicity-seekers find opportunities for interviews or other editorial contributions. Business and consumer magazines do not publish editorial calendars; see Chapter 17 for more on editorial calendars.

Contributing to staff-written articles is a fairly straightforward process: You identify the appropriate topic from the editorial calendar (or suggest one), contact the magazine at least five months before the issue's publication date (for monthlies) to get the name of the writer, call the writer to discuss his or her needs for the article, and provide the necessary information in the format that's needed—product information, how-to tips, interviews, and so on.

Bylined Articles

Securing a bylined article—one *you* write—takes more effort. You need to determine the topic, then find a home for it. And you have to be able to write well enough that your end product will need only minor editing—or you need to hire a ghostwriter who can do this for you.

Hitting on the right topic is probably the easiest part for most business owners—what do you know a lot about that you can share with others? A marketing consultant might write about how to market a small business effectively or the five most important questions to ask before hiring a marketing consultant. A manufacturer of security systems might write an article for a retailing publication on how to select the right security system.

While it takes longer to write an article than it does to be interviewed for one that is written by someone else, the value of the bylined article comes in its flexibility: The article you write for one industry publication can be tweaked and placed again in a magazine read by a totally different audience. The article on how to select the right security system, for example, can also be placed in a magazine targeting builders of commercial property, or for specific segments of the retailing industry—clothing retailers, drugstores, liquor stores, and so on. Just make certain that the magazines you're targeting don't have overlapping audiences.

Once you've used your target magazines' editorial calendars to help you identify appropriate article topics (it always helps to have a few in mind so that if your first idea is rejected, you can bounce back with another option), you can "pitch" (sell) your article by phone, by e-mail, or in a mailed letter. If your idea is accepted, the editor will give you guidelines on length and tone and provide a deadline. (Read more about pitching articles in Chapter 9 and about writing articles in Chapter 10.)

Case Histories

Case histories are articles with a problem/solution format. They focus on a particular company's problem while showcasing another company's solution. Trade magazines welcome case histories that are written in the publication's editorial style and are not overly self-serving. These "my problem and how I solved it" pieces allow publications to share valuable and often innovative ideas with readers without sending staff writers on expensive field trips.

Pitch a case history by summarizing your idea in a letter to the publication's editor; be sure to note that you have the cooperation of the organization that uses your company's product or solution. (For more information on key elements of a case history and how to write one, see Chapter 10.)

Who Speaks for Your Company?

If a reporter called your company today for a comment on a news story, who would your receptionist or switchboard operator give the call to? You don't want to bounce the reporter around from department to department, and you don't want just anybody talking to the press, either. In most businesses—even the largest—only a few people are authorized to talk to the media on behalf of the company, so there's no reason why yours should be any different. Once you've decided who that is (in small companies, it's often the president), make sure the switchboard operator knows that. Make sure everyone else in the company knows it, too.

Where Should You Begin with Consumer Magazines?

Think you don't have a chance for publicity in consumer magazines? Not necessarily. There's no question it is harder to get publicity in consumer publications than it is with trade magazines. But that doesn't mean it can't be done, and it certainly doesn't mean you shouldn't be targeting high-profile newsstand magazines. Go after these outlets with enthusiasm tempered with realism. Start by targeting the short news item sections common in most publications, usually placed in the front of the magazine or in the back. Do you have news, advice, or information that would interest readers of this section?

Consumer Media Exposure Opportunities

Publicity in consumer media outlets—newsstand magazines, newspapers, and radio and TV news and talk shows—is harder to secure than trade media exposure for many reasons. Most importantly, there is much more competition for these highly visible outlets. (Who *doesn't* want to be on *Oprah?*) In addition, consumer magazines rarely make their internal editorial calendars available, so it's harder for publicists to identify articles to contribute to. This forces publicity seekers to be more creative, developing article ideas or talk show topics that they can contribute to through interviews.

And while trade magazines welcome the free editorial content they get in the form of bylined articles and case histories, consumer publications prefer to write their own content. In addition, while an interview on a TV news program or talk show might do a lot for a company, it takes more skill to communicate key messages on TV in a very short period of time than it does to do the same in an interview with a print media reporter.

That said, consumer media opportunities include:

- General news and information
- New product (and book) news and reviews
- How-to/tips articles
- Expert or informational interviews
- Event coverage
- Opinion articles or columns

General News and Information

The types of general news and information your company might provide via press release or press conference (see Chapter 13 for information on press conferences) to consumer media outlets might be different from what you provide to the trade press. In addition, the information you're announcing isn't necessarily appropriate for all forms of consumer media. A local dating service announcing the results of its "Celebrity Dream Date" survey of single men and women in a single county will want to send a press release announcing the survey results to the local media—particular morning drive-time radio program producers or hosts—but not to the producers of the *NBC Nightly News*. Would the information be of interest to a trade magazine for the dating service business? Possibly. Would you want to send it to them? The answer is "yes" if you're looking to establish a reputation with a larger audience, perhaps laying the groundwork for franchising your operation . . . or "no" if you are totally focused on the local market.

Similarly, the media list used to announce the upcoming unveiling of the world's largest milkshake produced by your Dairy Queen franchise can extend beyond local boundaries and include the national media outlets that often cover such quirky news stories. National exposure can bring many unanticipated but positive opportunities for your company.

New Product News Items and Reviews

New product (and book) news items and reviews are also generated by press releases accompanied by photos and, quite often, product samples. They sometimes involve press conferences, too. A new product announcement can range from a small item in a newspaper lifestyle section to inclusion in a product category segment on *Good Morning America*. The consumer media you target with your press materials depends on a number of factors, including product type and availability.

How-To and Tips Articles

How-to/tips articles are mainstream media staples based on input from people like you who know a lot about the subject. You can generate them with a press release called a "tip sheet" that offers tips and advice, or through a letter to an editor or reporter suggesting an article that uses you or your company's expertise as a resource. Certain kinds of "how-to" information are also useful to local and national TV talk shows and news programs. One of the most successful tip sheets promoting a humor book on male behavior outlined tips for getting a good gift from a man during the upcoming holiday season. This tip sheet was used by newspapers coast-to-coast, and was the impetus for the author's appearance on a national cable TV talk show.

Expert or Informational Interviews

Secure expert or informational interviews with print or broadcast media outlets by using a pitch letter that suggests a specific article or broadcast segment idea, outlines your views on the subject, and reviews your expertise in this area (see Chapter 9 for more on pitch letters). An executive recruiter might want to build awareness for her business by convincing a local radio station to schedule an interview with her on a public affairs program to discuss "Six surefire ways to jump-start your career." She will also have to convince the producer that she can sustain a thirty-minute interview and will be an engaging talk show guest. To pitch herself as a guest to national business-oriented talk shows like those produced by the *Business Talk Radio Network*, she will need national credentials.

Event Coverage

Event coverage often hinges on the novelty or appeal of the event and is secured through press releases and who/what/when/where/why memos called media alerts. A well-executed local event with a media celebrity host or participant and a charity tie-in can generate newspaper, radio drive-time, and TV news exposure. Nonprofits are especially skilled at maximizing the publicity value of their fundraising events while small businesses are sometimes overly optimistic with their media coverage expectations. A nonprofit fundraising luncheon featuring a nationally known celebrity speaker and sponsored by a local business will probably generate publicity for the non-profit and the speaker, but not the local business that donated the speaker's fee unless the business made sure its sponsorship package included logo signage at the event and insisted that all media interviews and photos take place with the signage as a backdrop.

Other special events can be quite significant for your business but inconsequential in the eyes of the media. A ribbon-cutting ceremony at your

> Nonprofits are especially skilled at maximizing the publicity value of their fundraising events.

new facility, for example, is likely to draw yawns, not TV cameras, unless you include a dramatic or highly visual element (like the governor cutting the ribbon) or you're one of the area's largest employers. Your success will depend not only on the newsworthiness of your special event but on the size of your community, and what else is happening that day. One publicist saw his anticipated media coverage of a ribbon-cutting event disappear when a school bus with a complete passenger load collided with a truck thirty minutes before the publicity event. (Read more about publicity-generating special events in Chapter 14.)

Opinion Articles or Columns

Opinion articles or columns offer both national and local publicity opportunities for those seeking to influence public opinion or to establish credibility. Locally, the daily and weekly newspaper's editorial pages run "op-eds" written by members of the community and others outside the reporting staff on a regular basis. Some national magazines, including *Newsweek,* feature thought-provoking essays by readers. Opinion pieces for national magazines must address a topic of interest to a national audience while local newspaper op-eds or weekly newspaper columns need to zero in on a topic of local interest. In both cases, controversy helps. Contact the section editor to determine interest before writing and submitting your essay or column.

Internet Media Exposure Opportunities

Internet media opportunities mirror trade and consumer media possibilities and sometimes offer additional publicity opportunities like the following.

Exclusive Online Content

Both trade and consumer media outlets have Web sites. Some have very little content, some provide full access to content from the print publication, some provide password-protected access to content to subscribers only, and others provide exclusive online content. The "interactive" media sites—those that actually want to engage their users to enhance their

Finding E-zines

Want to get exposure for your company in e-zines but don't know what e-mail publications are out there? The world of e-zines changes daily, so it's hard to stay on top of which e-zines are new, which are still publishing, and which have folded. Start by entering "e-zine directory" into a good search engine such as Google. The options will lead you to sites that list e-zines by topic; your topic might or might not be on that list. A few of these sites include:

✍www.zinos.com/cool/zinos/ ezine_list.html

✍www.ezine-dir.com

✍http://ezine-universe.com

✍www.freezineWeb.com

If your topic isn't on that list, do a topic search, instead, with your search engine. Active e-zines should show up on your list of options. A recent test search for "pizza restaurant e-zine," for example, led quickly to a site for *The Pizza Lover* e-zine—what could be better?

content—make it easy for you to contribute articles or other content. The Web site for *Workforce*, a trade magazine for human resource professionals, posts its writers guidelines on the site so you know what material they would like to receive from you and how to submit it. Many other magazines, including *Fast Company*, do this as well. But others with exclusive online content, such as the consumer magazine *Family Circle*, don't even provide a "write to us" link so that you can help shape that content. When it's not clear how to contribute, send a note to the Webmaster asking who to contact, or use the old-fashioned approach—call the publication and ask for the information.

Interactive Message Boards

The *Workforce* Web site also features a "Community Center" that allows site members to chat with others. Mentoring and assisting others through interactive message boards is an excellent way to gain exposure for your business by showing, rather than telling, that you know your stuff. In addition, reporters looking for article resources often review these postings for experts to interview. Reporters also post messages asking for experts interested in being interviewed for articles.

E-zines

These specialty newsletters e-mailed to subscribers who register to receive the publications are often open to news, information, and tips from outside sources. As with all media outlets, the material you provide should not be overly self-promotional and should be focused on helping others. The best way to contribute to many e-zines, in fact, is by offering information based on your own experience. Most e-zines contain information on how to contact the editor at the end of the publication, or on a companion Web site.

Which Is Best for Your Business?

Whether your publicity plan targets trade, consumer, or Internet media— or a combination of them—depends on a number of factors, including the following:

- What your target market reads, watches, and listens to
- Whether you want to reach your target market in their workplace or off-hours
- The nature of your business, since not all situations lend themselves to consumer publicity opportunities
- The amount of time and money you can devote to a publicity program

You might want to reach all of the purchasing managers in a particular industry in the country. Reaching them at work through trade magazines is one option; reaching them at home through daily newspaper business pages is another option; reaching them through TV business programs is a third choice. If your sole objective is to influence purchasing managers, then reaching them through trade magazines should be your top priority. If your goal is to establish a reputation for your CEO among purchasing managers, then consider taking advantage of the celebrity-building power of television by adding TV business programs to your plan (and making sure your CEO has something newsworthy to say).

The planning and packaging that goes along with securing an appearance on a national TV show can be expensive, though, which brings us to your budget. Sometimes, the media categories you target will be influenced by your staff and financial resources. By the time you read this entire book, you will be well-prepared to "book" yourself on a national TV talk show, to get your business mentioned in newspapers across the country and in e-zines, and to be featured in articles in trade magazines. Doing this work yourself, or assigning it to a colleague, will be less expensive and perhaps more rewarding and less frustrating than paying an outside agency to generate your publicity. After all, you know yourself and your business better than anyone else. If you're promotion minded, you probably know all the angles that make your company newsworthy, too.

What Are Your Resources?

As you think about audiences, goals, objectives, and strategies, spend time thinking about what you can accomplish with the resources available. Ask yourself the following questions as you begin thinking about your publicity plan:

- What skills are needed for the work we need?
- Who has (or wants to learn) those skills?
- Is that person available?
- Will staff members need training?
- Can I do the work myself? Is this a good use of my time?
- If we use outside help, how much can we budget?

Keep the answers to these questions in mind as you select appropriate tactics for your publicity plan, but at the same time, don't let them scare you. Some of the most cost-effective publicity results are also some of the least time-consuming.

But will you make the time to do the publicity work yourself? If not, consider hiring an outside firm. But be prepared to spend enough time with this firm for its staff to grasp the various newsworthy angles inherent in your company and how it does business. And be prepared to spend money, even when you're working with a solo public relations practitioner (see Chapter 23 for information on working with agencies). Ultimately, your publicity media mix will be determined by your company's priorities and how much time and money you can put into the publicity process, which will still cost less than a comparable advertising campaign.

Tailoring Your Publicity Plans for Each Option

The tools you employ as part of your publicity plan will depend on your media mix. Some plans are built entirely around press releases. Others, particularly those involving broadcast media talk shows, involve researching a list of targeted media outlets, then sending pitch letters to generate interviews. Other plans might need special events, press conferences, media training sessions, and so on. The publicity tools you employ to reach the trade, consumer, and Internet media outlets will be shaped not only by what you have to say and how much you can spend to say it, but how these various outlets prefer to hear from you—or what gets their attention.

▶ **Chapter 3**

Defining Your Audience, Setting Goals, and Establishing Objectives

Part One

Part Two

Part Three

Part Four

Part Five

PART ONE   WHAT PUBLICITY CAN DO FOR YOU

Knowing Why You Need to Determine Your Goals and Audience

This chapter stops talking about target audiences and business priorities and starts getting you to put this information on paper. If you have a business plan and a marketing plan, now's the time to pull them out. Most of the information you need at this point in your publicity plan development should be in those documents. If your business hasn't evolved to the point where you have this information in writing, then you need to do it now.

This is where your company's publicity potential begins to unfold. And whether you run a manufacturing operation or you're a sole proprietor who consults, speaks, and sells books showcasing your expertise, you need to outline and prioritize your target audiences and determine your expectations—your goals and objectives—for communicating with your audiences through publicity. Keep these concepts in mind as you read through this book and learn more about the tactics and resources available to help you achieve your company's publicity goals and objectives.

What Do You Want to Accomplish?

Specifically, what is that you want *publicity* to accomplish for your business? Do you want to use publicity to sell more products? Do you need it to educate prospects about your product category first, then about your particular product? Do you want publicity to influence public opinion so that people are more receptive to your message, product, or service? Do you want to use publicity to establish you as an expert, so that you can then leverage that perceived expert status with your target audience? Do you need publicity to help your company recruit qualified employees? Do you want publicity to help shape your company's image in the community?

Publicity can do all of these things—and you may *need* it to do all of these things—for your company. But there are some things it can't do. It can't help you establish a reputation as a socially responsible employer if you aren't one. It can't help you communicate that you care about your community if you don't. It can't help you sell a product if you haven't created any news value for that product. It can't help you establish yourself as an expert if you're a phony. It can help you generate early interest in your product or service, but it can't save you if what you're selling is lousy.

Bottom line: Within reason, publicity can help you accomplish what you need to accomplish as long as you have something interesting to offer and as long as your company has some amount of integrity. Otherwise, your peers will be quick to discredit you . . . and the media doors will close.

Defining Your Audiences

The first step in developing an effective publicity plan is defining your audience. You can't develop your media list and select the tools and techniques you will use in your publicity plan without knowing who you need to reach. Many companies sell to multiple audiences. Lactation consultants, for example, must market their services to several audiences to generate customers and referrals—new mothers, health care professionals in private practice, hospital staffers in maternity wards, and so on. Target audiences aren't necessarily external, either. They can include employees, management, and board members.

Describing Your Target Audience

How do you describe your target audience? Brainlink International, a twenty-two-person company in New York City, provides technology solutions and services to health care, pharmaceutical, financial, retail, and new media industries. Many times, the services Brainlink provides to a retail business are very different from what it offers a health care operation. The job titles of the people the company works with in each industry vary, too. Because of these factors, Racheline Maltese, director of marketing communications, breaks Brainlink's target audiences down by industry and job

Confidentiality or Paranoia?

Businesspeople who aren't used to talking to the press tend to be extremely cautious about the information they share because they're afraid of "giving away company secrets." It's always wise to be concerned about proprietary information or tipping off the competition to something you don't want them to know. It's okay to be cautious, but it's not okay to be paranoid. Paranoid people don't offer any information, and that makes for a bad interview that wastes everybody's time. Make it your goal to strike a balance between sharing information that moves your company forward and offering information that gives competitors your secret manufacturing process. Many times, you'll realize that you aren't really telling a reporter anything he can't get elsewhere—you're just telling the reporter first.

title when she develops the company's publicity plan. She then develops different publicity programs for each audience.

For instance, the audience for Brainlink's work developing e-commerce sites includes large chain stores that need impressive, database-driven sites that will showcase their inventory to more potential customers. The key concerns of this retail audience generally revolve around security of customer information, ability to rapidly update product availabilities, and return on investment. When Brainlink targets this audience with publicity, its case histories become more critical because they provide the clearest illustration of the benefits of the company's offerings without drowning people in technical information. On the other hand, the company's communications with publications serving hospitals might focus on news releases explaining how Brainlink services help hospitals develop technology systems to protect patient privacy. Maltese knows that the more specific she gets with audience definition, the more likely she is to provide prospects with news and information that meets their specific needs, and the more likely these prospects are to be influenced by her publicity efforts.

After defining your audiences, prioritize them so that when it comes time to create your publicity plan, you will be clear on which audience is the most important and can plan accordingly, especially if there are time or budget limitations.

 ## Mass-Market Exposure

Don't abandon the "broad" audience concept. Mass-market exposure can also be quite valuable—and appropriate. A guest appearance by a newsletter publisher on a syndicated television talk show gave her the opportunity to include an address viewers could use to request a free sample copy. That opportunity generated 15,000 newsletter requests, thousands of which became paid subscribers. At the same time, ask yourself if you can handle this kind of exposure. Before your product can be mentioned editorially in *Better Homes & Gardens*, for example, your company has to prove it can fulfill the product orders this kind of publicity will generate. Make sure you're ready for the potential offered by mass-market exposure.

Determining Who Is in Your Audience

Sometimes your audience is obvious, sometimes it isn't. When developing your public relations plan, refer to this list of potential audiences described in the e-zine *ExpertPR* (✍ *www.mediamap.com*). How many of them does your publicity need to reach?

- Academic community
- Banks, insurers
- Board of directors
- Community groups
- Competitors
- Customers
- Dealers and distributors
- Employees
- Employees' family
- Government representatives (federal, state, local)
- International customers
- Investors
- Labor unions
- Managers and supervisors
- Online media
- Print media
- Radio media
- Regulatory agencies
- Special interest groups
- Stockholders
- Suppliers
- Television media
- Temporary employees
- Trade associations

Establishing and Reaching Your Publicity Goals

Business coach Hal Wright emphasizes the importance of goals in his book, *How to Make a 1,000 Mistakes in Business and Still Succeed*. "Strong goals create an irresistible force, because goals mean both motivation and direction," he writes. "Motivation gives people a reason to do something, and direction helps them determine what to do."

This applies to publicity plans, as well. You cannot know which publicity tactics to employ if you don't know where you want to go with your publicity efforts. Your publicity efforts will be much more effective and satisfying if you first establish well-defined goals.

Defining Goals

Keep in mind that a goal is a broad statement of direction that is determined by the needs of your organization. It must be in line with the overall

Publicity Goals Are Like Business Goals

Do you have business goals or personal goals? How do they influence the everyday decisions you make about the work you do, the assignments you take on, or even the phone calls you return first? Clearly defined goals provide much-needed direction in small businesses. One small business owner has as his overriding goal the desire to "be famous." It's that simple. This individual keeps this goal in mind every day as he makes decisions about business and personal priorities, asking himself, "Will this project help me become famous?" or "Will this task bring me closer to this goal?" He places a high priority on publicity tasks—those "to-dos" that keep his name in the news because he won't become famous if people don't know who he is. And he won't rest until he's on *Oprah*. So he's doing things that are worthy of an appearance on that show.

goals of your business and have management support. With good goals in place, you can look at each publicity element or tactic and ask, "Does this step help us achieve our goals?" If the answer isn't "yes," the tactic should be removed from the plan.

Setting Goals

Once you understand the purpose of goals, it will be relatively easy to put them on paper. Does your company already have goals as part of its business plan or marketing plan? Your publicity goals should support them; in some cases, they might be the same.

Looking at Sample Goals

Sample publicity program goals include:

- To generate target audience awareness of the quality of our company's products
- To position our CEO among key audiences as an expert in our company's industry
- To create awareness of our company's commitment to the well-being of the community
- To introduce product XYZ as the first of its kind, and to communicate its unique attributes
- To position our company as the most innovative in its field in our geographical region
- To show potential employees that we provide a creative work environment

Remember that goals are well-defined but are not specific or measurable. They tell you which direction you want to go in, while your subsequent objectives will tell you how you're going to get there.

Establishing and Reaching Publicity Objectives

People often confuse goals and objectives, and although they are related, they are not synonymous.

Defining Objectives

Unlike goals, objectives are measurable targets set within a specific time frame. Objectives grow from goals to help determine progress toward those goals. Put in different terms, goals tell you where you want to go; objectives tell you how you're going to get there. Publicity objectives must be stated in very specific terms if they are to be meaningful and useful. Objectives are specific and detailed, outlining the expected accomplishment, who will do the work to make sure the company succeeds with that accomplishment, when it will be finished, and how you will know the accomplishment has been achieved.

Setting Objectives

To establish your plan's objectives, review your goals, then ask, "How are we going to make this happen?" If your business has not taken advantage of the power of publicity before, your goal might be "To establish a system for sharing our company's news and expertise with the trade media read by our target audiences."

Looking at Sample Objectives

Sample objectives for the goal stated in the preceding section might be:

- By October 7, Mary Brown will survey key customers by telephone to identify the trade magazines they read.
- By October 30, Brown will research these magazines by obtaining sample copies and identifying regular features of the publications that include news announcements and interviews with companies like ours.
- By November 2, Brown will develop a grid that lists each target magazine and the editorial opportunities for our company.

Picture This

Staging a look-alike contest is a surefire way to attract media cameras. The new owner of a Canadian bed and breakfast, the Windsor House, staged a "Queen Victoria Look-Alike Contest" on Victoria Day as an excuse for opening the recently renovated establishment to the community, then admired the photos in the newspaper the next day. Kentucky Fried Chicken introduced a new menu option with a parade of Colonel Sanders look-alikes in downtown Louisville, Kentucky, the company's hometown. The scene was captured by a wire service photographer. Ringling Bros. and Barnum & Bailey recently used a Marilyn Monroe look-alike contest to promote the acquisition of jewels worn by Marilyn Monroe atop a Ringling elephant at Madison Square Garden in 1955. When properly promoted with publicity and advertising, a look-alike contest can draw colorful contestants, crowds of curious people, and media cameras to your establishment or event.

- By November 3, Brown will develop a contact database for all the target trade magazines that will be used to generate press release mailing labels or e-mail distribution lists; it will be used to record our contacts with these publications and the outcomes.
- By November 15, Brown will meet with Claudia Jones and Mark Smith to brainstorm what information our company can provide to these magazines, and whether this information should be distributed through press releases or article idea suggestions. She will then add this information to the publication grid.

Using measurable words and assigning specific responsibilities allows you to monitor the progress of your activities as you work to achieve your goals. Adding deadlines helps those who execute publicity plans prioritize this work with their other responsibilities.

What's Your Strategy?

After defining your goals and objectives, develop a strategy for your publicity plan. This summarizes the direction you'll take with your publicity efforts. It's the big picture for how you will proceed.

Looking at Some Sample Strategies

Your strategy might be to leverage the president's outgoing personality to secure more public exposure for your brand, or it might be to capitalize on the company's intellectual capital in a way that generates positive publicity. The strategy for a writer hoping to promote a nonfiction book could be to use excerpts from the book's content to generate sales-generating media exposure. The strategy for a new florist might be to call attention to the store's unique floral arrangement style. As you review your audiences, goals, and objectives, ask yourself how you will use this information to generate publicity, and you'll have your strategy in place.

Going from Strategy to Plan

Audiences, goals, objectives, and strategies are beginning components of your publicity plan. With these in place, you can begin thinking about the publicity plan tactics outlined in Part 2 of this book. You'll learn how to determine what's newsworthy in your organization and how you can use that information to complete your publicity plan (see Chapter 21) and achieve your publicity goals.

Extending Your Effort

As you think through your publicity goals and work to identify the media categories that will take you the farthest (see Chapter 2), begin thinking in terms of how elements from one category might feed or play off elements from another. A bylined trade magazine article, for example, might be the starting point for a booklet, which can then be offered free of charge to readers of several more publications through a press release mailed to those magazines and e-zines. It can also be used in your company's marketing newsletter and should absolutely be added to your Web site. Many daily and

Get Ideas from the Big Guys

When you're faced with a publicity challenge, study how the "big guys" have handled similar situations. What if you want to have a party to launch your newest product, but you want the launch to be as unique? Do what the publicity people at Coca-Cola did when they introduced Vanilla Coke. After giving the hosts of *The Today Show* the first media opportunity to sample the brand live that morning, they scooted off to a tiny, ninety-seat establishment called the Vanilla Bean Café in Pomfret, Connecticut (population 3,391), in the northeastern part of the state, a good hike from the closest major city, Hartford. (The Coke folks found the restaurant after doing an Internet search for restaurants with "vanilla" in the title.) It's an unusual approach in an industry known for splashy product introductions, but that's the point.

weekly newspaper business pages also like to let readers know when someone in their community has been featured in a national magazine; leverage that published article in your local press by sending a copy to your newspaper business section editor with an "FYI" note that could result in a short news item.

Similarly, maximize the impact of special events so that you reach as many audiences as possible. Introducing a new product at a trade show through a press event? Consider inviting customers and prospects to the event, too. And don't forget to tell the hometown press about the new product you introduced at the trade show in another city.

Much of the material you generate for publicity purposes has multiple uses. Plan to take advantage of this. You'll want to get as much mileage out of your publicity efforts as possible.

> **Chapter 4**

Finding Something Newsworthy to Say

Part One

Part Two

Part Three

Part Four

Part Five

PART TWO PUBLICITY PLAN TACTICS

■ **CHAPTER 4 Finding Something Newsworthy to Say** ■ CHAPTER 5 Getting Your Information to the Right People
■ CHAPTER 6 Using the Proper Format

What Is Newsworthy?

The tools and techniques you use to secure publicity are often referred to as tactics.

The tools and techniques you use to secure publicity are often referred to as tactics. All of them, whether they're press releases, articles, or special events, must have some news value in order to generate that free media exposure called publicity.

It is sometimes difficult for business owners to understand what is newsworthy and what isn't. That's why it's not unusual for a publicist to meet with a company president who is confused about why the daily newspaper hasn't yet profiled his business. When asked a few questions about what is interesting or different about his company that makes it newsworthy for the paper's business editor, the president responds, "We think our work is interesting, so everyone else probably will, too." That might be true, but the editor's attention can be captured only by specific examples of what's interesting.

Other times, a business owner will call a publicist because he sent the newspaper information about a new addition to his small staff, but the newspaper ran only a paragraph about the new employee. The president expects the publicist to talk to the newspaper editor about the mistake and encourage her to correct it by running a large article about this person and her new job with the company. Sometimes, by asking the right questions of company leaders or employees, the publicist can uncover information that shows there is publicity potential in this kind of assignment—and can then share the new information with the editor. But always, the first task is to help the business owner get a realistic sense of what *is* newsworthy and what *isn't*.

How the Media Determines Newsworthiness

Editors, reporters, and producers determine what is news or newsworthy based on their knowledge of the interests of their readers, listeners, and viewers. It doesn't really matter what we think is newsworthy if the gatekeeper at the media outlet doesn't agree. And when that individual *doesn't* agree, there's no point in arguing.

The best way to get a sense of whether your information is newsworthy is to imagine yourself as one of those readers, listeners, or viewers and ask yourself, "So what?" If you didn't work at your company, would you find this information appealing? Step outside your business and assess whether the information you want to share with the press will truly be of interest to the community.

In the situation above, where the newspaper only ran a paragraph on the company's new employee, it's possible that there really was a story there that wasn't shared with the paper. If the business hired the new person to take the company in a new direction that will allow it to hire fifty more employees in nine months, then this new hire might be newsworthy, because that person's position with the company could have an impact on the rest of the community. Or if this new hire has an important position within the company, yet lives in a city 1,000 miles away, that could be the basis of a newsworthy story about a trend toward virtual staffing. Without some kind of interesting "news hook," the new hire just isn't very newsworthy. Don't despair if the "So what?" process helps you determine that your information is not newsworthy, though. With a little bit of creative thought, you can often turn your ho-hum story into something unique and newsworthy.

Judging the Newsworthiness of Your Information

Many people have trouble being objective about what is and isn't newsworthy in their company. It's worth noting that just because it's worth putting in the company newsletter doesn't mean it will be interesting to the outside world. When looking for newsworthy material or information in your company, keep in mind that if your news can be told with any of the following words, it is probably newsworthy:

- Unique/one-of-a-kind
- First ever
- Significant impact on the local community
- Expert advice on a topic of interest to the media outlet's audience
- Atypical community service
- Trends
- Interesting or highly unusual applications of a product or service
- Brings national recognition to your company

What Is Not Newsworthy

Much of what we do in our businesses every day is very interesting to us but is not newsworthy to others. Sometimes, it's newsworthy for one media outlet but not for another. The fact that your company has moved to a new location might merit a two-sentence mention in your local newspaper, but it won't be newsworthy to the local radio and TV stations, or to trade magazines serving your industry. If you have moved to a facility that quadruples your existing space and allows you to greatly increase the size of your staff, it might get more coverage in the daily newspaper though, and it could interest a local TV news department.

Much of what small businesses do isn't newsworthy to radio news directors, either. Radio news broadcasts are very short, with barely enough time to keep up with the area's bad news—an overnight shooting, a big fire in progress, a local plant closing. That's why most news coming out of small businesses will not be covered on radio news broadcasts unless you are extremely creative. It is more typical for small businesses to secure radio publicity through interviews on public affairs program or during drive-time programming.

It is also difficult to secure local television news coverage without a strong, interesting, visual angle. A TV news department is not interested in the fact that you moved your office space unless that new space is visually impressive in some way—involving the restoration of a historic building, perhaps, or a facility that uses more state-of-the art technology than any other space in the community, for example—or unless that move has an economic impact on the local community, as noted above.

Similarly, a women's magazine is not interested in your personnel news even though you manufacture a product sold to women coast-to-coast. If you were a woman in Anniston, Alabama, would you be interested in knowing who is now working for a company in Bar Harbor, Maine? Unless the new hire is Martha Stewart, the answer is "no." Asking yourself "So what?" helps you realize that. So does studying the media outlets to learn what material they do and don't use.

Remember, what's news for one media outlet isn't necessarily news for another. Placing yourself in the shoes of the person controlling what news gets used by each outlet helps you determine what information to send where. It also helps you determine the missing newsworthy element in the information you want to share, and how you can add that element.

Using Press Releases to Announce Your News

Businesses use press releases—news releases—to announce news. Press releases are typed, double-spaced documents that answer the questions who, what, when, where, why, and how. (For specifics on how to write a press release, see Chapter 7). Beginners often make the mistake of sending a reporter a press release that contains no news. It might offer lots of information about how and why the company was founded two years ago, but it still has *no news*. Countless releases like this are thrown away in newsrooms across the country every day. A press release is pointless *unless it contains news*.

Other times, news releases are tossed in the trash because they are not relevant to the media outlet's audience. An editor for a weekly newspaper recently wrote an editorial about the volume and nature of press releases his paper receives but would never use. He cited headlines that ranged from "Hypnotist Helps Man Deliver Baby" and "Truth to Finally be Revealed in O.J. Case: O.J. Receives Amazing Offer on Fifth Anniversary of Being Charged with Murder," to "Larger, Firmer Breasts Through Self-Hypnosis," and "The Amazing New Popcorn Fork." Maybe there's an audience for this information, but it's more likely to be the *National Enquirer* than a small community newspaper. Because publications receive a great deal of inappropriate material, it's even *more* important for your releases to be interesting and on target.

What's Your Angle?

It's not easy to identify the news angle in your company information, but with a little practice and guidance, anyone can do it. First, make a list of what you believe is new and interesting in the company. Then walk away from it. Return to it the next day with new eyes—those of someone who reads or watches the media outlet you're targeting—and ask yourself "So what?" So what on this list would be interesting to newspaper subscribers? So what on this list would appeal to readers of my trade magazine? Does your neighbor care that you hired a new director of senior housing development? No. So the newspaper's business editor won't either. Always step outside your role in the company and view what you're doing through the eyes of the people who will hear about it in the press.

Six Great Reasons to Write a Press Release

Now that you have a very basic understanding of what press releases can offer you, consider these six automatic reasons for you to write and distribute a press release (see Chapter 7 for even more reasons to send a press release).

New Product or Service

When writing a press release that announces your new product or service or a line extension, make sure you include the following information:

- A description of the product or service
- A statement of why the product or service is being introduced
- An example of how the new product or service might be used
- Pricing information
- Product availability—is it available locally or nationally?
- A substantive quote from a company executive offering an opinion about the value or usefulness of the product, or its expected impact on its industry
- How readers can obtain the product or service
- A general statement or description about your company

Grand Opening

This announcement can be used by any business that sells products or services to the general public, including stores, health clubs, automotive services, doctor's offices, spas, and so on. The amount of publicity generated by this type of release depends on how newsworthy you make the grand opening itself. To secure the maximum amount of exposure, consider adding elements to the grand opening such as a celebrity appearance, product or service demonstrations that will appeal to TV news cameras, or a tie-in with a radio station that gets you a live remote broadcast from your facility. Door prizes, raffles, and giveaways work well to draw customers but will not enhance your event's publicity value.

A grand opening press release should include the following.

- A description of the facility that is opening
- The date, time, and place of the grand opening
- A description of the special activities taking place at the opening
- A statement of what makes this business unusual, special, or newsworthy ("This is the first independent bookstore in the eastern suburbs" or "This is the company's third franchise in the western part of the state")
- A paragraph that describes the business

Special Event Announcement

Are you hosting or sponsoring a special event, such as a charity golf tournament, a public demonstration, an effort to break a world record, a running competition, etc.? Special events have inherent news value, and like grand openings, you can enhance your media coverage by adding special features such as unusual stunts, celebrity appearances, check presentations, "world's largest" elements, and so on. (See a press release announcing a fundraising luncheon in Chapter 8.)

Special event announcement releases must include:

- A description of the special event
- The event's date, time, and place
- A statement about the special event's newsworthiness ("The golf tournament is expected to raise $3,000 for the Alzheimer's Association" or "The Taste of Cherry Creek showcases the talents of local restaurant chefs while raising money for three of the community's most needy charities" or "The Bozeman Health Center's open house will include free massages and other health-oriented demonstrations designed to showcase the benefits of preventive medicine")
- A description of special activities taking place at the event
- A paragraph describing the host or sponsoring organization

New Personnel Announcement

Most new personnel announcements are very straightforward, using no more than one sheet of paper. Do not include personal information, such as marital status and where the new employee lives, unless you are sending

Newsworthy Employees

What are your employees doing that might generate publicity? Mine them—and their hobbies—for feature story potential. The grandmother who goes to night school to get her college degree is a perennial May story; does she work for you? What about the accountant-by-day who morphs into the lead-guitarist-of-a-popular-rock-band-by-night? Sometimes the way your employees handle themselves on the job is newsworthy, too. The flight attendants at Southwest Airlines do their best to make sure they get the attention of even the most jaded travelers when presenting the scripted flight safety messages. Stories of attendants who play the ukulele while singing the message or do impersonations of Arnold Schwarzenegger were the basis of a wire service article. Give employees a stage and call a reporter. It could lead to publicity that distinguishes you from your competition.

the release only to a weekly newspaper. Daily newspapers and trade magazines do not use this information. (See a template for a personnel announcement release in Appendix A.)

A new personnel release should include:

- The new employee's name and job title with your organization
- A short description of the individual's responsibilities
- A short summary of the new employee's past employment ("Sarah Block was most recently customer service manager at Company XYZ and has ten years of customer service experience.")
- One sentence about the employee's college degrees or relevant education
- A paragraph describing your company

Large Charitable Donation

While your company probably doesn't donate money to charities for the publicity value, a donation often warrants a press release (the newsworthiness of the size of the donation varies from community to community; in a small town your business could donate $250 and receive mention in the newspaper, while in a large metropolitan area a donation much greater than that might have no news value at all). Note that even if your donation announcement releases do not get used by the local newspaper, they still serve a purpose by communicating to reporters that your company cares about its community. Later, when a reporter is researching a story on "local giving among small businesses," yours might be first on the list for an interview.

A press release announcing a charitable donation should include:

- An announcement of the amount of the donation, who made it, and the name of the organization receiving the donation

- A description of how the money was raised by the company
- A quote from the president of the donating company about why the company made the contribution
- A quote from the executive director of the charity about how the organization might use the donation
- A paragraph describing your company

Contest Announcement or Results

Many small businesses host promotional contests or drawings for customers and prospects. While designed to showcase a company's products or services or to generate traffic in a store, contests often give a business owner an excuse for generating a few lines of free exposure in a local newspaper or in a trade magazine. You can announce the contest first and the winner later.

Content announcement releases must include:

- A brief description of the contest and who is eligible to enter
- Entry guidelines or rules
- How people can enter the contest
- Where people can enter the contest
- A prize description
- A paragraph describing your company

"Worst Gift from a Man" Contest

To promote a newsletter that explains male behavior to women, we generated publicity by sponsoring a "Worst Gift from a Man Contest." We announced the contest in the newsletter and through a press release sent to daily newspapers and radio stations nationwide. The publicity generated hundreds of entries ranging from a camera for a blind woman to plastic corncob holders from a new fiancé. We got additional publicity through a press release announcing the contest winners and by using the information from the contest to develop a tip sheet for women on how to get a good gift from a man. The contest was a natural for television interviews, too, because the bad gifts (the woman who received the yellow plastic corncob holders actually sent them with her entry form) made good TV visuals.

What? No News? How to *Create* News

It's not unusual for a company to have, on the surface, *no news*. You aren't introducing a new, exciting, or unique product. None of your employees have interesting off-hours pursuits that could generate a feature story. You're certainly not making changes that will affect the local economy. And as a sole proprietor consultant operating out of your house, the only kind of open house you'll host is one designed to sell your residence when you don't generate enough income to pay the mortgage. Regardless, there are many things you can do to create news for your business, whether you're a home-based accountant or the owner of a manufacturing business that employs 175. Here are four more ways you can use press releases to generate media exposure for your business.

Offer Advice in the Form of Tips

You know a lot about what you do, don't you? Share it! Magazines, national radio syndicators, and daily newspapers all use how-to information or tips provided by small-business owners just like you every day.

Take a moment to consider what you know about your business or your customer's needs, then think about how you can offer it in the form of bulleted or numbered points in a "tip sheet." Still not quite sure what kind of tips you can offer? Here are a few ideas to get you thinking:

- **From a landscaper:** "The six best flowers to plant this fall for early spring blooms"
- **From a management consultant or coach:** "How to deal with difficult people"
- **From an interior decorator:** "Five ways to breathe new life into your home"
- **From a shipping products or services supplier:** "How to streamline your shipping operation"
- **From an organizational psychologist who consults:** "Ten tips for reducing stress at work"
- **From a nutritionist:** "The six nutrition tips that will change your life"

- **From a professional speaker and business consultant:** "Hate public speaking? Five ways to overcome your fear"
- **From a private investigator:** "Six ways to reduce workers' compensation fraud"
- **From a computer retailer:** "Four things every computer user must do to protect valuable data"
- **From a home security firm or a hardware store:** "Six low-tech ways to protect your home from burglars"
- **From a business consultant or coach:** "Three ways to reduce your overhead"
- **From a professional organizer or a computer software store:** "Five tools that will increase office productivity"
- **From a special event planner:** "Twelve surefire ways to make your special event a success"
- **From a trade show exhibit manufacturer:** "Seven ways to use your booth to draw trade-show traffic"

Because media outlets are so receptive to tip sheets, many small-business owners use them as their only source of publicity.

Conduct a Survey and Announce the Results

A survey is a particularly useful tool because it allows you to research customer needs or opinions while giving you information you can use to generate publicity. Before conducting a survey, give careful thought to whether the topic you're researching has news value.

Consider conducting a survey for its publicity value alone, too. Survey result announcements are surefire ways to generate media exposure. The Soap and Detergent Association built an entire national publicity program around a survey designed to determine whether men or women were doing the housework in American homes. Accountemps, a temporary staffing service, wanted to learn more about the excuses workers use when they don't show up for work, so it surveyed executives on the most unusual explanations they've heard. The answers, including "There was a bear in the street," were distributed via press release and used by a range of media outlets. Scan your local newspaper or trade magazines for news items linked to

> Before conducting a survey, give careful thought to whether the topic you're researching has news value.

A Sweet Idea

The National Confectioners Association (NCA) and the Chocolate Manufacturers Association grabbed a story on the front page of *USA Today*'s "Life" section when they announced results of their survey about where Washington insiders stash their office candy supply. The sister organizations sent questionnaires to all Senate and House of Representatives offices; 160 of the 535 survey cards were completed and returned. The article, which ran just a few days before the biggest holiday for candy sales—Halloween—listed several politicians, their favorite candy, and where it's hidden in their offices. The NCA also has surveyed teachers about whether they enjoy receiving candy as a gift, how often they receive it, and on what occasions they receive candy; it also quizzed consumers about "must have" candy for Easter baskets (chocolate bunnies and jelly beans). It's clear that candy makers understand that a survey is a sweet publicity tool.

survey results, and you'll get a sense of the effectiveness of these publicity tools and what types of topics get used by the press. A local hairdresser can survey the community for the city's "Five Top Local Celebrity Hairstyles" while a kitchen remodeler can survey homeowners about the "Three Changes I'd Make in My Kitchen."

Make a Local Connection to a National Trend or News Development

Local reporters are always looking for local connections to national news stories or national trends. Marcia Layton Turner of Layton & Co., a marketing consulting and public relations firm, recently secured a newspaper business feature for her client, a woman who "sculpts" eyebrows at a hair salon, by linking her client's services to a national trend. Turner wrote a press release that cited national statistics illustrating the growth in eyebrow sculpting and waxing services, referred to celebrities who had their eyebrows sculpted professionally, and described the work of her salon client.

Turner's press release on eyebrow sculpting was "evergreen," meaning that it could be used by the newspaper today, or six months from today, and still work. Most opportunities to provide expert commentary on a national news event or trend require quicker action if you want to capitalize on the opportunity. For example, an article in a recent *Journal of the American Medical Association* reports that obesity and diabetes have increased in the United States in the past decade. A nutritionist could capitalize on this immediately by faxing to the newspaper and TV and radio stations a short press release that summarizes the article's primary conclusion, offers tips for using nutrition to manage diabetes or to reduce weight, and concludes with a paragraph that summarizes her credentials as a nutritionist.

When faxing this information to local media outlets, include a cover note that states you are available immediately for interviews in your office or at their location. (If you can't be available for interviews, don't contact the press. Capitalizing on a breaking story requires you to be available that same day for interviews; taking advantage of a less urgent story allows for more time flexibility, but you still need to be accessible.)

A press release offering your expertise as a local connection to a national trend or news development needs to include:

- A statement of the trend or news item
- A summary of your expert response or a list of bulleted tips in response to the news item
- A paragraph that provides information about your expertise and credentials that allows an editor or reporter to determine if you are, indeed, qualified to provide an expert local view

Fax or e-mail this material to the appropriate media contacts if it's time sensitive, particularly if you're connecting your expertise to today's headlines.

Create a Holiday or Seasonal Tie-In

Holiday news articles are predictable. Each year, local TV news broadcasts in December include reports on coping with grief and loss during the holiday season, while magazines and newspapers feature articles showcasing "the best gifts for under $20." Memorial Day brings stories about the start of the grilling season or the beginning of summer vacation travel, while late summer generates stories about students returning to school. Each one of these predictable topics provides an opportunity for small-business owners to use their imaginations to secure publicity.

Take your cue from the big businesses, too. The folks that make Budweiser commissioned a survey to find out how adults acquire Halloween costumes; the results were used by *USA Today* in pie-chart form as one of the paper's trademark "USA Snapshots." A local costume shop can do this for local release.

Do you service autos? Offer tips for how vacation travelers can get their cars ready for a long trip. Does your store offer back-to-school supplies?

Write a release that predicts the five "must have" items for students heading back to school. Are you a caterer? Issue a release with tips for planning a summer patio party or a picnic with an unusual menu. The possibilities are endless, once you begin connecting the seasonality of your business with media coverage of those seasons.

Businesses that don't provide products or services to consumers can also take advantage of these opportunities. For example, a manufacturer might survey its employees about how they are planning to use their vacation time and use this information to pitch the newspaper on a story about ways local workers are spending their summer vacation days this year. Events like "Make a Difference Day" sponsored by the Sunday supplement *USA Weekend* also provide companies that sell services or products to businesses, not consumers, with publicity opportunities. All it takes is a press release summarizing how your employees plan to make a difference and information on how reporters can videotape and interview your employees while they're giving back to their community.

Holiday tie-in press releases should contain the following:

- A lead statement that suggests an appropriate article topic ("The festive winter holiday season is particularly difficult for people who have recently lost a loved one" or "For some families, 'holiday decorating' refers to Halloween, not Christmas, and a surge in sales of decorative items with a fall theme reflect that trend at XYZ store")
- An expansion on that theme with facts, statistics, etc.
- A quote that supports your premise and offers more information, particularly opinion
- A paragraph describing your company

Moving Forward with Your Newsworthy Event

Applying the thinking in this chapter to article ideas, case histories, special events, and the other tools you use to secure media exposure as well, will make the difference between whether your information is—or isn't—used. Which tools you use when sharing your newsworthy information are determined by your media targets, discussed in Chapter 5.

> **Chapter 5**

Getting Your Information to the Right People

Part One

Part Two

Part Three

Part Four

Part Five

PART TWO   PUBLICITY PLAN TACTICS

■ CHAPTER 4 Finding Something Newsworthy to Say ■ CHAPTER 5 Getting Your Information to the Right People

■ CHAPTER 6 Using the Proper Format

The Three-Step Process of Targeting the Right People

Publicity involves communicating your newsworthy messages and information through the media. Getting your information to the right people through the media is a three-step process:

1. Identifying which media outlets reach your target audiences
2. Determining which editors, reporters, or producers at those outlets will be interested in your news and information
3. Getting your information into their hands in the proper format

What Does Your Audience Watch, Read, Listen To? Targeting the Media

Determining the media your target customers watch, read, or listen to helps you focus your publicity dollars and energy so they are most effective. If you sell a product to teenagers, your campaign might focus on specific types of radio stations, but not weekly newspapers. If you provide a service to homeowners in your community, you will want to target the local newspaper, certain radio stations, and TV stations. If your customers are trainers at *Fortune* 1,000 companies, you'll want to reach them through the trade magazines they read.

You can approach it from another direction, too, asking yourself who reads newspapers and magazines, who listens to the radio (and when), and who watches TV news and talk shows. According to the Pew Research Center for the People & the Press, local television news and daily newspapers remain Americans' favorite news sources, with 64 percent watching their local news regularly and 68 percent reading a daily newspaper regularly. There are generational differences, however, in how Americans get their news. Only 26 percent of those eighteen to twenty-four years old reported reading the newspaper the day before they were polled by Pew. In contrast, 69 percent of those sixty-five and older read the paper the day before. But these generational differences are not as sharp for television news viewing and are nonexistent for radio. The youngest group spends an average of twenty-six minutes watching TV news, compared to forty-four minutes for the oldest group. Those under thirty spent fifteen minutes listening to radio news, compared to fifteen minutes for those over age sixty-five.

Americans ages eighteen to twenty-four are most likely to have read a magazine yesterday (42 percent) and spent a considerable amount of time doing so, too. Young people are the most enthusiastic users of online services as well.

While nightly network news viewership continues to decline, the Pew study shows that specialty cable channels are now major components of our daily news diet. Some 40 percent regularly watch one of the major cable news networks—CNN, CNBC, MSNBC, or Fox News Channel.

The National Association of Broadcasters reports that radio in general, rather than just radio news, reaches 95 percent of all consumers each week, with four out of five adults listening in their car on a regular basis.

When determining which media outlets to target, in addition to asking the outlets' advertising sales departments to provide you with demographics, keep in mind the following summaries from the Pew report:

- Among women, 48 percent watch one of the three network morning programs regularly, compared to 35 percent of men; these shows are most popular with women over the age of fifty.
- While 68 percent read a daily newspaper regularly, only 28 percent of those readers are under age thirty. Newspapers hold less appeal for minorities, those without a college degree, and those making less than $30,000 a year.
- Some 28 percent of readers say they read *USA Today*, while 16 percent read the *Wall Street Journal*, and 10 percent read the *New York Times*.
- More than one-third read *People* magazine, while 15 percent read a tabloid newspaper.
- On a typical day, a majority of Americans are reading the newspaper, watching TV news, listening to radio news, or logging onto the Internet for news from the beginning of the day until the late night hours. Midday is the most common time to get the news, primarily from television.
- More women watch TV news during the day, when more men listen to the radio.

- There is no age gap among those getting their news during the late evening hours—it reaches 60 percent of those eighteen to twenty-nine years old, 60 percent of those thirty to forty-nine years old, and 62 percent of those over fifty.

(For even more detailed information about our news habits, read the complete report at ✑ *www.people-press.org/med98rpt.htm.*)

Media Decision-Makers

Once you've determined which media you're targeting, you need to identify the decision-makers at each outlet—the media "gatekeepers." They have different job titles, but their mission is the same: To determine what goes into print or over the airwaves. This section explains who you need to get your

---

The Ten Top Newspapers and Who Reads Them

The following information about newspaper readers is posted on several Web sites, making it difficult to give credit to the brains behind this amusing analysis. And while the ten newspapers listed are not all in the *real* "top ten" for circulation, they *are* all in the top twenty-five.

1. *The Wall Street Journal* is read by the people who run the country.
2. *The New York Times* is read by people who think they run the country.
3. *The Washington Post* is read by people who think they ought to run the country.
4. *USA Today* is read by people who think they ought to run the country but don't understand *The Washington Post*.
5. *The Los Angeles Times* is read by people who wouldn't mind running the country, if they could spare the time.
6. *The Boston Globe* is read by people whose parents used to run the country.
7. *The New York Daily News* is read by people who aren't too sure who's running the country.
8. *The New York Post* is read by people who don't care who's running the country, as long as they do something scandalous.
9. *The San Francisco Chronicle* is read by people who aren't sure there is a country, or that anyone is running it.
10. *The Miami Herald* is read by people who are running other countries.

---

information to at each type of media outlet; the next section will tell you how to get actual names of the people you need to reach.

Newspapers

Most sections of the newspaper—local, lifestyle, business, sports, etc.—have individual editors. Those sections also have reporters that specialize in topics, or "beats." The local section of a daily newspaper typically has a reporter who follows education, for example. On a large paper, that might be her only assignment. At a smaller paper, she probably has other beats as well. Similarly, the lifestyle or living section has reporters specializing in food, entertainment, and so on, and the largest metropolitan daily newspapers have editors for these topics as well. Business section reporters focus on small-business topics, workplace issues, technology, and other areas of interest or companies that are unique to your community. For all sections, you can contact either reporters or editors. If you can identify the appropriate reporter, start there. If you can't, contact the section editor, who will know the best reporter to assign to your story if it's of interest.

Television Stations

At your local station, there is typically a daytime assignment editor, a nighttime assignment editor, and a weekend assignment editor. The assignment editor you send your information to is determined by the time of day, or the day of week, that you want news coverage. There is not much specialization in TV news reporting with the exception of health and sports. When you have a health-related or sports story, or news about another topic that you know a specific reporter has a special interest in, send your news to those individuals. If they think it's newsworthy, they will get buy-in from the assignment editor.

Your contact at local television stations for talk shows is the show's producer. Many network affiliates air news programs before *The Today Show* (NBC), *Good Morning America* (ABC), and *The Early Show* (CBS); these shows often include in-studio and on-location interviews that showcase special events of the day or offer early morning viewers timely advice.

Your contact at local television stations for public affairs programs is the public affairs director. About one-third of commercial television stations produce public affairs programs with guest interviews; they provide limited opportunities for small businesses to educate the public or to help shape public opinion.

Radio Stations

Your contact for radio news is the news director. Radio stations have short newscasts, so be selective about the information you give them. Unless you have something earth-shattering, very timely, or incredibly interesting, you'll have difficulty getting radio news exposure.

Your contact for a morning or afternoon radio drive-time program is the producer for the show, who may also be the host. The most popular radio stations in each market typically have a drive-time program with colorful hosts who do short interviews by phone with local and national guests or experts. They are good targets when you have fun or interesting information to share. They're also receptive to free samples. When a juice company introduced a line of fresh fruit beverages in the San Francisco area, for example, it used a messenger wearing a giant apple costume to deliver product samples to select morning drive-time program hosts. The oversized piece of fruit always got in the door—and the juice always received free, positive air time when the hosts tasted the juices on the air. It's a safe bet, too, that the Krispy Kreme new store publicity plan includes delivering warm, fresh doughnut samples to popular radio personalities while they're on the air.

Your contact for talk shows on talk radio stations is each show's producer. Talk radio is enormously popular, and producers need a steady influx of guests bearing information to keep these programs on the air.

Your contact for radio public affairs interview programs is the public affairs director. Radio stations serve the public interest by offering thirty- to sixty-minute public affairs programs. To sustain a program this long, you will need to demonstrate that you have enough to say, and that you can say it in an articulate manner. You also can suggest that the producer include other experts on the same topic, and provide contact information for those people as well.

Magazines, Newsletters, and E-Zines

Your contact at a consumer magazine is the editor of the section where your news or information belongs. If you are offering a free booklet to readers, send that information to the editor of the section that uses this type of information. Most magazines have some kind of news section—send relevant news to that section editor. If you are pitching an article idea, contact the articles editor, but if it's a health-related topic and there's a health editor or reporter, pitch it to him or her.

Likewise, your contact at trade magazines is the editor of the section where your news or information belongs. Many trade magazines have news editors who should receive your press releases; some even have new product editors. When offering to write a bylined article or a case history, or when suggesting an article idea, contact the editor.

Your contact for electronic newsletters (e-zines) is the editor. Keep in mind that e-zines are short, news-oriented publications, so tailor the information you send them accordingly.

Your contact for the online version of print publications—both trade and consumer—is the online editor. Note that this is not always the Webmaster, who is frequently the technician behind the site and is *not* the individual who actually determines what content is posted and what isn't.

Compiling a Media List

An accurate and comprehensive media list is the backbone of your publicity campaign; compiling it takes time, effort, and research, but it's not hard work. The resources you use to develop your list will depend on the scope of the project.

You have several options when developing a media list:

- You can compile it completely internally; this works best when the list is small.
- You can use media directories to compile a list that

Reaching Diverse Communities

As you determine what your audiences tune in to, it is worth noting that the best way to reach an ethnic audience might not be the same way you reach the general public. For example, radio reaches 96 percent of both the African-American and Hispanic populations, making it an ideal communications vehicle for these audiences. According to the Radio Advertising Bureau, African-American women ages twenty-five to fifty-four listen to radio slightly more than other age groups—radio reaches 97.7 percent of them weekly, and they tune in twenty-six hours per week. These statistics are similar to those for Hispanic listeners—radio reaches 97.1 percent of Hispanic women ages twenty-five to fifty-four, who listen to the radio twenty-five hours a week. Hispanics also tune in to Spanish-speaking radio stations.

you maintain and update internally; the directories are available for purchase but are also available as public library reference books.

- You can use one of the companies that publishes media directories to generate, maintain, and update your list for you; this is cost-effective if your list is large.

If you're contacting local media only, you can compile your list quickly with a couple of issues of the daily newspaper and a phone book. Review the newspapers for names of reporters and editors. If you can't find what you need, call the newspaper to get the appropriate names. (If the operator can't answer your question, ask for the newsroom.) Use the Yellow Pages to get addresses and phone numbers for radio and TV stations; call them for the names of the radio news directors and TV news assignment editors.

Similarly, the least expensive way to develop a targeted trade or consumer magazine database is to get copies of as many of the targeted publications as possible, and use their mastheads (the listing of staff by job title) and the telephone to identify the appropriate editors. Publication Web sites also can help you assess a magazine's content and identify editors, too.

Reviewing publications to pinpoint the best editor or reporter for your news is time-consuming, but the results are more useful and accurate than what you'll generate with a directory or service. Plus, a well-targeted list will save you time and money in the long run because you'll get your information in the hands of the best person immediately.

There are a number of media directories available as books or CD-ROM databases to help you compile your list, too. You can spend anywhere from $110 for one directory listing daily and weekly newspapers to $1,000 for a set of media directories covering most media outlets. One resource allows you to tap into its online media resource to generate and manage a media database, but with charges starting at more than $2,000 for just one media category (technology print media, for example), it is better suited for a public relations agency managing many publicity programs rather than a small business handling its own publicity.

Most small businesses work from the same media list all year. While you need to update the list regularly because of personnel turnover, you probably don't need in-house access to a directory that lists all trade magazines published in the country. Send an administrative person to the

> The least expensive way to develop a magazine database is to get copies of as many of the targeted publications as possible, and use their mastheads.

reference desk of the library to borrow a media directory. (The Bacon's directories published by Bacon's Information, Inc.—see ✐ *www.bacons.com/ directories/maindirectories.asp* for a description—are among the most popular.) The staffer can photocopy the relevant directory pages needed to build an in-house database. Other commonly used directories are the Gebbie Press *All-In-One Media Directory* and *Burrelle's Media Directory.*

An affordable alternative is to use the press release distribution services available from companies such as Bacon's and PR Newswire (see "Distributing Your News" later in this chapter for more detail). These organizations will generate, store, and update your customized media database for a fee; they will also reproduce and distribute your press releases and press kits. You pay a price for the service, but if your mailing list is long, it is often a more manageable way to keep your list current and to allow your staff to do more challenging assignments than stuffing press releases into envelopes.

Media Relationship Building

Good relationships with the media are important, but don't, under any circumstances, let your lack of relationships stop you from contacting the press with your story. An existing relationship with a reporter can open doors, but the doors are rarely closed to strangers like us who have a good story to tell. If you're calling the right person with a good story, you will get a chance to be heard.

Make an effort to identify the *most important* contacts on your media list, and cultivate relationships with these individuals. Do this in the same way you maintain relationships with other business contacts—by being helpful and a good resource. Make sure the information you send them about your company is truly useful and relevant. Don't send a personnel release, for instance, to the *BusinessWeek* reporter who covers your industry, because he won't use it and it serves no background information purpose.

Here are tips for building good relationships with the press.

Do As Much of the Work for the Reporter As Possible

When suggesting article or talk show segment ideas, include names and phone numbers of other individuals who can be interviewed on that topic. Provide background information and statistics, or direct the reporter to sources of that information. Anything you do to save a reporter time will bring you closer to your goal—that interview or article.

Help Reporters Do Their Jobs By Sending Relevant News Items or Suggesting Article Ideas

These news items may come from trade magazines they might not see; article ideas don't need a connection to your business. This helps establish you as a friend and resource, further developing that relationship. The "FYI" information you fax or e-mail to them might never be used, but it shows you have an understanding of their job and are trying to be helpful.

Set Aside Time for Face-to-Face Contact

Whenever possible, take a key local reporter to lunch, even when you're not looking for media coverage. Ask questions about what he or she is currently working on, and what he or she might be developing for the future. Can you open any doors for the reporter? How can you help the reporter do his or her job better? If your trade media outlets are based in one city, travel there and schedule a day of desk-side briefings so you can provide useful background on your industry, your company, trends, projections, and so on. Schedule meetings with writers and editors at trade shows.

Be Available to the Media and Respond to Inquiries Quickly

Returning calls immediately is important because reporters and producers are usually working against deadlines, and if they don't hear back from you in a short period of time, they will move on to the next resource on their list, and you will miss your opportunity for an interview. Respond quickly even if their call is to ask for your help identifying a resource for a story that has nothing to do with your company. If you don't have the information they need, tell them you'll get it and call them back. Your job with the media is to be as helpful and resourceful as possible. That's how you make friends.

Distributing Your News: Mail? Fax? E-mail?

Even well-established practitioners have different views on the best ways to distribute your news to the media. There are advantages and disadvantages to all approaches, and you're most likely to use more than one approach over the course of a sustained publicity campaign.

Faxed publicity material was once considered the newsroom equivalent of junk mail—and that's probably why the *Miami Herald*'s city desk uses a 900 fax number (an income generator for the paper). More recently, many media outlets have started asking publicists to send materials via e-mail or fax. In general, unless you're dealing with technology publications, don't e-mail press releases or links to online press kits without getting the reporter's permission first. Don't assume that everyone has the same access to e-mail or comfort level with it that you have either. In fact, many journalists still prefer to receive information through the mail.

Because of computer viruses, don't send press release or press kit attachments. Instead, when using e-mail distribution, be more thoughtful with your e-mail message space, using it for a condensed version of a more typical print press release. Use the subject line for your attention-getting press release title (see Chapter 7 for more information about writing press releases), then summarize your point quickly in the message space. Get the journalist's attention with your lead, then immediately introduce your connection to the topic. Your message/release should be just a few paragraphs with a link to your Web site for more information, including a longer, more detailed press release and background information.

Try to send each release individually, rather than mass-mailing your release. When you must send it to several recipients at once, send it as a "bcc" so that the journalists on your distribution list don't know it was sent to others.

Many editors appreciate the immediacy of a pitch letter

Are You Ready for the Big Time?

When a regional manufacturer of windows and doors was featured on the PBS show *This Old House*, it was flooded with inquiries about its products and services from all over the country. The national inquiries supported the company's planned expansion beyond its northeastern roots by giving it the right kind of exposure to one of its targeted audiences—homeowners interested in renovation. It could have been a bad experience, though. If the company didn't want to serve other regions or didn't have the manufacturing capacity to support the sudden interest in its product, there could have been a backlash among potential customers—and frustration among its more than 100 employees. Before you pursue these exciting opportunities, make certain you can survive the best-case scenario. If you can't, it might turn into the opposite.

sent via e-mail. When you paste the text into the body of the e-mail message, make sure you include your address, phone number, and URL. Some editors say they prefer to receive ideas through the mail, though, so ask first.

While many publicists are now distributing press kits by sending messages with links to the kits online at their Web sites, there will still be times when you want to use the mail for press kits—especially those with product samples. Notify the recipient that it is coming, and add a label to the package that says what's in it and how to reach you with any questions. Make sure you let them know how they can get the same material electronically, too. When you can't use the mail—when you're offering yourself as an expert interview for a breaking news story, for instance—do fax or e-mail supporting material, but keep it short and to the point. A six-page curriculum vitae is not only hard to evaluate, it's also overkill; a one-page narrative bio is helpful.

Many news distribution services use a broadcast fax approach to distribute your press materials, and by pricing their services according to the length of your release, you have an incentive to keep it short. Newsrooms know that and like it. They also recognize that the material they receive from these services will always contain a mix of useful and useless information, so they *do* sift through it to find the good nuggets. Bacon's Media Distribution and PR Newswire are the most commonly used services; they can also deliver your information via e-mail.

Press Release Distributor Sites

You can often distribute your press releases completely electronically using the services of companies that specialize in that service. But visit the Web sites of several news release distribution companies—✎ *www.bacons.com,* ✎ *www. prnewswire.com,* ✎ *www.usnewswire.com,* ✎ *www.prWeb.com,* ✎ *www. usanews.net,* and ✎ *www.XpressPress.com*—to compare their services and determine which best meets your needs (if at all). Some specialize in trade media only while others focus on technology media. Make sure the service you select reaches the media gatekeepers to your target audience. (To find more options, type "press release distribution" into your search engine.)

Distributing Your News: In-House, Print, and Electronic Distribution Services

Once again, the best distribution option depends on the size of your list, the nature of your news, whether you're targeting local media outlets or a large group of trade magazines, and so on. Here are a few things to consider:

Consider Producing and Distributing Your Press Releases Internally

If you plan to develop and manage your media database in-house, you will probably want to produce and distribute your press releases internally, too, especially if the size of the mailing is manageable.

Keep Electronic Distribution Narrow

The electronic distribution services have broad reach—sometimes too broad. Focusing your mailing list with these sources can be a challenge. Handpicking editors can be almost impossible. Electronic distribution is an acceptable option for large-scale distribution, but not the approach to use if your publicity plan emphasizes establishing personal relationships with the media.

Merge Your Mailing List with That of an Outside Service

An outside service can mail to a list that includes your media contacts as well as theirs. The specific reporters you have relationships with might not be part of the media list an outside company generates to your specifications from its database, so these companies will always merge your list with theirs for the most comprehensive coverage possible.

> Chapter 6

Using the Proper Format

Part One

Part Two

Part Three

Part Four

Part Five

PART TWO   PUBLICITY PLAN TACTICS

■ CHAPTER 4 Finding Something Newsworthy to Say   ■ CHAPTER 5 Getting Your Information to the Right People

■ CHAPTER 6 **Using the Proper Format**

Understanding Publicity Formats

While the press release is the most versatile and common format for your news and information, you can and should communicate with the media in other formats designed to generate specific kinds of publicity. The most widely used formats are:

- Press releases
- Tip sheets
- Media alerts
- Backgrounders
- Fact sheets
- Press kits

- Pitch letters
- Articles
- Case histories
- Opinion pieces (Op-Eds)
- Public service announcements (PSAs)

While several of these formats have their own chapters in this book, it will help you to understand the purpose of each now.

Using Different Formats for Different Purposes and Audiences

Each format exists because it is an effective way of meeting the editorial needs of the media, but not all the media use information from all of the formats listed above.

For example, all of them use information from press releases, but TV talk shows have no need for case histories. Public service announcements—PSAs—are broadcast media formats. Opinion pieces, referred to in newspapers as "op-eds," are tools for print publications. Case histories are limited to trade magazines. Understanding the purpose—and limits—of each will help you determine which formats to use as you develop your company's publicity plan.

Press Releases, Tip Sheets, and Media Alerts

These three types of publicity tactics are all used to alert the media to a newsworthy piece of information (see Chapter 4 to find out what makes an item newsworthy). This section covers each briefly.

Press Releases

The press release is the most common, most versatile, most useful, and most abused format. Use it only to announce news. When an editor, reporter, or producer gets a press release, that individual scans it quickly for news. When he finds none, he tosses it in the trash, or recycles it by writing interview notes on the back of it. Many press releases are loaded with information but contain no news. Many press releases have news, but it's buried at the end of the release, after glowing descriptions of the company. (Learn how to write a killer press release in Chapter 7). If you don't have an announcement to make, examine the other formats to decide which might be most appropriate.

Press releases are printed *double-spaced* on your letterhead with a contact name and telephone number for more information in the upper right corner, below the letterhead. Place a release date or the words "For Immediate Release" in the upper left corner, directly opposite the contact information. See examples of press releases in Chapter 8.

Tip Sheets

Tip sheets are a specific type of press release, one that offers a list of tips or nuggets of advice. They contain a catchy headline, an introductory paragraph that summarizes the issue or topic, and a numbered list or bulleted points that share information. They can be distributed alone as press releases, or included in a press kit. Chapter 4 includes a list of tip sheet topics. Wisconsin publicist Joan Stewart, who says, "It's easier to promote one of your products or services with a tip sheet than it is with a longer article," offers these examples:

- Eight ways to encourage your kids to save for college
- Seven ways to save money on your taxes
- Six ways to have a better sex life

Tip sheets are printed like a press release—double-spaced on your letterhead with a contact name and telephone number for more information in the upper right corner, below the letterhead. See a sample tip sheet in Appendix B.

Format Cheat

Here's the short course on what format to use to get your information to the press. When you have news to announce, use a press release. If it's a big announcement, break it down into several components and create a press kit. When you have a story idea, use a pitch letter, regardless of whether you want to write the story yourself or not. Use a pitch letter when you're pitching an idea for a segment to a radio or TV talk show producer, too. When you're trying to get TV coverage, use a media alert. If you want your opinion heard, write an op-ed. To showcase your company's successful application, use a pitch letter to propose a case history article.

Media Alerts

A media alert is essentially a memo informing the media of an event taking place soon. The "who, what, when, where, why, and how" approach is the most efficient format for telling the recipient what's going on and why they'll be interested. When the media alert is going to TV stations, make certain to accentuate the event's enticing visuals. In all cases, make it clear who is available on site for interviews and why these people are appropriate choices for interviews.

Media alerts are designed to inform the press of something that is going to happen, not give them the language they will use to write a story. That information comes from press materials sent separately or made available at the event and through on-site interviews. Use them to remind the press of upcoming events you have already described in press releases they've received, too. Fax them typed single-spaced on letterhead. See a sample media alert in Appendix B.

Backgrounders and Fact Sheets

Backgrounders and fact sheets provide factual information for clients, news media, and so on.

Backgrounders

Backgrounders provide exactly that—background information. They can be attached to pitch letters as additional information but are most often found in press kits. Backgrounders can provide biographical information about the management team, a company's history, a product category overview, a campaign description, or anything else that is useful background information but does not contain "news" or an announcement. Backgrounders are double-spaced and printed on plain paper (not letterhead). See a sample backgrounder in Appendix B.

Fact Sheets

A fact sheet is a list of bulleted points containing specific information expanding on general information provided in a press kit, or features background information in a bullet format. Fact sheets are attached to pitch letters as background information or used as press kit elements. A press kit announcing a new product might include a fact sheet that includes a brief product description and its dimensions or size, price, availability, the distribution points, etc. Similarly, a press kit announcing the details of a merger might include a fact sheet highlighting key points, including the name of the combined company, names and titles of the top leaders, and so on. Fact sheets are printed single-spaced in a bullet format on plain paper. See a sample fact sheet in Appendix B.

Photos

Sometimes your story is best told in a photo. Publicity photos range from head shots to product shots to action shots. Smaller daily newspapers, weekly newspapers, trade magazines, and some consumer magazines appreciate receiving "submitted" publicity photos that meet their editorial needs

Stay on Top of the News

The best way to learn what's newsworthy and how it's reported is to monitor media outlets constantly. Read your daily and weekly newspapers cover to cover. Listen to talk radio in the car once or twice a week on the way to work and back. Watch the local evening news every day without being loyal to one station—watch all of them regularly. That's how you'll understand what they cover and what they don't cover. It's also a good way to identify those less-obvious publicity opportunities—the segments the local stations call "bright spots" or "news you can use"—that aren't listed in media directories.

To be informed about what the nation's TV networks are reporting on, get the short course at *www.tyndallreport.com*. There, media analyst Robert Tyndall summarizes the amount of air time given to the top ten stories on the ABC, CBS, and NBC nightly newscasts.

and are of good quality. With the exception of head shots, larger daily newspapers and large circulation consumer magazines tend to assign their own photographers when they cover a story with pictures.

Both newspaper publishing and photo technology have evolved in recent years to the point where the technology has changed the rules for how we submit publicity photos. With more and more newspapers printing color photos on certain pages, we're throwing out the rule that says publicity photos should most often be shot with black and white film, and now submitting color photos. Today, unlike years ago, publications can turn a color photo into a black and white print without losing quality, so by submitting the photo in color, the publication has more options for how it is used—which increases your chances it *will* be used. In addition, with the proliferation of digital cameras, scanners, and e-mail, photo prints are almost obsolete. They still serve a purpose, particularly in press kits (see Chapter 12), but are increasingly being replaced by electronic submission of photos as JPEG files. (For more information about publicity photos, see Chapter 7.)

Press Kits and Pitch Letters

Press kits are usually folders that contain any number of the elements discussed in this chapter, including photos. Pitch letters are one-page sales letters that strive to interest an editor or reporter in a story idea, or a producer in a radio or TV talk show guest interview or feature.

Press Kits

A press kit is used when a subject is too complicated for a single press release or when there is a great deal of information to share. A press kit always contains at least one press release and at least one other element. Many have several documents—there were so many press releases, backgrounders, fact sheets, and photos for the introduction of NutraSweet, the revolutionary nonsugar and nonsaccharin sweetener, that the press kit was a three-ring binder.

Press kits are a useful packaging device for small businesses providing media contacts with background information to keep on file. A "here's information about us for your files" press kit should contain the company's most recent release, a backgrounder on the history of the company, a backgrounder with short bios of the organization's key leaders, a fact sheet that summarizes key points about the company, and reprints of previously published articles about the company.

A consultant seeking to establish credibility with reporters as an expert source might include a tip sheet-type release, a list of topics the individual is qualified to address in an interview, a one-page bio, a "head shot" (portrait), and reprints of articles quoting the consultant. (Find out more about other uses of press kits in Chapter 12.)

Pitch Letters

Pitch letters, which often accompany press kits or other background information used to support your idea, are printed single-spaced on letterhead using a traditional letter format. They need to be enticing but to the point. They have to sell your media contact on your idea, which often requires proving that it will interest readers, listeners, and viewers. Chapter 9 goes into greater detail about how to write compelling pitch letters. See a sample pitch letter in Appendix B.

Publicity Bolsters Plastic Surgeon's Bottom Line

One Long Island plastic surgeon relies heavily on publicity to bring in new clients. Here's how he does it: He has one very interesting topic to discuss: He provides buttocks implants. How's that for an attention-getting topic? If you provide an offbeat service or product, as this physician does, it will be easier for you to generate publicity than it is for another entrepreneur who doesn't. Imagine the veterinarian who offers pet owners a workshop on preventing heartworm and another one on how to communicate with animals. Which one should she promote to the press? As you explore your company's publicity opportunities, wander down that path that takes you toward your more unusual endeavors or products, and think of how you can shine the spotlight on them to call attention to your entire company.

What Some People Don't Understand about Articles

A small business in the Pacific Northwest recently threw its publicity money out the window when its public relations consultant spent valuable time writing a long feature article to send to large daily newspapers and consumer magazines, including *Family Circle*. The money was wasted because the (must be) inexperienced publicist didn't realize that consumer publications rarely use feature articles written by publicists. Daily newspapers and magazines like to do their own feature writing. And while a submitted article might inspire a newspaper reporter or magazine writer to pursue the idea, publicists can save a great deal of time—and the client's money—by summarizing the idea in a pitch letter and by providing the journalist with names and phone numbers of appropriate people to interview for the article.

Articles and Case Histories

Articles and case histories refer to written items you have likely seen in trade and consumer magazines (see Chapter 2 for the differences between these two types of publications). Even if you do not have strong writing skills, consider these useful tools for gaining publicity.

Articles

You are probably familiar with the article format because you read articles in the newspaper, in magazines, and on Web sites. When promoting your business, there are two types of articles: Those you write yourself (bylined) and those that others write that use information you provide. Both have merits, so which format is most valuable for your business? As with everything else, the answer is "it depends." Consumer publications—newspapers and newsstand magazines—do not use promotional bylined articles written by outside experts. If these are your target publications, you must direct your efforts toward generating articles that others write based on interviews with you and other sources. On the other hand, trade magazines use a combination of staff-written articles and those written by outsiders. Your work with them should include contributing to articles written by staffers and writing articles based on your unique knowledge and expertise.

Articles are usually submitted electronically, with the editor's approval, according to the publication's specifications for style and length. See a sample article in Appendix B; learn more about article writing in Chapter 10.

Case Histories

Case histories are articles with a problem/solution format. They focus on a particular company's problem while showcasing another company's solution. Quite often, the "solution" is a product, method, or systems application. You must have your customer's cooperation to write a case history that showcases your product application, and you must be careful to place the emphasis of the article on your customer's needs. Regardless of how much useful information you pack into a case history, it will be rejected if it mentions your product or company too many times and comes across as overly self-serving.

Case histories often include photos and are submitted electronically with the editor's approval, according to the publication's specifications for style and length. See a sample case history in Appendix B; learn more about writing case histories in Chapter 10.

Opinion Pieces (Op-Eds) and Public Service Announcements (PSAs)

Neither opinion pieces or public service announcements need be newsworthy (as defined in Chapter 4), which makes them fantastic tools for your publicity plan. They should, however, be relevant to your audience. Both tactics are described in this section.

Opinion Pieces (Op-Eds)

Opinion articles, usually referred to as "op-eds," are short, biased articles written in the first-person style. They express the writer's opinion on a current topic. They are usually written to influence public opinion and policymakers, and to stimulate change. All newspapers use op-eds and some trade magazines run them, too. Consumer magazines use them in the form of first-person essays, but many of these essays are designed to entertain or stimulate thinking rather than to influence the opinions of others.

Op-eds can be submitted electronically with the editor's

Editorial Board Meetings

When using publicity to support a specific issue or cause—as opposed to product—it is possible to influence your newspaper to take a stand in your support on the op-ed pages. Schedule a meeting with the paper's editorial board to present your position, educate the board about the issue, and encourage a board member to write an editorial in support of your cause. Before scheduling such a meeting, make sure you know how the newspaper has covered your topic in general—in both news and opinion pages. Be clear on how the paper has covered related issues, as well, and whether it has taken a stand on them. Bring to the meeting a fact sheet that summarizes your position as well as related background information that will help board members better understand the issue. Provide them with names and phone numbers of people they can talk to who share your perspective.

News Exclusivity

It's not unheard of for a local media outlet to request exclusivity on a news story, especially in communities where competition among media outlets is fierce. What should you do if that happens? The answer depends on your audiences, which media outlet is most important to you, and how likely the other outlets are to use your news. Consider a situation in a community where the business section of the daily newspaper competes with a weekly business magazine. The daily, with its larger circulation, pushes for exclusivity so it can be the source of all breaking business news in the community. The weekly also likes to receive exclusive stories of interest to its readers, who tend to be owners of small to medium-size local companies who are very interested in local business news. Deal with the "exclusivity" issue by answering this question: Which one of these publications does a better job of reaching your target audience? That's the one that gets the exclusive—if you want to offer one.

approval, according to the publication's specifications for style and length. See a sample op-ed in Appendix B; learn more about writing op-eds in Chapter 11.

Public Service Announcements (PSAs)

Public service announcements—PSAs—are popular publicity tools because they do not need to be newsworthy. The Federal Communications Commission (FCC) defines PSAs as "any announcement . . . for which no charge is made and which promotes programs, activities, or services of federal, state or local governments . . . or the programs, activities or services of nonprofit organizations . . . and other announcements regarded as serving community interests." PSAs, which promote a specific social message aimed at increasing public awareness or having listeners take action about a specific issue, lend themselves easily to nonprofits and small businesses sponsoring events that raise money for nonprofits.

Typically, PSAs run free-of-charge on a radio or TV station as a community service. They are supplied to stations either as scripts, audio recordings, or videotapes of sixty, thirty, twenty, or fifteen seconds. See a sample PSA in Appendix B; learn more about writing PSAs in Chapter 11.

Writing a Killer Press Release

The Anatomy of a Press Release

A press release is a document that uses a specific format to tell the press that you have newsworthy information that "deserves" free media exposure. Both a commonly used and overused tool, it is the basis of any solid publicity program. All good press releases have a few things in common (see Chapter 8 for samples).

Contact Information

Who should a reporter or customer call for more information after reading your press release? For the reporter, place a contact name, phone number, and e-mail address at the top of the first page, on the right side. Many times, however, the individual to call for more product or event information, or to make a purchase, is not the media contact person. In that case, include the name and phone number of the person to call for more information at the appropriate place in the text of the release.

Catchy Headline

A reporter or editor looks at your press release headline first, and if it doesn't grab his attention, he tosses it into the recycling bin quicker than you can shout, "Wait! This is really interesting!" *Do* agonize over your headline. Show it to others and get their reactions. Does it make them want to read on? Does it pull them to your opening paragraph? "Expert reveals five secrets for breathing new life into a home" is more compelling than "Painter gives advice for homeowners." And "New product from Acme Manufacturing will revolutionize the kanooter valve industry," is more interesting than, "Acme Manufacturing announces new product." When writing headlines use an active voice—"introduces" rather than "plans to introduce"—and colorful or energetic words. Make it exciting, but don't exaggerate.

Do agonize over your headline. Show it to others and get their reactions.

Attention-Getting Lead

Craft an attention-getting lead—your first one or two release sentences—without worrying about including all the details. When the subject lends itself, use a clever lead. For example, are you launching a series of workshops on how to deal with change? The lead, "The only kind of change some people like is the kind that jingles in their pockets," is more interesting than, "Simpson Consulting announces five workshops on how to deal with change," because it describes the problem the sessions will help solve.

Leads should be based on facts, but sometimes facts aren't enough. When publicizing a program that taught disadvantaged students how to use computers, the press release writer knew that the facts were boring. A fact-based lead would have read, "The County Department of Social Services has partnered with a nonprofit agency and a training firm to execute the Summer Youth Employment Program, which teaches computer skills to disadvantaged students, builds their self-esteem through entrepreneurial experience, and fosters a sense of community service and leadership." Yawn . . . That lead is straightforward but long, and not as interesting as it could be. Instead, to communicate to the media the *significance* of the youth training program, the writer put it in the context of a national issue. The result? "As concern over the 'digital divide' continues to grow nationwide, one summer city youth employment initiative today showcases its efforts to make sure fifteen disadvantaged youths don't slip into the resulting crevasse." This version generated a story in the daily newspaper and a TV news report.

Kirk LeMessurier, former online editor for Expert PR, a publicity resource at ✎ *www.mediamap.com,* offers this example of how to write a good lead in his online article, "Six Steps for Building the Better Press Release." He writes, "Pop Quiz: To illustrate, which of the following would you rather read?

(a) Cheap Tickets today announced an unprecedented savings program that would enable the traveling public to leverage their buying power to maximize savings on a number of airfares.

(b) Summer's almost over, but Cheap Tickets is offering super savings to keep the heat on."

"Needless to say, it's (*b*) right? It's shorter, less formal, and more relevant to you." Version (*a*) is real and it's typical and it's got lots of good marketing buzzwords like "unprecedented" and "leverage" and "maximize." But it has too much hype and is too wordy. You'd never read a sentence like

A Life-Altering Release

Several years ago, a press release announcing a subscription newsletter I created for women, *The Do(o)little Report*, changed my life, transforming me from a publicist to a relationship expert, book author, and keynote speaker. It made me an international television talk show guest and the darling of radio drive-time producers from coast to coast. It even won me a national award.

I sent the release with the first newsletter issue to a carefully crafted media list of nearly 400 outlets. The resulting chain reaction, including articles in *USA Today* and the *Wall Street Journal*, a wire service story referring to me as a "genius," an appearance on *Eye to Eye with Connie Chung*, and multiple daily interviews on radio stations coast-to-coast, amounted to at least $4.5 million in media exposure in ten months. The cost to my business? Less than $5,000. (See Chapter 8 for a copy of the release.)

that in a newspaper or magazine, so don't write one like that in your press release, especially as your lead.

Press Release Style

A press release always has a title in bold-faced letters, and a name, telephone number, and e-mail address for the person to contact for more information. Include at the beginning of the first paragraph the city and state you are sending it from, followed by the release date. Both these items should be in capital letters. Indent each paragraph five spaces. While there is a trend toward typing press releases in a single-space format, the "old" double-spaced format is still preferable because it leaves room for editors to edit and because it's just easier to read. You can save a tree by copying a two-page release on the front and back of one sheet of paper, but if you copy on just one side (again, the "old" style), environmentally conscious journalists will recycle the blank side of the paper by using it for interview notes. Put a page number on everything but the first page and at the end of the release, add "# # #" or "-30-" (both without the quotation marks) so the reader knows he or she has hit the end.

Making Your Press Release Stand Out

Beyond the basics of what every press release contains, you can make yours stand out—and lead to free publicity—by applying the tips in this section.

Use Statistics and Facts

When possible and appropriate, use statistics and facts to support the premise of your press release. If you're announcing a new product, add statistics about the size of the product category to underscore your product's potential for success. Are you introducing a new service? Offer industry research that supports the need for this service.

For the press release on educating disadvantaged youths described earlier, the writer searched the Internet for statistics illustrating the impact of the digital divide. This provided material for a quote from the trainer that illustrates the impact of the training program on the local community: "Linda Keefe, president of Shared Results, adds, 'Studies show that a working person who is able to use a computer earns 15 percent more than someone in a similar job who cannot. By teaching these students how to use computers, and by giving them the confidence that comes with success, we are making sure they have the skills needed in the New Economy.'"

Include a Quotation

A quote from a company leader or expert is appropriate for most press releases, especially those announcing new products or services, research or survey results, and tips or advice. The quote can amplify information already presented, or express an opinion, but it should add to the story.

After you write the quote, read it out loud to make certain it sounds natural, not stiff. Ask yourself, "Is this how this person really talks?" And if the person quoted used incorrect grammar when you interviewed them to get information for the press release, improve the language. In some situations, you might even need to create the quote for the leader or expert—and if you do, make sure you get their approval on the comment before the release is distributed to the media.

Use Numbered Lists or Tips

If your release is a "tip sheet" offering advice, follow the lead of magazine covers—"Five ways to lose weight before June" or "Top seven mistakes shoppers make"—and list your tips in a numbered format. This is much easier for an editor to read than a paragraph format that separates the tips with commas. Bulleted points also work well for tips and for product features and attributes. In general, when your release needs to make several consecutive points, use bullets for readability. When tips are listed in a bullet format, editors can quickly scan them to see if they would be useful to readers—or not.

Include a Paragraph about Your Company

Always conclude your release with a paragraph that describes your company without hype or exaggeration. Here's an example: "Interwest Home Medical, with sales of $43.3 million during the fiscal year ended September 30, 2000, provides rental and sales of home oxygen and respiratory equipment and other home medical equipment. Interwest Home Medical has twenty-five branch locations in Utah, Arizona, Idaho, Nevada, Colorado, Alaska, and California and employs over 400. Interwest Home Medical has preferred provider agreements with more than fifty health insurance companies to provide home medical services to their covered beneficiaries. More information on Interwest is available on the Internet at ✑ www.iwhm.com."

This is an accurate, factual, neutral description of the company that tells the reader the basics about the company's products or services. Avoid the temptation to share your company's mission or vision statement—it is not relevant or appropriate. Do not include your company's goals. "Widget Wonders aims to be the top supplier of widgets in the country by 2010" will not be used in a news article, but "Widget Wonders is one of the top ten suppliers of widgets in the country" could be.

How to Describe Your Company

Writing a short paragraph about your company to include at the end of your news releases can be a challenge because, quite often, there's a lot to say about what you do—more than you can put into two or three sentences. But this is not the place for specifics and details. This is where you describe your business in broad terms. When writing this paragraph, think in terms of where your company fits into the industry or community ("Acme Pipes is the third-largest manufacturer of pipes used by the water treatment industry") or with the type of customers or assignments you would like to attract in mind ("Country Kitchens, the largest kitchen designer in Marshall County, specializes in new home construction"). Read the company description paragraphs at the end of the many press releases online at the Web site of PR Newswire (✑ www.prnewswire.com/news/).

Remembering the Five Ws and One H

In the same way that friends often talk for a few minutes about the least interesting details of their lives before they get to the *really good stuff*, beginning press release writers often "bury the lead" by providing a great deal of detail up front without getting to the real point of the release until the third, fourth, or even fifth paragraph. To avoid this, work to get the five Ws and one H—who, what, when, where, why, and how—into the first two paragraphs.

Placing this essential information in the beginning of the release is important because reporters edit press releases by cutting from the bottom up. They assume that you, like them, put your least important information near the end of the release or story. If you've saved the best for the last, you're in trouble, because they might not notice. Or they might not want to do the work that's required to rearrange the information in a press release, turning instead to one from a competitor that's more usable.

Do make certain you get to the news by the second paragraph and do make certain that you actually have something newsworthy to offer. Here are the first two paragraphs from an actual release (the "expert's" name has been changed to protect her): "Summer is the season for weddings and their accompanying wedding showers. Cathy Frank suggests turning the traditional bridal shower into a couples shower by including the groom-to-be. Frank suggests a pantry theme for couple showers. Gifts to help stock the kitchen can range from spices and pot holders to window cleaners and non-perishable food items." The paragraph goes on to suggest ideas for a bathroom shower.

What's the news here? That summer is the wedding season? I don't think so. Is a couples shower a new or newsworthy idea? No. And who is Cathy Frank and why is she making these bridal shower suggestions? You have to read a couple of more paragraphs to find out who she is and to discover that she does not have the credentials you'd expect for someone giving advice on wedding planning. This is the kind of release that gives publicists a bad name. You can do better than that.

Using Newspaper Style

Just as a press release should contain certain elements—contact information, a catchy headline, an engaging lead, the important facts, a quote from a company source, and a description of the company—it should be written a certain way, too. Write a press release using the style you see in your local daily newspaper. Train yourself to do this by studying several newspaper news items before you sit down to write your release. You will discover that newspaper news is written in a direct, "just the facts, ma'am" style. Sentences are relatively short—or, at least, a lot shorter than your college English term paper sentences. Try writing as if you were talking to a family member, especially one who doesn't know as much as you do about the release subject.

Avoid Complicated Language

Keeping this relative in mind as you write also will help you avoid complicated phrases or language. Limit your use of industry jargon to press releases going to trade magazines in your field. It's okay to refer to "hindered amine light stabilizers" in a publication read by those in the painting industry, but it is not appropriate for a press release offering tips on how to select the right paint for your home that is sent to newspapers or consumer magazines. Avoid hyperbole such as *superior*, *dynamic*, *impressive*, or *extraordinary*. These words express opinions, not facts, and opinions are only acceptable in the quotes used in your release.

> Limit your use of industry jargon to press releases going to trade magazines in your field.

Keep Your Release Short

Using a direct style will help you keep the press release short, too. The preferred standard is no more than two double-spaced pages. If you find yourself going onto three or four pages, go back and cut out unnecessary detail. You won't be fired if your release is longer than two pages, but a reporter probably won't keep reading after one or two pages, so why waste your time and paper?

Make It Clear and Complete

After you've written your first draft, re-read it for clarity and content. Does it read smoothly? Or does it contain a lot of jargon in long sentences? If you were a stranger receiving this release, what else would you want or need to know? Is any important information missing? Don't expect a reporter to call you and ask, "What time does this event start?" or "What's the price of this product?" Like you, reporters are busy people. They don't have time to call everyone who omits important information from a release. It is much easier to toss out a release with holes than it is to call for details.

In fact, if your release is newsworthy, interesting, and relatively well-written, don't expect a call from a reporter at all. Your goal is to provide a document that contains everything the reporter needs to share your news. Sending a complete release saves time for you *and* the reporters.

Fact Check, Proofread, and Check Again

Reporters rely on press releases and media alerts for the basic facts about your news. They assume that what you've given them is honest and accurate. This is one reason why it's crucial that you fact check all the information in your press release and media alert. Is the product or event name spelled properly? Are the date, time, and place of an event included and correct? Are the product specifications accurate? If you're the owner of a microbrewery introducing your community to your first product, you will be disappointed if the product name flashed on the TV screen during your launch party interview is spelled incorrectly because there was a typo in your release.

Your releases won't be discarded if you used *that* instead of *which*, but if your company is to be viewed as a credible source of information, you need to make sure that your releases are, too.

Print versus Broadcast Media

If your press release is targeting just broadcast media—radio or television news—it should be shorter than a release written for newspapers or magazines. Typically, a broadcast reporter covering your event or announcing your news will use the release for the bare-bones facts only, relying instead on interviews with your spokesperson for the guts of the story. In that situation, the person interviewed becomes the "content" of the press release and needs to be prepared to share that information succinctly in an interview (see Chapter 19).

If your release targets both print and broadcast media—typical of a release promoting a special event—summarize the key information for TV assignment editors and radio news directors in a supplemental "media alert" document. This "who, what, when, where, why, and how" format on one sheet of paper allows a TV assignment editor to determine quickly whether you have the "visuals" he needs to assign a crew to your story. Similarly, it allows you to show radio station news directors that they will be able to secure an audio interview to use in their news broadcasts. A media alert is preferable in these situations because it allows you to speak directly to the needs of the people making the news decisions in ways that press releases don't.

When a company wanted to publicize an open house at its new inner-city computer training facility, its publicist knew there was not a good newspaper story in the event, but that TV stations might be interested in attending because there were good visuals. So in the "why" section of the media alert (see the entire document in Appendix B), the writer included this language, which would not have been appropriate in a press release: "Because of its affiliation with a number of local social service agencies, the training center serves as an example of the community's efforts to assist youth in becoming lifelong learners with the skills for success in the job market. This is a 'good news' story with great visuals. You will be able to interview students. In addition, you will be able to speak to Nydia Benitez, the new receptionist and bookkeeper at the training center, who was hired as a result of her participation in training provided by Shared Results under contract with the Rochester Welfare to Work program."

This extra information prompted two TV stations to attend the open house to interview high school students trained at the center and tape them showcasing their new computer skills at a terminal for reports that aired on the news.

Electronic Press Releases

Electronic press releases are shorter versions of print releases (see Chapter 5). They are designed to do the same thing as a traditional release—get attention while explaining your connection to the topic—but they do it with less detail and are therefore often "teasers" for longer releases you provide upon request, or are used to sell a story idea rather than generate news coverage directly from a release. Format your short electronic press releases—those distributed as e-mail messages, *not* attachments—so that they are readable by all e-mail software programs. Use standard Courier ten-point type and type only sixty-five characters per line by using the return key when you reach sixty-five or so characters. Otherwise, your message will scroll across the screen and frustrate the reader, who will delete it rather than copying and pasting the text into a Word window where it's easier to read.

Deciding Whether to Send Photos

Most media outlets prefer to take their own photos because they can do it better than we can. Even weekly newspapers covering stories or events take their own pictures. When newspapers or magazines use submitted photos, they are usually product shots taken by a professional photographer in a studio. They also will use submitted photos of prepared recipes done by studio photographers for food pages. So if your release is about a new product or something else that lends itself to professional studio photography, then do include a photo.

If your press release is about an event or news with great photo possibilities, don't put your energy into taking a photo of the event and submitting it to the press after the fact. Instead, work to get a news photographer to cover the event by pitching the publication's photo editor. If you are hiring a photographer to record the event for other purposes—your company newsletter or Web site, for example—then consider hiring an off-duty newspaper photographer who freelances. Ask him to shoot the type of photos that he would take on assignment for the paper and provide you with one that you can e-mail with a caption to the newspaper quickly for consideration.

How to Make Sure You Don't Get Publicity

There are plenty of things you can do to stay out of the media limelight. The best way to avoid that valuable free exposure is by *not returning calls promptly*. A journalist often starts an assignment with a list of potential resources representing the mix he needs to present a balanced story. He calls people on the list, connecting with sources or leaving voice-mail messages. Once he has all the information he needs to write the story or produce the segment, he's done, even if he hasn't spoken to you yet. If you call back after the research has been completed, you won't be included in the piece.

Another way to avoid exposure is to *minimize the amount of information you offer in an interview*. You've seen bad guests on *Late Show with David Letterman*, right? When you're incommunicative or difficult to work with, a journalist will find another information source to fill in the blanks.

► **Chapter 8**

Sample Press Releases

Part One

Part Two

Part Three

Part Four

Part Five

PART THREE ELEMENTS OF A PUBLICITY PLAN

■ CHAPTER 7 Writing a Killer Press Release ■ **CHAPTER 8 Sample Press Releases** ■ CHAPTER 9 Writing Pitch Letters That Get Results ■ CHAPTER 10 Writing Articles and Case Histories ■ CHAPTER 11 Writing a Column, Op-Ed Piece, or Public Service Announcement (PSA) ■ CHAPTER 12 Preparing a Press Kit ■ CHAPTER 13 Calling a Press Conference ■ CHAPTER 14 Planning a Special Event ■ CHAPTER 15 Sponsoring an Event, Group, or Person

■ Upcoming Events

This section contains sample press releases for three very different upcoming events.

Organized American Lawn Mower Racing is 10 Years Old!
2001: A LAWN ODYSSEY
10th ANNIVERSARY STA-BIL NATIONALS, CHAMPIONSHIP RACE FOR
RIDING LAWN MOWERS, HIGHLIGHTS LABOR DAY WEEKEND FESTIVITIES

Glenview, IL—Aug. 17, 2001—Who would believe it? Organized American lawn mower racing is 10 years old!

The U.S. Lawn Mower Racing Association (USLMRA) will present the 10th Anniversary STA-BIL Nationals, Championship Race for Riding Lawn Mowers during Labor Day weekend, Saturday, Sept. 1, in Mendota, Ill.

"It goes to mow, you don't ever know," quipped Bruce Kaufman, president of the U.S. Lawn Mower Racing Association. "When we hosted the first STA-BIL Nationals as a promotional stunt 10 years ago there was no organized nationwide lawn mower racing and we hoped people would show up. Now we have local clubs and state associations across the country, a network television series, international events in England and Canada and more than 600 sod warriors coast-to-coast. But I still don't own a lawn mower."

The STA-BIL Nationals will consist of riding lawn mowers racing in four road track classes and three drag racing divisions. All cutting blades are removed for safety. Racing classes include Stock (10 mph), IMOW (25 mph), Prepared (50 mph), and Factory Experimental (60 mph) as well as Pro, Super, and Top Grass Eliminator (75 mph).

Racers competing in the STA-BIL Nationals include The Lawn Ranger, Turfinator, Geronimow, Sodzilla, Mr. Mowjangles, Prograsstinator, Mowdacious, and Weedy Gonzales.

The STA-BIL Nationals is the final points races of the 15-city 2001 STA-BIL National Lawn Mower Racing Series, also known as *2001: A Lawn Odyssey.* Sod warriors from 25 states, ages 16–82 will compete. A sense of humor is not required but is strongly encouraged.

There is no purse money, as racers compete for trophies, glory, and bragging rights. The STA-BIL series is sanctioned by the USLMRA, which has more than 600 members across the United States as well as Australia, Canada, England, and New Zealand.

The STA-BIL Nationals will air on the Speedvision Network as part of a seven-race series beginning Oct. 14. Contact the USLMRA at 847-729-7363 or visit *www.letsmow.com.*

# # #

Heart Disease Biggest Health Threat To Women

BETHLEHEM, Conn. — More than a quarter of a million American women will die of heart disease this year, five times the number that die of breast cancer. Yet most women—and their doctors—still don't recognize the threat this disease poses.

The need for focus more attention to the problem of heart disease in women is the purpose behind National Women's Heart Health Day. Observed each year on Feb. 1, National Women's Heart Health Day is an opportunity to spread the word about heart disease, the nation's biggest killer of women.

"Cardiovascular disease—heart disease and stroke—kills half a million women each year. That's twice the number of women who die of all forms of cancer combined. But most people don't realize this, and the results can be tragic," says Charlotte Libov, the award-winning book author and heart patient who founded National Women's Heart Health Day three years ago.

Libov cited a 1996 Gallup survey which showed that half the doctors polled incorrectly cited other diseases, such as breast cancer and osteoporosis, as the greatest health risks for women over 50.

"Breast cancer is indeed a deadly disease, but because there is so much attention paid to it, little is paid to heart disease," said Libov.

The national Gallup survey commissioned by Washington Hospital Center in Washington, D.C., Libov notes, found that nearly two-thirds of the primary care physicians polled did not know that heart disease symptoms, warning signs, and diagnosis are different for women.

These results were similar to a national Gallup survey undertaken a year earlier, which found that not only doctors, but women themselves, were unaware of the facts about heart disease.

"It's not surprising that women are unaware," Libov said. "For years, all of the public education campaigns on heart disease were aimed at men. The tragedy is that even when women do summon up the courage to bring their concerns to the doctor, their doctors dismiss those concerns because they don't know enough about the problem either."

She also helped to create and was featured in the PBS documentary *Women's Hearts at Risk*, is a frequent guest on television and radio programs, and lectures throughout the country on health issues. Libov has received awards for her volunteer work on behalf of the American Heart Association.

For more information about Women's Heart Health Day, visit *www.libov.com* or contact Libov, 555-555-5555.

# # #

NAWBO announces keynote speaker
for Oct. 24 annual gala

ROCHESTER, N.Y.—Sept. 6, 2000—The Rochester Chapter of the National Association of Women Business Owners (NAWBO) has announced that local businesswoman and author Jane Plitt will be the keynote speaker at the group's annual gala luncheon Oct. 24.

The "Women Mean Business" fundraising and awards event is Tuesday, Oct. 24 at the Rochester Riverside Convention Center at noon. Tickets for the luncheon are $50; tickets for the 11 a.m. pre-gala reception and luncheon are $75. A table of 10 for the luncheon is discounted to $450. For more information, contact the NAWBO office at 716-262-2410.

Plitt, a founder of Rochester's NAWBO chapter, will talk about "Profiting Through Your Passion." The author of *Martha Matilda Harper and the American Dream: How One Woman Changed the Face of Modern Business* and the force behind a movement to get Harper on a U.S. postage stamp, Plitt ran a thriving business consulting practice until she became enthralled with Harper. Now a visiting scholar at the University of Rochester, Plitt has authored articles and lectured internationally on creative marketing, economic development, entrepreneurship, and women's rights.

The luncheon includes presentation of the annual Active Community Entrepreneur—ACE—Award recognizing a female business owner's outstanding entrepreneurship and community contributions. The ACE winner is selected by a panel of judges representing women business owners and prominent Rochester organizations.

Proceeds from the luncheon are shared with the Women's Foundation of Genesee Valley, which manages a permanent endowment fund to perpetuate grant-making that explicitly benefits women and girls. The luncheon is made possible by generous support from community organizations, including M&T Bank as presenting sponsor and award sponsor Mercury Print Productions. Other sponsors include FASTSIGNS; Generations Child & Elder Care; 1st-Air.Net, Inc.; Fleet Small Business Services; Nixon Peabody LLP; and Van Bortel Subaru. For sponsorship information, contact Bridget Shumway, 716-254-8160.

NAWBO is a national organization dedicated to supporting the achievement and professionalism of women-owned businesses. The Greater Rochester Chapter promotes the success and growth of women-owned businesses in the Rochester area. It has approximately 120 members representing a range of businesses, from services to manufacturing.

# # #

■ Company Anniversary

This release turns an event that has little meaning for the customer (the thirty-year anniversary of a company) into a reason to visit the location.

Beefsteak Mining Company Celebrates
30 Years of Service to Rochester Patrons

ROCHESTER, N.Y., Feb. 15—In March, the owners of Beefsteak Mining Company Restaurant, Judy and Bill Marean, will mark their thirtieth year in business. In an industry where few businesses survive past the fifth year, Beefsteak is a standout, having been serving friends, family, and neighbors from their location on East Ridge Road in Irondequoit since 1969.

For three decades, customers have come to this location to celebrate birthdays, anniversaries, and other important milestones. Today, younger family members are returning to make their own memories.

"We've been here long enough to now have the next generation of our regular families coming here for dinner. It's a festive, celebratory place," said Bill Marean.

Beefsteak Mining Company has earned a reputation for its wide selection of steak, poultry, and seafood entrees, but its signature all-you-can-eat hot and cold salad bar is what customers frequently remember. The free dessert bar is an added bonus for many patrons.

In addition to serving lunches and dinners daily, Beefsteak also serves as host to area organizations that choose to schedule meetings in the restaurant's Golden Nugget Banquet Room. The banquet facilities were added four years ago to accommodate large parties, such as weddings, professional groups, and civic organizations.

The owners attribute their success in part to the outstanding staff they have retained during the last few decades. Five members of the staff at Beefsteak Mining Company have been employed there for more than 15 years. "Two members of the waitstaff, as well as the head cooks and manager, have been with us for most of their careers," said Judy Marean.

That says a lot about the way Judy and Bill treat both their employees and patrons. "You have to like people to stay in this business," advises Judy.

The Beefsteak Mining Company is located at 716 East Ridge Road, in Rochester, N.Y. The restaurant features a bar, dining room, and party room, where meetings and banquets can be held. For more information, call 544-8410.

\# \# \#

■ Grand Opening

This press release tells customers about a new location of a new entertainment venue.

Jillian's rolls onto the scene at High Falls

ROCHESTER, N.Y., Feb. 22—Jillian's, the nation's leader in all-encompassing interactive entertainment, is pleased to announce the opening of its latest location at 61 Commercial Street in downtown Rochester. Renovations are nearing completion on Jillian's twenty-third location, and the grand opening and ribbon-cutting ceremony will take place Thursday, March 18. Jillian's will be open to the public at 11 a.m. on Saturday, March 20.

The 45,000-square foot entertainment complex will feature a Sports Video Café and Bar, with more than 35 giant screen TVs. Perfect for watching in-your-face sports action! Play pool in the "Nine Ball Lounge" featuring eight Brunswick Gold Crown billiard tables and darts. There will also be a 10,000-square-foot game room (complete with its own bar) with a large selection of the latest electronic simulation games, such as linked downhill ski racers and NASCAR. Jillian's also features a private lounge complete with two billiard tables, giant TVs and leather club couches. It is perfect for corporate functions and private parties for groups of 10 to 1,000 people.

There is something for everyone at Jillian's, including dancing! A highlight of the Rochester location will be "LoveShack": dancing to the music of the '70s, '80s, and '90s! Experience the tropical sensation, feel the heat, and dance to the music you want to hear!

Jillian's will also feature its newest creation: Hi-Life Lanes, an over-the-top multimedia bowling experience including 15 lanes, seven giant video screens, a Video Disk Jockey, a theatrical light show, a megawatt sound system, and a Retro Lounge. Hi-Life Lanes is guaranteed to be bowling like you've never experienced.

"Jillian's is synonymous with total entertainment, and we are taking that one step further with our newest creation, Hi-Life Lanes," states Steven Foster, Jillian's founder and CEO. Foster notes that "Jillian's is all about fun interaction, and our Hi-Life Lanes captures that in the bowling experience. We are delighted to be bringing Jillian's and the Hi-Life Lanes to Rochester."

# # #

■ New Publications

The press releases in this section are all discussing new publications: a newsletter and a new book.

New newsletter tackles problems of male/female relationships with a smile.

ROCHESTER, N.Y.—A unique newsletter created to help women cope with the men in their lives is now available nationwide.

The Do(o)little Report is designed to give women the information they need to understand the men they live or work with, according to its creator and editor, Sandra Beckwith of Beckwith Communications, Fairport, N.Y.

"We've spoken to a lot of women about their relationships, and they're confused about why men do what they do, or don't do what we want them to do," Beckwith observes. "*The Do(o)little Report* provides answers and explanations. By offering insights into the male mind, we'll help women cope better."

The publication's name was inspired by *My Fair Lady*'s Eliza Doolittle; the subtitle—"Answering the universal question, 'Why can't a man be more like a woman?'"—pokes fun at the movie's song, "Why Can't a Woman Be More Like a Man?"

Features in the premiere issue include, "Male support groups: A solution to women's problems?" about one way to deal with relationship issues, and "Do they really have to tape games they attend?" offering explanations from two men who believe they do.

Each issue includes "Women want to know," a male-authored column covering topics such as this issue's "Why do men zap channels" about how the TV remote control has become the power tool of the '90s. Real-life anecdotes, including "My problem and how I solved it" and "True stories," address parenting, housework, and other topics relating to daily coexistence. Book reviews report on new titles addressing relationships, gender differences, and communication.

"We believe that maintaining a sense of humor is important in any situation, so while we offer useful information, we've also crafted every article to make readers smile," Beckwith says.

The eight-page newsletter is published every other month, six times a year. To subscribe, call 800-836-4467, or send a check or money order for $12.95 to *The Do(o)little Report*, PO Box 1121, Fairport, NY 14450.

# # #

New Book Covers Networking from the Small-Business Perspective

Denver, Colo.—There are perhaps as many books on networking as there are networks. What this new book from Top Floor Publishing offers that all the others don't is a look at networks from a small- or home-based business perspective. *Poor Richard's Home and Small Office Networking: Room to Room or Around the World* ($29.95, ISBN 1-930082-03-7) shows how a small company can set up a network and run more efficiently without spending lots of time or money.

"A home office or small business can no longer afford to ignore the cost savings, collaboration, and outreach benefits of networking," explains the author John Paul Mueller, who has written more than 45 computer books. "If you're not connected, you aren't working at maximum efficiency."

Whether you're in the next room or across the world, *Poor Richard's Home and Small Office Networking* offers lots of different ways to stay in touch and share data. The book explains how to use inexpensive alternative networks such as house-wiring systems and telephone cables. It also covers the best ways to use the Internet for file sharing, conferencing, and remote communications.

Administration and maintenance are vital to the success of a network. This book shows how to maintain a small network with minimal time and effort and how to fine-tune a network to run more efficiently.

A small network isn't simply a scaled-down version of the networks used by large businesses; it's an entirely different entity. Small networks can serve businesses in ways that the large corporate networks never could. *Poor Richard's Home and Small Office Networking* explains how a small-business network can become a profit center rather than a cost to list at the bottom of a financial report.

The goal of this book is to help the small business get the most from networking. It looks at the benefits of being a small business with a network and explains in a geek-free, easy-to-understand language how to design, protect, and maintain that network.

The associated Web site, at *http://www.TopFloor.com/pr/homeoffice/*, contains links to useful resources, a full Table of Contents, sample chapters, and readers' comments.

Poor Richard's Home and Small Office Networking: Room to Room or Around the World, can be purchased for $29.95 directly from the publisher, by calling toll-free 877-693-4676 or by ordering online at *http://www.TopFloor.com/*. The book is being distributed to bookstores by Independent Publishers Group, a major book distributor (800-888-4741).

# # #

■ Product or Service Introduction or Release

This section gives you two types of press releases for products: a new addition to a product line and an imported product that's new to the United States. You can use a similar approach if your company markets new services. Both types of press releases are fantastic ways to spread the word about your company's products and services.

TLR Set to Release New Office XP Guide Series

FAIRPORT, N.Y., June 6—On the heels of Microsoft's release of Office XP, its newest software application, local computer publishing company Technical Learning Resources, Inc. (TLR) is set to release its newest training guide series—Microsoft Office XP 2002. TLR began development of its step-by-step tutorial guide for the Office XP applications (including Word, Excel, Powerpoint, Outlook, and Access) in February 2001 after receiving the beta version of the software from Microsoft.

TRL is one of several companies developing training materials for Microsoft XP. It has worked with Microsoft since 1994, when Microsoft Press hired TLR to develop a step-by-step training guide for its Visual Fox Pro 3 for Windows.

Since 1993 TLR has been writing self-paced training guides for the small office/home office market. "At that time, we were the only courseware developer that had identified this niche market and were designing guides specifically for this segment. This differentiation enabled TLR to be on the same playing field with the largest courseware vendors in the industry, explains TLR's president, Kathryn Hogan. Industry giants such as Intuit, Hewlett-Packard, CompUSA, and Gateway have all relied on TLR's expertise, engaging the company to create branded software training materials. TLR expects its release of Office XP will continue to fuel the company's double-digit growth.

"It opens up several large, significant new markets for us; corporate America and small- to medium-sized businesses are just the beginning," says Hogan.

Some added amenities of the Office XP software application are designed especially for these larger organizations, helping employees to connect with each other and communicate more effectively. Specific features include the ability to access information on the Web quickly and conveniently while working within a document, enhanced formatting options, improved e-mail options, including combining multiple addresses to be accessed and collected from one centralized mailbox, and improved security and reliability.

# # #

Frankenheim Alt–German Brown Ale
Comes to the U.S.

CINCINNATI—Dec. 31, 2001—WARSTEINER Importers Agency, Inc. (WIA) will introduce the refreshingly dry, full-flavored classically brewed Frankenheim Alt–German Brown Ale to import-loving Americans in February 2002.

"Beer drinkers are increasingly interested in trying new, unique, and flavorful beers, and we're eager to tap into that trend," explains WIA president Greg Hardman. He adds, "The acceptance of brown ales by U.S. consumers has led to significant sales increases over the past few years, and we believe that Frankenheim Alt–German Brown Ale will fill a need in this growing segment, for consumers, retailers and wholesalers."

Brewed in Duesseldorf by Brauerei Frankenheim since 1873, Frankenheim Alt–German Brown Ale is the top-selling "alt" beer in that region of Germany, where brown ales are preferred. *Alt*, which means "old" in German, refers to the original and classic method of brewing with top-fermenting yeast. The dark roasted malts used to make Frankenheim Alt–German Brown Ale give it a distinctive rich, amber color and hoppy nose.

Frankenheim Alt's introductory packaging—30L kegs and six-pack bottles—reflects consumption trends in Germany, where 60 percent of the beer is sold in barrels. It will be supported on-premise with a full complement of point-of-sale materials, including tap handles, coasters, table tents, t-shirts, banners, and unique cylindrical glasses that enhance enjoyment of the beer's nose. Off-premise establishments will receive static cling sheets, display cards, and shelf-talkers. Frankenheim Alt–German Brown Ale will be available initially in the top imported markets.

WARSTEINER Importers Agency, Inc. imports a full range of premium beers, including WARSTEINER Premium Verum, WARSTEINER Premium Dunkel, WARSTEINER Premium Fresh Non-Alcoholic, Isenbeck Premium Dark and now Frankenheim Alt–German Brown Ale. For more information about WIA brands, call 513-942-9872.

# # #

■ Announcing Results

Whether you run a for-profit or nonprofit company, your business can get the exposure it needs by sharing results of research, surveys, or initiatives. This section gives you two examples.

FOR IMMEDIATE RELEASE

Summer employment program for city students narrows the "digital divide"

ROCHESTER, N.Y.—Aug. 17, 2000—As concern over the "digital divide" continues to grow nationwide, one summer city youth employment initiative today showcases its efforts to make sure 15 disadvantaged youths don't slip into the resulting crevasse.

Three teams of city students who have learned how to use computers while developing virtual businesses as part of a six-week "Computers and Entrepreneurship" employment program will make PowerPoint presentations about their concepts to a group of supporters at the Ibero American Action League's training center this morning.

Funded through Monroe County Department of Social Services and implemented by Ibero and Shared Results, Inc., this summer 2000 Youth Employment Program was designed to teach computer skills to disadvantaged students, build their self-esteem through entrepreneurial experience, and foster a sense of community service and leadership. In addition to providing computer training, Shared Results facilitated inspirational conversations with successful local entrepreneurs and hosted field trips to technology-related entrepreneurial businesses.

Citing a 1999 National Telecommunications and Information Administration report indicating that there is still a significant "digital divide" separating American information "haves" and "have nots," Julio Vázquez, Ibero's president and CEO, emphasizes the importance of this endeavor. "Our community needs to do as much as possible to narrow the digital divide in Rochester so that all of our youths—regardless of their home or school resources—can capitalize on the tremendous employment opportunities available in the information technology industries," he notes.

Linda Keefe, president of Shared Results, adds, "Studies show that a working person who is able to use a computer earns 15 percent more than someone in a similar job who cannot. By teaching these students how to use computers, and by giving them the confidence that comes with success, we are making sure they have the skills needed in the New Economy."

# # #

Hospital Staffs Still Mostly Unaware
of HIPAA Regulations

Brainlink International Advocates
Extensive Education as the Critical
First Step in HIPAA Remediation

New York, Aug. 20—In an informal survey of over 25 New York metro area hospitals, Brainlink International has discovered a surprising lack of awareness when it comes to the extensive HIPAA regulations that all large health care organizations are required to comply with by early 2003.

Brainlink staffers found that most organizations had not yet appointed a compliance officer, and that staff of HIPAA-critical departments in both information services and administration were usually unfamiliar with the existence of the regulations.

"Staffers asked us to explain HIPAA repeatedly and few had any idea what department would handle HIPAA issues once they were explained," says Raj Goel, Brainlink's CTO. "We were transferred all over some hospitals, trying to find staff we could talk to about their HIPAA plans. Our calls were directed everywhere from admitting to the security guard stations."

When Brainlink staff were able to locate hospital employees familiar with HIPAA they were almost always in the hospitals' legal, risk management, or information services departments.

"While those hospitals where the legal and technical teams are familiar with HIPAA have a good start on meeting these regulations, facility-wide education is the critical first step to a successful remediation plan," says Goel.

HIPAA, which stands for the Health Insurance Portability and Accountability Act, has a number of objectives, including protecting the privacy of confidential patient information and streamlining the processes by which hospitals and health insurance companies interact. Because most hospital staff come into contact with patient information, it is important that HIPAA education be extended throughout the entire organization, both to ensure compliance and to make sure employees understand compliance's benefits to both the hospital and its patients.

Once hospitals start exploring the HIPAA regulations, many are struck by their complexity and the degree to which they affect every aspect of a hospital's operation. While Brainlink agrees the regulations are complex, the company discourages hospitals from viewing the regulations as an obstacle or nuisance.

"The HIPAA regulations actually provide a great opportunity for hospitals to upgrade their technologies as well as their security," says Goel. "This can help improve business and reduce liabilities, while making sure an organization doesn't face the significant penalties of HIPAA noncompliance."

"There are several steps to making a hospital HIPAA compliant. Our telephone survey underscored that hospitals must start with education, so that everyone on their team is aware of these regulations and understands their importance and usefulness. While the staff is being educated, we can see where their current policies and technologies fall short and develop a strategy for moving the hospital into compliance and keeping them that way."

Brainlink's HIPAA process emphasizes education at every step. The company begins by developing a gap assessment document outlining all the areas in which the hospital is not currently within compliance. That document is then the basis for a strategy session between Brainlink and key hospital staff. During the strategy session the team ascertains the best way to close gaps and the priority in which various problems should be addressed. Once this plan of action is developed, Brainlink begins the remediation process, targeting specific solutions to systems, procedures, and policies. Afterward, Brainlink remains involved to ensure that the hospital keeps up with changes to the HIPAA regulations and is vigilant in maintaining and enforcing its security improvements.

Brainlink International is a multi-service technology firm specializing in providing innovative solutions to the health care, pharmaceutical, financial, retail, and new media industries. With expertise in Web site and application development, intranet and extranet design, and security implementations, Brainlink uses its structured service method to help its clients improve their businesses. A HIPAA specialist, Brainlink works with an organization's technical, legal, and medical staff to efficiently bring them into compliance with these government regulations.

For more information on Brainlink and its HIPAA remediation services, visit *www.brainlink.com/services/hipaa.html* or contact *hipaa@brainlink.com.*

# # #

► **Chapter 9**

Writing Pitch Letters That Get Results

PART THREE   ELEMENTS OF A PUBLICITY PLAN

■ CHAPTER 7 Writing a Killer Press Release   ■ CHAPTER 8 Sample Press Releases   ■ CHAPTER 9 Writing Pitch Letters That Get Results   ■ CHAPTER 10 Writing Articles and Case Histories   ■ CHAPTER 11 Writing a Column, Op-Ed Piece, or Public Service Announcement (PSA)   ■ CHAPTER 12 Preparing a Press Kit   ■ CHAPTER 13 Calling a Press Conference   ■ CHAPTER 14 Planning a Special Event   ■ CHAPTER 15 Sponsoring an Event, Group, or Person

Moving from Press Releases to Pitch Letters

Many small businesses and fledgling publicists communicate with the media exclusively through press releases. This is a mistake. Press releases are designed to communicate news or make announcements, and not all of your publicity opportunities involve news. When you want a reporter to write a feature article, when *you* want to write an article for a magazine, when you want to secure a print or broadcast media interview, and when you want to highlight the story ideas in a press kit, the most effective tool is a "pitch" letter.

A pitch letter is a pithy, one-page document that provides the media with good story ideas based on current issues, trends, useful information, and other newsworthy topics. It summarizes the story idea, explains why it will be of interest to the media outlet's audience, and outlines how your organization can contribute to the story. Like the press release, it is a powerful tool for generating publicity for your business.

> A pitch letter is a pithy, one-page document that provides the media with good story ideas based on newsworthy topics.

A Pitch Letter Is a Sales Document

You've likely received or even sent direct-mail packages that contained a compelling sales letter designed to stimulate interest in the product and to motivate you to take action. A pitch letter does the same thing. It's a sales letter targeting the media. Pitch letters are used to sell the media on:

- A specific story or broadcast talk show segment idea,
- An interview with a specific individual about a specific topic,
- Saving attached information on your organization in an "experts" file for future interviews, and
- Summarizing why the news and information in an accompanying press kit will be of interest to the outlet's audience and suggesting ways to use the information.

Drafting a To-the-Point Pitch Letter

While direct-mail sales letters tend to be long-winded, motivating you to action over the course of at least four pages, pitch letters need to get to the point quickly in just one page. Each letter should contain most of the following elements in a traditional business letter format:

1. An attention-getting first paragraph
2. An indication that you are familiar with the publication or media outlet
3. For television segment ideas, the story's visual elements
4. Research or statistics that support your story idea
5. Suggestions for other sources of information for the story
6. Appropriate credentials for the suggested interviewee (or article writer, if you're proposing a bylined article)
7. A concluding statement about who will do what next

Write an Attention-Getting First Paragraph

The first two to three sentences need to hook the reader immediately in the same way that you're hooked when you read a newspaper article or hear the lead-in to a story on TV news. This is the most important part of your letter, so spend time crafting a lead that will capture attention.

There are a number of ways to do this, and the approach you use will depend on the topic and the media outlet. Let these different types of approaches get you thinking about how to deal with your topic:

Use a startling, little-known fact to catch attention: "According to one industry report, fraudulent workers' compensation claims cost American businesses anywhere from $1 billion to $20 billion annually."

Use an anecdote: "Having built the largest limousine service in Texas, John Ferrari is still looking for ways to go that extra mile."

Ask a question: "If your father suddenly became seriously ill and couldn't communicate, would you know what kind of care he would want to receive?"

Be intriguing: "It's not the kind of bank with an ATM, but a withdrawal from this savings and loan could save a child's life."

Take a straightforward, sincere approach: "I will be speaking to the Omaha Women's Network on October 18, and I believe that the advice I will offer this group about six ways to achieve a healthy lifestyle today will be of interest to your readers, too."

Avoid This Pitch Letter Mistake

Too many pitch letters are sent to inappropriate media outlets because the senders are using mass-mailing lists that are not targeted to specific categories. If you're pitching a story involving your company's cleaning products, for example, and you want newsletter exposure, send your idea to newsletters read by people who are interested in this topic, not *all* newsletters published in the United States. It takes a little work to figure out which newsletters might be appropriate, but it's worth it because you'll stop alienating the journalists who receive your junk mail. Don't make the mistake of thinking that because a service customized your letter with a merge mailing that you'll trick a journalist into thinking he or she is the only recipient of that letter. The first clue that it's part of a mass mailing is the fact that you've sent a letter to an outlet that is obviously inappropriate.

Compare the following two approaches to an actual pitch letter lead paragraph. If you were an editor, which one would hook you?

Version 1: Dr. John Smith, former director of the National Cancer Institute's $20 million "Designer Foods" program, believes you can be what you eat.

Version 2: An expert on foods that prevent or cure disease will be in New York next week to share with editors the latest research on this topic and how it will affect consumers.

Version 1 is good. But the letter took nearly two pages to get to the point, which was that the scientist would be in New York City to meet with editors individually the following week. Version 2 says "here's why I'm contacting you" quickly while also communicating the topic.

Use Clear, Clean Language

Avoid buzzwords (like "designer foods" in the preceding example) or industry jargon, because your reader might not understand it. Also edit out unnecessary or redundant language. The "grammar checker" feature of your word processing software can help with that.

Using clean language also helps you keep your letter to one page. Busy people won't read more than that, especially considering your letter is unsolicited. If an editor is interested in more information, he or she will read the background material you've attached that goes into greater detail about the topic or any of the concepts you've presented in your letter.

Get Familiar with the Media Outlet

A recent survey of television newsrooms by D S Simon Productions revealed that in the opinion of those surveyed, only one-third of the public relations people pitching a TV news program are knowledgeable about that program.

Give yourself a distinct advantage in this competitive arena by becoming familiar with the media outlet you're pitching, whether it's a local TV newsroom or a national magazine. That means studying a few back issues of the magazine you're targeting, or watching several days worth of the TV talk show you'd like to appear on as a guest. Make sure you communicate in your letter that you've done this by showing, rather than telling, that you're familiar with their needs. With magazines, note in your letter which section in the magazine you think your article idea is best suited for. Let the talk show producer know you're familiar with the format with an appropriate statement, such as "I've noticed that your hosts enjoy taking opposite sides on a controversial topic, and this topic is ideal for that." There are a number of ways you can communicate your familiarity so if you've done your homework, prove it, and move a step ahead of your competition.

When you're sending a personalized letter via mail merge to a large category of publications (food editors at daily newspapers in the top 50 markets, for example), include a reference that indicates that you are familiar with the general editorial needs of the category. For example, "Most newspaper food sections are interested in information on trends in home food preparation, and a well-researched article on that topic should include the latest in high-tech stoves" accomplishes that objective in that pitching situation.

Support Your Statements

Facts, figures, research, and statistics help you prove your point. You don't need research or numbers from your own organization. It can come from almost anywhere as long as you provide source attribution. And thanks to the Internet, it's a lot easier to get this kind of information than it used to be.

Use data to support a need for the information you're offering. If you're pitching a "how-to" segment, search for statistics proving how many people don't know how to do what you're going to teach them through an article or interview. ("According to the National Association of Hardware Stores, there has been a sharp increase in the sales of sophisticated power tools.

At the same time, the Association of Emergency Room Physicians reports a marked increase in injuries caused by power tools. At Joe's Hardware, we hope to reduce the number of emergency room visits by offering your readers six power tool safety tips.") Even if you did a little "armchair" research ("I spoke with a handful of my neighbors who were not aware that there are natural alternatives to chemicals used to treat their lawns"), go ahead and include it.

If you're making claims about your product or service, support your claims with persuasive facts. If your letter positions your product as "the best," answer the question, "Says who?" before it gets asked. Don't use superlatives you can't support.

Provide Other Information Sources

Imagine yourself in the shoes of the editor or talk show producer considering your story idea. Who else would you need to interview to present a well-rounded story? Provide contact information for those additional sources.

This is particularly important if your story can't be told completely without an interview with an end user—a customer. As the *Wall Street Journal* illustrates every day in countless articles that start with a personal anecdote, reporters need to put a "face" on a story. When you help them do that by leading them to customers or others, you're closer to closing your media sale.

Other resources to offer a reporter in a letter include trade associations, authors of books on the topic and others in your field.

Give Credentials and Background

If you want to be interviewed for the story, state why you are a good source of information. If you want to *write* the article, state why you are the best person to write it. Mention where you've been published before, even if it was an editorial in the local weekly newspaper. If you want to be interviewed on TV or radio, summarize your broadcast interview experience if you've been interviewed before. A reporter needs to know that you are a solid source of information, so provide that reassurance.

It is often appropriate or necessary to attach appropriate background information to the pitch letter. This is most often a press kit, press release, fact sheet, backgrounder, or sales literature. Sometimes it's even a product sample. If you are including background information, make a reference to it and why you've included it.

Knowing Who Does What Next

Reporters, editors, and producers are just like us—they're busy people with good intentions, short attention spans, and memories that could use a little help. That's why you should follow up your letter with a phone call to remind the recipient of your great story idea, determine interest, and ask what other information you can provide to help them make a decision or to pursue the story. Say you will do that in your last paragraph—"I will call in the next ten days to determine your interest and answer any questions."

If you expect the recipient to take the next step—"Please call me at your convenience to discuss this idea"—then say it. Omitting this important final point—who is responsible for the next step in this communication process—gives the recipient an excuse to do nothing with your idea, and that's not what you want to have happen.

Getting Feedback

After you've written the best letter you can, ask someone you trust to review it as if he or she was an editor or reporter. Does it get her interested? Does he have any important questions that should be addressed in the letter, but aren't? What about suggestions for improvements? Feedback is almost always useful.

How to Find Supporting Data

Need industry statistics or other data to support your pitch but don't have any? Never fear, the Internet is here! Library searches for statistics that used to take hours—even days—can now be accomplished in a fraction of the time with a well-worded Internet search. If, for example, you need to find out whether people really do cut themselves a lot when slicing bagels, type in "bagel injuries" on a search engine and find a site with a quote from a *New York Times* article saying that "bagels are the most dangerous food in the nation." What a great lead that would make for a pitch letter! Tap into industry associations as well. Many post data on their Web sites. If that doesn't yield anything, call an association's public relations department and ask for help.

Using a Pitch Letter to Market Your Own Articles

Although you can use pitch letters for nearly any part of your publicity plan, one of the best ways to use one is to pitch your own ideas for a bylined article, discussed in Chapter 10.

Understand Which Types of Articles You Can Pitch

Grab the nearest trade magazine and flip through it. You'll see many types of articles with a byline—an author credit. You are in a position to write only a few of these types. You won't be writing a category round-up or a question-and-answer piece. You probably won't write a feature article, either. You are most likely to write a "how-to," "self-help," "service," or "case history" article. These are what trade magazines need from you the most.

> You are most likely to write a "how-to," "self-help," "service," or "case history" article.

- A "how-to" article tells the reader how to do something better: "How to select a law firm."
- A "self-help" article is similar to a "how-to" piece because it, too, tells how to do something better, but it focuses on human behavior or psychology topics: "Six ways to tell if your daughter has an eating disorder."
- A "service" article gives the reader a range of choices that helps him or her make a better decision: "Moving your business? The ten most manufacturing-friendly cities in the country."
- A "case history" uses a problem/solution format, focusing on a particular company's problem while showcasing another company's solution: "New strapping technology lets newspaper publisher get papers out the door in less time for less money."

How-to articles and case histories are the types most in demand from companies. At the time of this writing, for example, an editor for the online magazine *Signindustry.com* reports in a media newsletter that the publication is looking for both types: "For a series of case studies, I'm looking for unique sign projects—e.g., the restoration of the Paramount Theater marquee in New York City's Times Square. I'm also looking for how-to type articles about fiber optics signs, electric signs, flexible face signs, and awnings that cover techniques, new products, technologies, trends, etc." This is a great opportunity for a manufacturer or installer of these products to get free media exposure that can be leveraged with customers and prospects. Similarly, *Bank Marketing Magazine* is "looking for an expert who can write an approximately 1,250-word article about the latest trend(s) in the marketing of financial trusts." Trade magazines want to hear from you.

If you're too intimidated to write an article yourself (see Chapter 10), you can still reap the benefits of this exposure by hiring a ghostwriter who will transform your knowledge and expertise into a polished product. Similarly, an outside writer can do the interviewing and writing necessary for a case history article. Writers are usually not as expensive as the other specialists you might work with in your business, including lawyers and accountants.

Find an Idea

The article-writing process begins with an idea. What's yours? Flipping through a few back issues of the magazine you're targeting is certain to inspire you. Go online to the publication Web sites and review their editorial calendars (these are usually identified with an icon or included in the section with advertising information). Targeting a Web site or e-zine? The process works the same way. Whether you want your article to appear in a trade magazine, a local business monthly, or a content-heavy Web site, study what each uses and let that guide your brainstorming process.

Bringing a few colleagues into the brainstorming process can help. Ask them, "What does this company do better than anyone else, and how can we turn this into a magazine article?" Or ask them, "What article did you read lately that made you think, 'We could have written that!'" (You can pitch it to a competing magazine.)

Explore ideas you can generate around your unique selling proposition—you're already trumpeting this in your marketing materials, right? But don't let this concept of honing in on what you do best lead you to write an article about how fabulous your company is. There's no market for that article outside your employee newsletter because learning how great you are doesn't help anyone else sell more products, save money, or do a job better. Instead, use your unique selling proposition to stimulate ideas for ways that you can show, rather than tell, that your company is exceptionally knowledgeable, experienced, or competent. Let your service-oriented article suggest more subtly that your company is a trusted resource.

Consider a "lessons learned" article; magazines like to hear from people who have faced hardship and learned from it. Has your company overcome adversity in a way that might help others? There's an article in that "we survived" a hurricane/bankruptcy/loss of a leader/flood/scandal story. This can be harder to write because it often involves admitting that your company made mistakes, but it can also be a powerful testimonial to the quality of your product, service, and staff.

What advice can you offer in an article? Can you tell potential customers how to select a specific product or service? Can you tell them how to do something faster, smarter, or better? Do this, and do it in a way that says, simply, "Here's what our company has learned on this topic. We hope it will help your company, too."

You must also find the "angle" behind the idea. An article about "kiosks" is just an idea; an article for a banking magazine about how kiosks can be used to train customers for online banking is an idea with an angle. An article about trade show exhibits is an idea; an article about ten ways to design your exhibit so it generates more solid sales leads is an idea with an angle. Your pitch letter needs to be specific about your angle for an article.

Determine Whether There Is a Market for Your Idea

Never pitch an article until you determine whether there's a market for it. You must have a confirmed market—an interested publication—in mind before you can write because your article must reflect that publication's style and the interests of its readers. This is worth repeating: Do not write your article until you make certain a publication is interested. Otherwise, you will waste time and money, as one small business owner did recently. She hired a fledgling writer to "write and place an article about the company," but the writer was having trouble interesting a publication. That's because the article wasn't written for a specific magazine. Each publication has its own needs and style. You must cater to them individually.

How do you find out if there's a market for your article idea? You ask. The simplest way to do this is to query the editor on the telephone, but most people aren't comfortable doing this. A phone call to say, "Here's my idea, are you interested?" is comparable to a cold sales call, and most people would rather shop for clothes with a teenager than make sales calls. But pitching on the telephone saves time. The secret to success is practicing your pitch ahead of time to make sure it sounds appealing and to the point. Present a one- to two-sentence summary and offer to send a more detailed letter if the editor finds the idea intriguing. A phone pitch for an article for *Consultants News* about cold-calling might be: "Hi, my name is Georgia Brown. I'm a sales consultant with a record-breaking track record, and I would like to write an article for your readers about how they can boost their consulting businesses by using more successful cold-calling techniques. Would you be interested in seeing more information on this article idea?"

Sometimes, the editor will want to discuss the idea in greater detail on the phone. Just as often, though, she will ask the caller to expand on the idea in writing, and send it to her with background information. But when she says, "That doesn't sound right for us," never, *ever* argue with her. It is her job to know what's best for her publication and readers. It is arrogant of anyone else to think that he or she knows more than the editor does about the relevance of the article idea. Unfortunately, maybe the article *is* perfect for her readers, but it wasn't presented it in a way that allowed the editor to see that.

Pitch Your Idea for the Article

You can send your pitch letter for your proposed article via e-mail or snail mail. Many people prefer e-mail because of the potential for instant

Cold Feet on the Phone?

If you're too uncomfortable pitching on the phone, you can use a short e-mail that does the same thing, in the same words. Get the editor's e-mail address and send a quick note that says, here's my idea, would you like more information on it? If you're lucky, you'll get a response back within 24 hours. If you're unlucky, you won't get a response at all. Don't interpret that as a "no." Interpret it as a "maybe," and move on to the next step, which is to write and submit a pitch letter that offers more detail than your short e-mail note.

Publicity Visuals

Some publicity documents can be supported and enhanced by visuals such as charts or graphs, but not all need them. First, decide whether a chart or graph is appropriate. If it is, give a great deal of attention to how you present the information in that format so that it supports, rather than confuses, your message. For tips on which chart or graph format to use, turn to the advice built into Microsoft Power-Point. As you scan the types you can create—bar, line, or pie, for example—the description box on each tells you whether the chart is appropriate for the information you're presenting. After you've selected the best format for your data, work to simplify the visual by eliminating unnecessary information and focusing on what's most important—just a few pieces of data instead of a dozen.

gratification. But a response *can* take up to four weeks. If you don't hear back within a month, follow up on the telephone or via e-mail and ask about the status of the idea. Is he interested? Can you provide anything else that will help him decide? Sometimes it's necessary to add a deadline, as in, "If I don't hear back from you by May 15, I'll assume you're not interested and I'll take the idea to another (insert industry here) magazine."

If your idea is rejected, submit it elsewhere. Don't just type in a new name and address, though. Reevaluate your pitch in case there was vague language that made it hard to understand your idea or other confusing information. Even if you still think it's perfect, retool it to reflect the needs of the new magazine you're pitching. It's important that your letter target a specific publication. In addition, anything you can do to communicate that you understand the magazine you're writing to will bring you closer to success.

Because in most cases you will be pitching your ideas to trade magazines and small local business magazines, it is likely that as long as you communicate your idea clearly, you will have a decent success rate. Trade magazines rely on *free* input from experts like you to meet their editorial needs. Every article you write for an understaffed trade magazine is an article the editor doesn't have to assign internally. If you're pitching newsstand magazines such as *Entrepreneur* or *Popular Science*, prepare yourself to be frustrated. They are inundated with article ideas from professional writers as well as content experts like you, so they can afford to be very selective. With few exceptions, bylines in the best-known magazines will be those of professional writers.

Trade magazines are open-minded about outside submissions, so do consider submitting articles for publication. Suggest a focused idea and deliver an article on time and in the right format, and you have a very good chance of seeing your name in print.

➤ **Chapter 10**

Writing Articles and Case Histories

PART THREE   ELEMENTS OF A PUBLICITY PLAN

■ CHAPTER 7 Writing a Killer Press Release ■ CHAPTER 8 Sample Press Releases ■ CHAPTER 9 Writing Pitch Letters That Get Results ■ CHAPTER 10 Writing Articles and Case Histories ■ CHAPTER 11 Writing a Column, Op-Ed Piece, or Public Service Announcement (PSA) ■ CHAPTER 12 Preparing a Press Kit ■ CHAPTER 13 Calling a Press Conference ■ CHAPTER 14 Planning a Special Event ■ CHAPTER 15 Sponsoring an Event, Group, or Person

Utilizing Even a Little Bit of Writing Skill

Most books on "do-it-yourself publicity" ignore the enormous potential in bylined articles and case histories, probably because they require more writing skill than the other publicity tools. But that shouldn't stop you from writing and placing articles that showcase your expertise or products. Magazine editors don't expect perfection from people who don't write for a living, so they plan on editing articles coming from topic experts who are not professional writers. And capturing your thoughts in a logical, readable way is easier than you think, especially with the tips offered in this chapter. Keep in mind that entire books are written about writing magazine articles, so it's impossible to tell you everything you need to know in a single chapter. This chapter, though, will give you enough information to write the type of article you'll be submitting. See Chapter 9 for more information on writing articles; specifically, on writing a pitch letter for your article idea.

Beginning with a Vision

This section could also be titled, "Be Careful of What You Wish For, It Might Come True." It's one thing to propose an article . . . it's another thing to have to write 1,200 or 1,500 words about your idea! But if you like putting puzzles together, this is where the fun begins.

You have the assignment: The editor of the most important trade magazine for your target audience has asked you to write a 1,500-word article in 30 days (or more, rarely less). How do you start the article writing process? By focusing.

What Do You Want to Accomplish?

Begin by thinking about what you want the article to accomplish. What is your goal? What is the point of writing this article? You might want the article to help generate new customers. Or you might want to correct misconceptions in the industry that make it difficult for you to do business. Maybe you need to position your company as an industry leader. Once you know what you expect from the publication of your article, it will be easier for you to determine what should—and shouldn't—be included in your article.

How Can You Encapsulate the Idea?

When your goal is clear, get more focus by writing a one-paragraph summary of the article. This information might already be in your pitch letter (see Chapter 9). If it is, pull it out and put it on a separate sheet of paper. If it isn't, write it now. For the article idea mentioned in the previous chapter for *Consultants News* on cold-calling techniques, the one paragraph summary is: "This article will help professional consultants understand the importance of cold-calling to generating new business for their firms. Readers will learn five specific techniques for turning a cold-call into a warm call, and will feel more confident the next time they pick up the phone to call a prospect."

Once you have an overview of what you want your article to do for the readers, you are better able to begin determining whether you have enough information to write it—or what information is missing and needs to be gathered.

Outlining the Article

Move from your article summary to an outline that allows you to organize your thoughts and determine if you need to do additional research. Start the outline with your idea for how to begin the article—your idea for the lead (sometimes spelled "lede") paragraph.

Using your own logic as a guide, list subsequent concepts in the order they will appear in the article. Since it's likely you will be writing a "how-to" article offering both information and advice, your outline might follow a "do this, then do this" format.

The outline for a case history—a "my customer's problem and how I solved it" kind of article—will be different from what you write for a regular article. Most case histories can rely on the following broad generic outline.

Reviewing Some Writers' Guidelines

Let's assume you've interested an editor in your article. That editor will expect you to deliver an article that matches the publication's tone and style. You do that by studying back issues of the magazine. You also do that by reading the magazine's writers' guidelines. These documents, available from most publications, explain the types of articles they want to receive from outsiders, how they want them written, the length requirements (usually in terms of word counts), and so on. They're often available on the magazines' Web sites; if not, just phone the publication's editorial department and ask an assistant to fax the guidelines to you.

In addition, talk to the editor about your article idea once you're given the go-ahead. Ask about the mechanics—how long does the article need to be, what's the deadline, do they need photos or other artwork—but also ask the editor for guidance on what he or she is expecting.

- A statement of the problem ("Acme Manufacturing needed a faster way to install kanooter valves")
- An explanation of the options available
- A description of the solution chosen and why
- A review of how the solution works, the cost involved and how it was used (including problems it created and how they were solved)
- A summary that emphasizes the outcome and how everybody is now much happier

If your company has learned lessons about providing good customer service by first providing bad customer service, the outline for your article, "Five ways to use bad customer service to alienate your best accounts," might look like this:

Lead

The lead is an anecdote about how my best customer called me personally to cancel his account, saying my company's exceptionally bad customer service was the reason.

Body

The body is made up of the following:

This was my "wake up call"; I knew we had problems, but I hadn't allowed myself to accept how bad they really were. I had to address the problem: I called other customers and quizzed them about our service.

Using this research, we completely revamped our customer service department; here's what it looks like now.

Here's what we did wrong; don't make the same mistakes we did:

- Make sure customer service is the last option on your automated phone system ("For customer service, press 23"). Better yet, make sure they get a busy signal before they even get that far.
- Once they punch the right number into their keypads, keep your customers on hold for a long time.
- Encourage your customer service representatives to be argumentative.

Who says the customer's always right?

- Don't train your customer service representatives on the products you sell. The less they know, the easier it is for them to play dumb with angry customers.
- Don't empower your customer service representatives to solve problems quickly.

Transition out of the "bad tips" by describing how much better we're doing now; refer to high scores on a recent customer satisfaction survey.

Conclusion

The conclusion is as follows: looking back, that angry call from my best customer was the best thing that ever happened to my business. I hope it has helped yours, too.

Doing Research—Moving from Outline to Article

When your outline is finished, review it to determine the information you have to go looking for. The writer of the customer service article outlined above, for example, might need to ask a colleague for transcripts of conversations with clients about their customer service experiences so she can quote from them. Or she might need to do a telephone interview with the company's new customer service consultant for a quotable summary of the initial problem areas.

If you're writing a case history (an article that uses a problem/solution format, focusing on a particular company's problem while showcasing another company's solution), you will have to do more research, interviewing several people and taking careful notes that record those interviews. (It's okay to use a tape recorder.) Many times, a case history writer starts out with just a general understanding of the customer's problem and the resulting solution, and has to fill in

How to Interview Someone

You've been given the job of interviewing a colleague for information you'll use to write a press release. You can use the press release writing worksheet in Appendix A, but chances are, you'll still have to come up with a few questions of your own to ask so you get all the information you need for your assignment. Begin by avoiding "yes" or "no" questions. You want to use questions that generate a lot of information so you begin to know the topic almost as well as your source. Instead, focus on open-ended questions related to your press release topic, such as "Tell me what's behind this product." "Where did the idea come from?" Ask about interesting stories or anecdotes connected to the announcement. Inquire about research or studies that support this news or development. Be brave and ask about the politics involved.

Use Quotes Effectively

Most press releases can be enhanced by an interesting quote from the company's leader or the person behind the news being announced. But many beginning release writers make the mistake of using that powerful space between the quotation marks to just repeat information already presented in the body of the release. Mollie Katz, a senior associate at Burness Communications, a public relations firm that works with nonprofit organizations, cautions press release writers to use a quote to express an opinion, not repeat a fact. "Save the quote for something more interpretive," she says, "so it has greater impact." Katz adds that colorful, provocative quotes are more likely to be used in news stories than factual, but uninteresting, statements. "You'll know you've done it right when you see your quote used word-for-word in quotation marks in the news article," she adds.

all the blanks in between.

Case history research involves learning as much as possible about the product or application used by the customer. If you know the product inside and out already, you're a big step ahead in the research process. But you will also need to interview key customer staff about the problem (going on-site for this is preferred, but not required) and the process staffers went through to find an acceptable solution. It might involve interviewing product specialists within your company to learn more about why your product or application was the ideal solution for the customer's situation, or to talk about initial failures your company might have had with this specific situation before finding the right solution. It means asking questions that will get you the information you need to provide a good description of the obstacles everyone overcame to solve the problem.

It also means asking questions that will provide the balance editors look for in a case history. They don't like stories that shout, "We're the greatest!" Instead, they look for articles with a certain amount of drama or tension—articles that suggest that the problem was harder to solve than you first thought, or that it should have been straightforward but wasn't, and so on. If your case history doesn't address barriers to improvements, it will be less appealing than one that does.

Whether you're writing a bylined article or a case history, make a list of the missing pieces and indicate what you need to do to get those pieces. Who has the report you will cite? Where will you find the statistics you need? Who will you interview? Few of us can write articles without some kind of additional research, even though it might just be checking the spelling of somebody's name. The time to discover what research is needed is when you're fleshing out the article. You want all the information in place when you begin to write. Use the article writing worksheet in Appendix A to help you organize your thoughts and shape the direction of your article.

Organizing Your Information and Writing the Article

You have an idea with an angle, you've pitched it and an editor is interested, you've read the magazine's writers' guidelines and received additional input from the editor, and you've outlined the article. Now it's time to start organizing your information and writing.

Put your notes and research into the format that works best for you. Schoolchildren assemble school reports by putting their research on note cards, then arranging the structure of the report by grouping note cards together. If it works for them, it can work for us! If you type your notes while interviewing people, print them and use a highlighter to mark the blocks of information you plan to use in the article. In certain situations, it can help you to mark the chunks of text with a shorthand, such as "intro" or "wrap-up," so you can identify what you're looking for more quickly as you wade through the writing process. If you write reports or proposals, you probably have an information organizational system that works for you already—apply it to this process, too.

Crafting a Compelling First Paragraph

The beginning of this chapter observes that entire books are written about how to write articles. There are books written about how to begin and end articles, too. But these books are written for serious writers, people who want to get paid regularly to write magazine articles with well-crafted first paragraphs. As an occasional article writer for trade magazines, here's all you need to know: Your opening paragraph has to draw people into the article.

The best type of opening paragraph is the one that's appropriate for the magazine you're writing for. You discover what's appropriate by studying similar article types in that magazine, and uncovering a pattern, or what's common, among all of the first paragraphs.

For example, most of the *Wall Street Journal's* front page features start with an anecdote or personal story that shows how the issue being reported on affects one individual—who could be you or me. A recent story about bioterrorism titled "The Military, Microbes and Secret Tests Using the U.S. Public" began this way: "Fifty-one years ago, Edward J. Nevin checked into a San Francisco hospital, complaining of chills, fever and general malaise.

Three weeks later, the 75-year-old retired pipe fitter was dead, the victim of what doctors said was an infection of the bacterium Serratia marcescens." The article went on to explain that Nevin was the victim of a secret Army experiment to see what might happen in a real germ-warfare attack.

Obviously, if you had an assignment to write an article for the *Journal*, you would make sure you started it with an anecdote. Otherwise, it would be rejected. On the other hand, *Presentations*, a trade magazine that accepts submissions from readers, began an article by a reader in this straightforward manner: "If you're looking for ways to improve the appearance of your PowerPoint presentation, take a closer look at the charts you are using." It's a nice summary of what you'll expect to find in the article written by a woman who creates custom-designed presentations. It tells you what to expect, and that helps you decide if you should read on. If you were writing for that publication, you would consider using a similar approach for your lead.

Your challenge is to intrigue the reader with that opening paragraph in the same way you captured the attention of the editor when you sent a pitch letter proposing the article idea. Quite often, in fact, pitch letter leads are suitable as article leads. The lead for a letter sent to *American Painting Contractor*, "The most successful business owners in any community often have celebrity status achieved through media visibility. This prominence in the local newspaper, on radio talk shows, or on TV news generates greater

Ways to Begin an Article

You can begin your article in a number of ways. Your best approach is to study the magazine you're writing for and look for article-opening trends, but here are a few different approaches to get you thinking: an anecdote or story that puts a face on the subject being discussed, an interesting quote from someone interviewed for the article, a straightforward summary of what the article's about, or a question that summarizes the article's direction (such as, "What's the biggest problem facing your business today?").

Keep in mind that the best one for your article is one that matches the magazine's style and the information you have available.

awareness for the business's products or services—and that exposure leads to business success," followed the anecdote used to open the article.

Work to avoid ho-hum or self-serving leads. Here's a bad lead for the article described above for the painting magazine: "I know a lot about publicity and I'm going to share it with you in this article." Nobody cares how much the writer knows about anything. What the readers of this magazine care about is whether what the writer knows will help them do their job better, faster, or smarter, or whether it will help them sell more products, make more money, and so on.

Don't leap immediately to the content of the article, either. "Here are six ways to reduce overhead in the shipping department," as a lead gets to the point a little too quickly. First explain why readers need to know why they should reduce overhead in the shipping department. Consider this approach, which leads up to your six tips in a way that's informative but still to the point (and, by the way, is total fiction): "A recent survey by *Shipping Room News* reveals that 85 percent of the nation's shipping department managers do not shop around for the best prices on equipment or supplies, preferring instead to purchase from vendors with a long history with the company." If you're a shipping department manager reading this lead in a trade magazine, you might wonder if you've been making a mistake and could save your company money. And gee, here are six ways for you to begin that process!

As you write your opening paragraph, don't worry about whether it's Pulitzer Prize–winning material. Instead, focus on capturing readers' attention with an interesting lead, telling readers something about what they will expect to find in your article, and making certain that your lead uses an approach favored by the editor of that magazine.

Making Sure the Article Flows and Transitions Well

With your lead in place, you write the rest of the article working from your outline. There are many, many ways to construct a magazine article, but for bylined trade magazine articles, the easiest and most appropriate format is called the "building block." This is the format most often used for instructional articles. It starts with the simplest elements, then adds more complex material.

A case history, on the other hand, should use the "cause and effect" format. Typically, the "cause" is the customer's problem while the "effect" is the solution presented by your company. This "if A, then B" approach provides you with a framework that helps you determine how and where to use the information you've gathered for the article. Using the appropriate format or framework is important because your thoughts, advice, facts, quoted information, and all other content must flow logically in your article.

Writers also achieve "flow" through transitional sentences that link one paragraph to another. A lack of these transitions is a common problem of beginning writers; it's a problem reminiscent of the friend everyone has who talks without using transitions. She leaps from topic to topic, but as you listen, and don't hear a connection between the two subjects, you're forced to say, "You just lost me. What does this have to do with that?" The friend explains the transition that was in her mind, but not in her words.

As you write, remember that readers don't know as much about your subject as you do, so you will need to hold their hands through the process, showing them how one great thought connects to the next one. Study an article written by a staff writer for the magazine you're targeting, looking for transitions from paragraph to paragraph and from section to section. You'll see that the last sentence of one paragraph almost introduces the first sentence of the next paragraph. Here's an example from a sample case history by public relations writer Bob DeRosa. DeRosa's transitions are underlined.

> Remember that readers don't know as much about your subject as you do, so you will need to hold their hands through the process.

"Impurities in electrical power are like impurities in drinking water—they can sicken and even kill the 'consumer.' <u>Power that's 'dirty' with surges, spikes, noise, and other transients can negatively affect computers and other chip-driven devices</u>, as well as any other appliance it flows through.

"For the average business, <u>dirty power causes erratic operation</u> of computer networks, telephone systems and other appliances, sometimes creating downtime. For a hospital using sensitive telemetry equipment like heart monitors and testing equipment like EEGs (electroencephalographs) and EKGs (electrocardiographs), it can be disastrous, causing false readings, distorted waveforms, and sometimes, complete equipment failure."

DeRosa presented the general concept of "dirty power" in one paragraph, then transitioned to the next paragraph by explaining the problems dirty power can cause in hospitals.

After writing your article, read through it carefully for these transitional sentences. As you do so, remember that you know more about the subject than the person reading your article—that's why, after all, they're reading your article—so look for sections where you might have forgotten to explain the logic between thoughts.

Concluding Your Article

Just as your article needs a solid beginning, it needs a solid conclusion, too. Your last paragraph should tie everything up for the reader into a nice package. And just as there are a number of ways to begin an article, there are also a number of ways to close it, too.

In general, one of the best ways to conclude an article is by linking it back to your introduction. The conclusion of the *Wall Street Journal* article on bioterrorism mentioned above uses this approach. It starts with the story of Edward Nevin, whose death was caused by a germ-warfare experiment, and ends like so:

"Partly as a result of Mr. Nevin's death, says Lucien Canton, director of San Francisco's emergency services, 'one thing we now know is that it takes an awful lot of stuff to produce casualties, especially in a place like San Francisco that always has a stiff breeze.'"

The *Journal* article actually combines two ending techniques—it links the conclusion to the beginning, and it ends with a quote. Using an interesting quote to wrap-up your article is effective with a case history, especially if the article begins with a quote. If you use a quote for your conclusion, make sure it makes the right statement. You want it to sum up the message of your article. If the point of your case history is that your product saved your client a great deal of time or money, your concluding quote should be those words in your customer's mouth.

It's (Almost) Done!

After writing the first draft of your article, use the "word count" feature of Microsoft Word software to make sure you've met the editor's length requirements. (On the top toolbar, click "Tools" then "Word Count" from the drop-down menu.) Do you need to add information, or, more typically, have you written too much? You can get rid of a lot of words by tightening up your sentences and removing repetitious thoughts, but sometimes you'll need to remove chunks of precious copy that you labored over.

Edit the Article

To edit, print your article double-spaced and grab a pen with dark ink. Reread your article carefully for clarity of thought. Imagine yourself as the typical reader of that magazine—would your article be easily understandable to someone with less knowledge of the subject than you? Many writers imagine they are writing for a particular friend or family member who doesn't know a lot about the topic. This helps them avoid industry jargon or buzzwords the individual might be unfamiliar with. It also helps you identify a lack of transitions or concepts that need additional explanation.

Sleep on It

After your first round of editing, sleep on it. Walk away from your article for at least a day to clear it out of your mind. Then look at it again. You are certain to spot awkward or vague language that you missed before.

Ask a Friend to Review It

Make your corrections and give the article to someone you trust to read and edit. Ask that person to look for an interesting lead, a logical flow of ideas, awkward language, and a conclusion that reflects the message of the article. Then graciously accept the suggestions offered by your volunteer editor. Review the suggestions carefully before incorporating them into your finished article. Are they changes that improve your article, or are they just changes? You might find that you've tapped into a colleague who really can help you fine-tune your article.

> **Chapter 11**

Writing a Column, Op-Ed Piece, or Public Service Announcement (PSA)

PART THREE ELEMENTS OF A PUBLICITY PLAN

■ CHAPTER 7 Writing a Killer Press Release ■ CHAPTER 8 Sample Press Releases ■ CHAPTER 9 Writing Pitch Letters That Get Results ■ CHAPTER 10 Writing Articles and Case Histories ■ **CHAPTER 11 Writing a Column, Op-Ed Piece, or Public Service Announcement (PSA)** ■ CHAPTER 12 Preparing a Press Kit ■ CHAPTER 13 Calling a Press Conference ■ CHAPTER 14 Planning a Special Event ■ CHAPTER 15 Sponsoring an Event, Group, or Person

Why Write a Column, Op-Ed Piece, or PSA?

Columns, opinions, and editorials (both known collectively as op-eds) are particularly useful tools for influencing or shaping opinions of the general public and policymakers, while public service announcements (PSAs) can stimulate action. Publishing a column or op-ed also can showcase your expertise or bring valuable free exposure to your business; placing a PSA, primarily a tool used by nonprofit organizations, can educate your target audience.

Above All Else, Be Stylish

Journalists can recognize a bad press release pretty quickly. It's the one that capitalizes most of the words in the first few sentences. Overcapitalization means the release was probably written by an advertising copywriter who might know lots about the subject, but isn't an expert in *understatement*. All those capital letters will get the release tossed out pretty quickly, so save yourself that aggravation by using a journalistic style when writing press materials. Buy a copy of *The Associated Press Stylebook and Libel Manual* (available in the reference section of most bookstores) and use it regularly for all your writing, not just your press materials. You'll learn that you should use initial capital letters on a person's title only when the title appears before the name (President John Mooney or John Mooney, president), when and how to abbreviate state names, and how to refer to advanced degrees when describing an individual's education. It will soon become your most valuable reference tool, and will probably even settle a few office disputes, too.

Fact Check Your Press Material

A *Wall Street Journal* reporter received a press release from a public relations firm that quoted industry statistics "proving" the growth in popularity of an unusual procedure offered by the firm's client, a plastic surgeon. The reporter called the source of the statistics, the American Society for Plastic Surgery, for verification and learned that the figures offered in the release did not apply to the procedure they were supporting. "We don't even track that procedure . . . ," a society spokesperson told the reporter.

This misrepresentation, explained by an agency staffer as "a typo," influenced the direction the reporter took with a story about the firm's client, *and* it was described in the resulting article as an example of what lengths some will go to generate publicity. The lesson for publicists and business owners alike is to *fact check, fact check, fact check.* Don't assume anyone else has done it already. If you've hired a publicist who uses statistics in a release—generally a good idea—ask that person to provide you with documentation. If you're doing your own research and writing, make sure you aren't putting a spin on the numbers that isn't valid—call the source of the information and verify that your interpretation will stand up to a call from a reporter or anyone else. Always present information you can stand by. If you don't, your reputation—and your business—could suffer.

Does It Cost Anything?

Writers usually ask, "How much will I be paid?" while business owners say, "Do I have to pay the magazine anything to print my column or op-ed piece?" That's because nonwriters are more likely to think in terms of the advertising value of that column, which, like all other publicity material, has far more credibility than a paid ad. Except in very rare situations, you don't pay a magazine to run your column. It's a reader service and they are grateful to be able to offer your expertise to readers. Most publications are willing to pay at least a nominal amount for your column—often as little as $10. Web sites are notorious for paying nothing, but that's okay—you're not writing for the money. You're writing for the exposure.

In a way, you are actually paid to write the column through the promotional biographical text that appears at the end of the column. Most media outlets that are willing

How to Get a Correction in the Media

Finally getting that publicity hit in a key magazine or in a local TV newscast can be pretty exciting—until you discover that the reporter made a mistake about your company. The glow of success quickly wears off and is replaced by the glow of anger. If the mistake is minor, forget about it. For major mistakes, you can do a few things to turn the situation around. First, calm down. You won't fix anything when you're annoyed. Next, if the mistake is on a television newscast, call the news department immediately. Explain the problem and ask them to update the report and air a correct version with the next newscast. When the mistake is in a print publication, write a friendly letter thanking the media outlet for airing news of your company. Then politely point out the error and ask if the magazine or newspaper can make note of the error in their next publication.

to run your column are also willing to run a short paragraph that describes your credentials, your business, and how to reach you.

What's a Column?

One dictionary defines a column as "any of a series of feature articles appearing regularly in a newspaper or magazine, by a particular writer or about a certain subject." Let's expand that definition by noting that unlike a news article, a column can express an *opinion*.

Some of the most popular newspaper columnists—Dave Barry, Molly Ivins, and Ellen Goodman, for example—are read coast to coast because people enjoy the columnists' perspectives or appreciate their opinions. But these writers could not incorporate their views or attitudes into news articles because opinions aren't appropriate in news coverage unless you're quoting *someone else* expressing an opinion. The job of a news story is to inform, not influence. But a column can do both.

Columns are designed to educate, and sometimes entertain, readers. Barry's columns are far more entertaining than they are useful, while the columns of syndicated personal finance columnist Michelle Singletary inform readers about important topics such as 401(k)s, but rarely generate belly laughs. And because these writers are columnists, not reporters, they

Valuable Knowledge

Jane Grant Tougas, a professional writer in Middletown, Ohio, advises writers to begin by asking themselves, "What knowledge do I have that is valuable to the readers of this magazine?" Tougas adds that we have to frame our knowledge in a way that makes it useful to readers. "You have to be clear about the issues of interest to the readers of the publication," she says. "Every industry has priorities and issues that come and go, and they all have hot topics. If you can tap into one of those, and how what you're doing or what you're selling makes the readers' lives faster, better, or cheaper, then you have a message they want to hear. Otherwise, your column is nothing but an ad and it won't be used by the editor," she cautions.

can incorporate their personal experiences into their writing in a very direct way, providing advice or offering guidance. If Singletary thinks every employed person should put money into a 401(k) before paying the rent, she can say so in her column. A reporter cannot.

That's one reason we read columns—for advice and information we can apply to our lives. It's the same reason columnists who write about a particular topic—technology, cars, or parenting, for example—must have the credentials to do so. (General newspaper columnists who write about everything from raking leaves to things that annoy them need journalism credentials.) If you know a lot about something and can prove it, then you might have the right credentials to write an informative column.

A column, unlike a news story, shares the opinions and knowledge of one person—the writer. And because you control the content of the column, it can be a more powerful communications vehicle for your organization than a news article that quotes you and others.

What's in It for You?

Writing a regular column in a media outlet that reaches your target audience is a surefire way to establish yourself as an expert and a local celebrity (and celebrity status brings all kinds of unexpected opportunities to a business). A locally published or Internet column can be leveraged in a number of ways for marketing purposes. The status that comes with name recognition, for example, brings invitations to speak before a wide range of local or regional audiences. And if you discover you enjoy writing, a local column can be the launch pad for a more widely published column through self-syndication—if it makes sense for your business.

Column Frequency

Columns come in two types—a one-time deal, or a "regular" column that focuses on a specific topic. One-time columns are less common than regular columns, which can appear weekly or monthly, depending on the publication, its space availability, and its reader interests. Frequency can also be determined by how much *you* have to say about your subject and how much time you can devote to writing your column. Can you come up with fifty-two ideas for a weekly column on gardening as a way to promote your garden center? Or would you be better off negotiating for a monthly column?

Who Uses Columns?

Web sites, daily and weekly newspapers, and trade and consumer magazines all use columns written by people like us. Bosshotrods.com is so hungry for online columnists that it will send tape recorders to "industry pros" so they don't have to write out their thoughts—they just speak them into the recorder and send the tape back to the magazine for transcription. MacSpeedZone.com is looking for "talented and enthusiastic people to write columns on our sites on a one-time or ongoing basis." Even the *Denver Post* is seeking columnists from the community for its "Colorado Voices" column.

It's easier to secure a column assignment with a weekly newspaper than with a daily, so start there first if your topic addresses a consumer audience. (National consumer magazines usually work only with nationally known experts with household names.) Local weekly and monthly business publications are usually hungry for content that will serve readers at no cost to the editorial budget, making them a likely target for consultants and local entrepreneurs looking to share wisdom. Trade magazines and topic-specific Web sites are markets for certain business and industry topics. A restaurant trade magazine, for example, might feature a regular column on the human resource aspects of running a restaurant.

Because a column expresses your opinion, it will most likely be used on the editorial page of a weekly paper. With space dedicated to opinions from readers either as columns or letters, weeklies welcome input from the community. "Weekly newspapers are always looking for ways to feature local people and to fill their pages with good, local information," explains Bob Matson, executive editor of Messenger-Post Newspapers, a nine-paper chain in Western New York. "We welcome columns that are well-written and thought-out."

Your Regular Column Topic: Sharing What You Know

A one-time column requires you to know 500 to 800 words about a topic. A regular column requires a lot more know-how, but for that same

> It's easier to secure a column assignment with a weekly newspaper than with a daily, so start there first if your topic addresses a consumer audience.

reason it provides a rewarding experience for someone who wants to teach through writing. Sharing what you know—what you've learned from experience, what you know others should avoid—can be both personally fulfilling and good for business.

So what is it that you know a lot about that others will want to know, too? And what's not already being covered in the media served by your target audience? Newspapers are interested in service pieces that touch many readers and tell them how to do something better. Money, health, careers, and family are perennial topics. But what's hot today that you can write often about? The owner of a city's only independent record store could write a music column for a daily or weekly newspaper. A handyman could write a homeowners how-to column—so could a hardware store owner. An accountant specializing in serving small businesses could write a column on small-business finance topics for the local monthly business magazine. A manufacturer could write a column about small-business management for an industry trade magazine or for a local business publication.

While most daily newspaper columns are written by staff or syndicated journalists, there are noteworthy exceptions. A registered dietician can write a nutrition column, a realtor can answer reader questions in the weekend "home" section, and a local technology guru can pen a computer technology question-and-answer column. Opportunities abound if you can (a) verify that you have the knowledge to write a regular column, (b) prove there's a need for the column or a strong reader interest in the topic, and (c) make a good pitch to the publication or Web site's editor.

Placing a Column

You "place," or secure, or sell a column in the same way you place the bylined article or case history we discussed in Chapter 10: You make a compelling case for your topic and your expertise. Here's what you need to include in the package that will sell your column idea:

- A solid pitch letter (see Chapter 9) that proves readers will be interested in the column ("After your newspaper profiled my business, we received fifty phone calls and e-mails asking for advice" or "We receive about ten inquiries per day on this topic"),

- A short narrative biography that summarizes your experience with the topic (*not a resume*),
- A list of twelve to fifteen future column titles that represent what you'll write, and
- Your first three columns (you have to write a few columns as part of the sales process to prove you can do the job).

E-mail or mail this information to the appropriate editor at the publication (the section editor of a daily; the editor of a weekly newspaper, a trade magazine or a Web site), then follow up with a phone call two weeks later to explore interest.

Writing a Column

Write a column using the same approach outlined in Chapter 10 for writing articles: Be clear on the single message you want to communicate, outline your thoughts, write an interesting lead, and use your conclusion to wrap it all up into a neat package. As with all of your writing, edit your writing over and over again until it is clear and readable.

Keep in mind that unlike bylined articles, your column can let more of your personal voice show through. Just remember that as you share advice and information, you need to use a tone that is both friendly and humble—pompous or all-knowing won't fly, even if you are both.

Column length depends on the publication's requirements, but newspaper columns are no more than 650 words long. Figure out the length requirement of the publication you're pitching by calling and asking, or by counting the words in a column it's currently running. Remember to include your name, address, phone, and e-mail information at the top of each column you write.

Start small with your initial effort—don't pitch your first column idea to the "My Turn" section of *Newsweek*—and don't call Universal Press Syndicate for its writers' guidelines yet. Get some experience promoting your business and building your reputation as a local expert before taking your columns to the biggest markets.

What's an Op-Ed?

Op-eds—opinion pieces—are similar to columns but always appear on a publication's opinion page and are one-shot opportunities. Op-eds are short, biased articles written in the first-person style that express the writer's opinion on a current topic. They are usually written to influence public opinion and policymakers, and to stimulate change. All newspapers use op-eds and some trade magazines run them, too. Consumer magazines use them in the form of first-person essays, but many of these essays are designed to entertain or stimulate thinking rather than to influence opinions or initiate change.

Some businesses have no need to write and place op-eds, while others will find them to be one of the most valuable tools in their toolbox. They are widely used, for example, by nonprofit agencies. They certainly aren't limited to nonprofits, though. Business owners seeking to influence the outcome of proposed community initiatives or regulations, such as changing zoning restrictions, will want to write and place op-eds expressing their views on the issues.

The op-ed's purpose is to provide informed, thought-provoking, and educational commentary on an important and timely community issue.

The op-ed's purpose is to provide informed, thought-provoking, and educational commentary on an important and timely community issue.

Writing Your Op-Ed

As with all other forms of writing described in this book, begin by determining what single message you want to share. With room for just one point of view, you'd better be certain you know what it is. Your topic, and your opinion, should provoke discussion. With your message in mind, create an outline to follow when writing.

Op-ed length varies from 500 to 800 words, depending on the publication. The average length for a newspaper is 600 to 750 words—about three double-spaced pages. At first, this might seem like a lot of space to fill, but most people who feel passionately about an issue soon discover it's not nearly enough space to express their views. That is why it is so important to be focused when writing such a short piece. You'll need to use only the facts, figures, and information that make the greatest contribution to your case.

As with other articles, there is no hard and fast format or formula for op-ed writing. But beginning op-ed writers will do well to follow this general outline:

- Begin your op-ed by illustrating how the topic or issue affects readers,
- Follow with a statement that illustrates the broader scope of the issue ("Nationally, there were 32,061 fatalities in vehicle crashes in 1999, and the National Traffic Safety Council estimated 9,553 of those people would have survived if they had been buckled up"),
- Describe the problem and why it exists,
- Offer your solution to the problem and explain why it's the best option, and
- Conclude on a strong note, by repeating your message or with a call to action.

Avoid rhetoric and jargon. Keep your sentences and paragraphs short. Support your assertions with facts—don't make sweeping statements without the facts to back you up. Because you don't have much room to make your point, remember to focus, focus, focus.

Type your op-ed double-spaced with your name, company name, address, phone number, and e-mail address in the upper left corner of the

How to Begin Your Op-Ed

Because op-eds often address complex issues, it is wise to begin your piece with a one- or two-sentence vignette that puts a human face on your topic. If you're lobbying for a traffic light for the busy intersection near your business, begin with a description of an individual hurt in an accident because there was no light. Supporting a reduction of the county sales tax? Describe the person who will suffer most if it doesn't happen. Are you a pediatrician concerned about recent studies revealing that parents are lax about using seatbelts with children? Start your editorial with the story of a child who was seriously injured because he wasn't buckled in.

first page. Include a title and a byline ("By Mary Smith"), and two to three sentences of biographical information at the end of the article. Keep the biographical information brief and limited to your role as the writer of that editorial on that topic—it should suggest why you are qualified to address the topic.

Distributing Your Op-Ed

You might write your op-ed for a single magazine or a single newspaper, or for multiple newspapers. If you want to influence readers in a region—several counties, a part of the state, the entire state, or even the country—you can do this by sending your op-ed to non-competing newspapers. It works the same way with magazines—you can submit it to several as long as their circulations don't overlap.

Make an effort to send it to the proper editor. At a daily newspaper, it's the editorial page editor. At a weekly newspaper, it's the editorial page editor, if there is one, or the editor. At a trade magazine, it's the editor. Send it to the person by name (call the publication and ask who is responsible for selecting editorials) with a brief cover note that explains how to reach you.

Electronic submissions are easiest for editors because they don't require retyping (call to get the appropriate editor's e-mail address). When sending your op-ed via e-mail, attach the file, but also paste the text into the body of the e-mail message in case there are virus concerns or system compatibility problems. You can also send your op-ed via the mail or fax, but if you do, indicate whether you can send the file electronically if it's accepted for publication.

If you haven't heard from the editor in two weeks, follow up with an e-mail note or a phone call. If the issue is timely and can't wait two weeks, call before then. Read a sample op-ed in Appendix B.

What's a PSA?

Public service announcements—PSAs—are popular publicity tools for certain kinds of organizations because they do not need to be newsworthy. They are useful to nonprofit organizations or businesses that sponsor events that benefit nonprofits.

The FCC defines PSAs as "any announcement . . . for which no charge is made and which promotes programs, activities, or services of federal, state or local governments . . . or the programs, activities or services of non-profit organizations . . . and other announcements regarded as serving community interests." PSAs promote a specific social message aimed at increasing public awareness or having listeners take action about a specific issue. The most famous PSA icon is Smokey the Bear, who pointed his finger and said, "Only YOU can prevent forest fires." A younger icon is McGruff, the crime dog who encourages us to "take a bite out of crime."

Typically, PSAs run free-of-charge on a radio or TV station or in unsold newspaper advertising space—"remnant" space—as a community service.

Formats to Use

Supply them as scripts, audio recordings (for radio), or videotapes (for TV) of sixty, thirty, twenty, or fifteen seconds; or for print, as camera-ready ads. Many radio and TV stations will help produce a local PSA if you provide a script. You can also partner with a local advertising agency or public relations firm to produce them; many agencies will do the work at no charge as a public service and as a way of showcasing their creativity or expanding a portfolio. Note that it isn't necessary to provide radio stations with recorded PSAs; many will work from just a script, which is often the best approach because it takes far less time to write a script than it does to produce a finished product.

► **Chapter 12**

Preparing a Press Kit

Understanding What a Press Kit Is

A press kit is a package of news and background information presented in a format that reporters need and relate to. Understanding this can make a difference in whether your company does or doesn't get the publicity it deserves. It can also help you determine whether you even need a press kit for your business (not every company does). When a reporter asks you to "send a press kit," he's asking you to send a package of news and information he can use for story ideas or as background information, and he's expecting the contents to be written in a journalistic style and presented in a specific format. He doesn't want to read through brochures or product flyers or to try to work through advertising copy to figure out what your company does. He wants you to make all of that obvious to him.

When to Use a Press Kit

When you have a lot of information on a single topic to share with representatives of the news media, you put it all together in a press kit, a collection of news and background material presented in the form of news releases, backgrounders, fact sheets, and so on. (The publicity police won't arrest you if your press kit contains a brochure, but it's a waste of money,

It's Not About Sales Literature

I listened to a professional speaker lecture about the importance of having "a great press kit" at a "promote your business" round table event for other speakers not long ago. I was very interested in examining the samples she passed around—and just as disappointed by what I saw. Instead of information the press could use in formats they like to receive it in, her representative press kits were packed with brochures and other sales collateral, speaker portrait photos, and reprints of articles profiling or quoting the speakers. It was not appropriate for me to correct the speaker, but I was disappointed that the entrepreneurs gathered around that table walked away thinking that the most important thing to remember about press kits is that the color of the folder should match the collateral tucked inside. This misunderstanding could cost these people valuable publicity exposure.

because reporters loathe digging through the hype of promotional material for facts.)

Your press kit should be downloadable from your Web site, available in hard copy, and created in a format that you can e-mail. The easiest, simplest, and most cost-effective approach for the hard-copy kit is a pocket folder designed to hold the materials, but other approaches are often wise or appropriate. Downloadable kits can be available as PDF files or Word files, but if you chose a PDF format, make certain that the text can be copied from your document and pasted into the user's articles.

Use a press kit when, quite simply, a stand-alone press release is not enough. This includes when you are:

- Introducing a new product (including a book)
- Attempting to educate the media on a complex topic or issue
- Introducing an individual to the media as an expert resource to interview in the future
- Announcing a newsworthy event
- Announcing a significant change in your business, such as a merger or acquisition
- Making any kind of significant announcement that effects the community, including a plant closing

Press kits can contain a great deal of information, especially if the topic is complex and needs to be broken down into smaller units, and they can contain just a few elements. To promote an expert to a group of trade magazines, you can use a cover letter detailing how the expert might be useful editorially, a press release offering tips or advice on the topic from the expert, a biography of the expert, and a head shot. That's a pretty slim folder, but it's enough to get the expert a solid place in a writer's files. To introduce a juice in a test market through in-person media interviews with the brand manager, for example, assemble a press kit that includes an

Media Tours

A media tour is a series of scheduled, individual meetings between journalists and your company spokesperson. You often hear about them in reference to well-known authors crisscrossing the country to promote their books or with celebrities visiting New York and Los Angeles for a series of interviews hawking their latest movies. But many other products, services, and business situations lend themselves to media tours, as well. Publicists use media tours to introduce key journalists to a company's newsworthy material, presented in the form of the press kit, in the journalist's office or at another mutually convenient location (restaurant meals are popular). The journalist can review the press kit, ask questions, and take notes for an article or news item, or use what is learned in the briefing for background information. A media tour is particularly useful when most of the publications serving your market are based in another city from yours.

Press Kit Case History

Press kits should contain factual information that helps a reporter write a story about your organization's news. When the Medical Society of the State of New York worked with county medical societies to plan a series of press conferences and rallies across the state to call attention to the need for legislative tort reform, it provided the medical societies and reporters with an essential press kit that explained the group's position. Developed in conjunction with three state medical specialty societies, each press kit included:

- A "post-rally" press release reporters could use to describe what happened at each event
- A fact sheet with statistics regarding the issues
- A backgrounder that analyzed four bills that would expand wrongful death awards, expand the current statute of limitations, increase contingency fees, and award prejudgment interest.

announcement release, a backgrounder on the company, a product photo and caption, a product fact sheet, and a brief biography of the brand manager.

Press Kit Elements

We present information to the media in a format they expect and can work with. Press kits can combine any number of the following elements—and can contain other less common elements as well. Here are the most typical document formats and how to use them.

Press Releases and Tip Sheets

Press releases are described in great detail in Chapter 7, but here's a quick overview. Press releases—also called news releases—are news announcements that answer the questions who, what, when, where, why, and how. They also answer the primary question a reporter, editor, or producer will ask, which is, "Why will my readers/viewers/listeners care? What's in it for them?" In addition to providing newsworthy information, a press release makes a case for the topic's relevance to the media outlet's audience.

Tip sheets are a specific type of press release, one that offers a list of tips or nuggets of advice, usually in a bullet or list format. A press kit must have a press release or a tip sheet—if there's no news, there's no reason for the press kit.

See a sample of a press release used to announce a new book as part of a press kit in Chapter 8. The release can be downloaded with the rest of the press kit from the publisher's Web site.

Backgrounders

Backgrounders provide exactly that—background information. They can provide biographical information about the management team, a company's history, a product category overview, an advertising campaign description, or anything else that is useful background information but is not "news" or an announcement. The backgrounder's job is to tell the reporter or researcher more about a specific subject, providing in-depth information that is not appropriate for a press release. It's additional information for those needing it. Imagine putting one aspect of your story under a magnifying glass—that's a backgrounder.

Announcing a new product in a relatively unknown category? Include a category backgrounder to update reporters. Encouraging the trade media to call you in the future for articles addressing your areas of expertise? Include a one-page biographical backgrounder written in the third person. Announcing a new advertising campaign? Add a backgrounder on the history of your company's advertising programs.

See a sample backgrounder from a press kit in Appendix B.

Fact Sheets

Fact sheets are easy to write. As Sergeant Friday used to say on *Dragnet,* they're "just the facts, ma'am." A fact sheet is a list of bulleted points that contain specific information that expands on general information provided in a press kit. It also can feature background information in a bullet format. Here are typical topics covered by fact sheets in press kits:

- Detailed product information
- Commonly asked questions
- A company's new structure
- Key facts about a company
- Special event details
- Statistics
- Background on issues

Don't confuse a fact sheet with a backgrounder, which is written in prose and paragraphs. A fact sheet should contain bulleted points that provide useful information in anticipation of a reporter's questions.

See a sample fact sheet from a press kit in Appendix B.

Photos

Not all press kits require photos, but they are a wise addition for certain types of situations. Include a photo when it makes sense—when, for example, you think the coverage of your story would be incomplete without a photo illustrating your announcement. Typical—and appropriate—press kit photos include:

- Head shots of the people quoted in the press release
- Head shot of the expert the kit is promoting
- Product shots, especially for new product launches
- Recipe illustration for food publicity
- The new building (actual or artist's rendering) when announcing a significant move to a new location or new headquarters construction
- Action shots of the end users of your product, showing how people will be using the product or service you're introducing

Clippings

Clippings are reprints of articles that quote you or an individual at your company, or refer to your company. (See Chapter 24 for more on clippings.) Include clippings only if they are relevant to the topic covered in the press kit. For example, a new product announcement press kit might include a trade magazine article about the expected explosive growth in that product category, and a press kit promoting an individual as a topic expert could include reprints that showcase the expert's knowledge while illustrating that other reporters have found this person knowledgeable enough to do an interview. Note that copyright laws require you to get the publication's permission to reprint an article for distribution. This often requires paying a fee. The Copyright Clearance Center at ✍ *www.copyright.com* streamlines the process, but contacting the publication directly for permission is also advisable, especially when the clipping is from your local newspaper or a magazine you have a close relationship with. (The permissions process applies to use of a publication's clippings on your Web site as well; you can get around this by providing a link to the clipping at the media outlet's Web site rather than reproducing the clip on your site.)

Do not include:

- Clippings of routine personnel appointments
- Clippings just because you read about them in this chapter—they must contribute to the story in some way
- More than four reprints
- Badly photocopied, hard-to-read clippings
- Clippings that do not have the publication name and date included

For print reproduction, prepare your clippings by trimming them neatly and mounting them on plain paper on which you've typed the publication name and date. Don't copy copies of copies—they are too hard to read and look amateurish.

Sales Collateral

Journalists ignore collateral (brochures and other sales material) tucked into press kits, but marketers include it anyway. If you feel your world will end if you don't include sales literature, then limit it to one piece, perhaps a company brochure or product spec sheet substituting for a fact sheet. Don't use sales collateral as a substitution for press releases, backgrounders, or fact sheets, because reporters don't have the patience required to dig through the marketing-ese for useful information.

> Don't use sales collateral as a substitution for press releases, backgrounders, or fact sheets.

Cover Letter

The cover letter ties your package together by explaining why you're sending the press kit and suggesting ways the recipient might use the enclosed information. Sometimes it's a pitch letter, but sometimes it isn't. Clip it to the front of the press kit or tuck it in the inside right pocket.

If your press kit positions an expert source for future interviews, state that in the cover letter and suggest article topics the expert can contribute to. If the kit contains background information on your company that you would like the reporter to add to her files, say so, and let the reporter know how she can reach you, or the appropriate contact, when she needs more information from your company. If the press kit announces a new product introduction, say that, and explain why you think the readers/viewers of that media outlet will be interested. If your press kit contains background information about an expert you are pitching to a television talk show producer, make sure your cover letter acts like a pitch letter and suggests interview or segment topics that are unique to the personality of that specific show.

See a sample press kit cover letter in Appendix B.

Press Kit Packaging

All you need is a two-pocket folder. Don't let your advertising agency talk you into putting a chunk of money into printing special die-cut, foil-stamped, one-time-use folders that will do absolutely nothing to encourage a reporter to look inside. This is one situation where packaging *isn't* everything. Reporters are not the kind of people who are impressed by extravagant folders. What impresses them is solid information they can use with little effort. If you're already producing sales folders as part of your marketing campaign, then by all means produce extras for your press kit materials, too. In general, though, when budget is an issue, put your money into content, not packaging.

Going Postal with a Press Kit

Many years ago, when Spiegel wanted to communicate that its catalog was no longer a Sears wannabe and had turned itself into a marketer of pricier brand-name apparel and home furnishings, it used a mailbox for a press kit. Stuffed with luxurious, upscale items carefully selected to showcase its new image and merchandise, the press kit was the highly successful focal point of a media tour with major consumer magazines in New York City. The company spokesperson conducted in-person interviews with key fashion and home furnishings editors at their offices, giving each a mailbox customized with appropriate catalog merchandise along with a packet of press material about the company's makeover. It generated media coverage of the "new" Spiegel while introducing editors to a new source of fashion and furnishings merchandise for photo layouts.

Making Sure Your Kit Gets Noticed

Schwinn once included an appropriate attention-getting gimmick—a bicycle horn—with its press kit folder. There was probably internal discussion about whether it was wise to send the bike horns, since so many editors say they don't like these kinds of "tricks" or that they're not allowed to accept gifts. But the cute little honkers did the job—the recipients were both intrigued and charmed enough by the gimmick to open the press kit to discover why Schwinn sent both.

These kinds of attention-getters often do what they are supposed to do, which is to get the media materials noticed. This helps with your follow-up calls, because reporters remember those materials. They're a good idea when the topic lends itself to an attention-getting device, and when there's budget for it. Press kit packages might become obsolete because more reporters, editors, and producers are becoming comfortable with e-mail and Web sites. The fate of printed press kits remains to be seen, but in the meantime, when using the mail or other services to deliver them, make sure the contents are clearly labeled outside and that you include information on how to reach you with questions on the outside of the package.

At the same time, remember that face-to-face meetings with media representatives will always be important ways to introduce them to your company and services, and you'll want to hand them relevant background material at those meetings. You'll need hard copies for press conferences and special events, too.

For instance, when poet Maya Angelou was the keynote speaker at a nonprofit's annual fundraising dinner, publicists distributed a press kit on-site to the media covering her appearance at the dinner. The press kit explained the depth and breadth of the community's connection to the event, providing several angles for news coverage. It included:

- A press release announcing Angelou's appearance
- A press release announcing and describing a one-of-a-kind commissioned glass sculpture created by a local artisan as a gift to Angelou for presentation on behalf of a local business sponsor
- A press release announcing that several local businesses donated

seats to several deserving middle and high school students and teachers

- A two-page backgrounder on Angelou
- A backgrounder on the nonprofit
- A head shot of Angelou
- A photo and caption of the glass sculpture
- A list of the sponsors of the dinner

Press kit packages will never disappear completely, but one of the challenges of the public relations industry will be to identify new and innovative ways to get the media's attention if media mailrooms close their doors. In the meantime, realize that attention-getting devices are useful at doing just that—getting attention. But if the content of your press kit isn't relevant to the media outlet's audience, it won't get used, no matter how cleverly you presented the material. Make relevance and clear communication your priorities, and your message will be heard.

What to Avoid in Your Press Kit

Here are press kit "don'ts":

Don't Assume You Need a Press Kit

Don't assume you need a press kit just because you want to get publicity for your business. Not every situation lends itself to these collections of information. More often than not, all you'll need is a press release—or a series of press releases—to generate publicity.

Don't Overdo It

Don't pack your press kit with sales literature. It's a waste of money.

Don't include any more information than is necessary to communicate your story or message. For example, don't include executive bios if those people have nothing to do with the press kit topic and will not be available for media interviews.

Don't Spend Too Much Money

Don't spend a lot of money on press kit material packaging unless you need to convey a certain image for your company, product, or service. A provider of upscale products will want to make certain that the folder and paper look and feel expensive, but a heating and cooling contractor doesn't need to worry about that.

Don't Forget to Look for the Story

Don't forget to look hard for the story in your press kit, and make sure it's obvious to the recipient. If your press kit is strictly background information for a reporter's files, clearly identify it as such with a cover note and perhaps even a label. Otherwise, the recipient will wonder momentarily why you sent it before tossing it in the recycling bin.

What to Do in Your Press Kit

Here are press kit "do's":

Do Your Research

Do check the pulse of the media you're targeting by making a few phone calls to find out if your contacts prefer a hard copy of a press kit or an electronic version.

Stick with Facts

Do stick to the facts in your press kit. Remember, a press kit is designed to communicate both news and background information. Superlatives and hype are never appropriate.

Virtual Press Kits

Virtual press kits—press materials that reside online on your Web site—are increasingly popular as journalists become more Internet savvy and technology tools become more available to them. Make sure your Web site includes a press room with all of your press materials—most recent and older material as well. When you're releasing a press kit, it's not enough to just upload the press kit elements to the press room, though. Instead, make sure you label it appropriately so reporters can distinguish that new material from older items already posted. The label—or name—you use on the Web site should match the label you use in the e-mail message you send to reporters when directing them to the online materials (this will eliminate problems identifying the material later if the reporter loses your message with the URL link). Remember, too, that not all reporters are working with speedy Internet connections or the latest computers.

Include a Cover Letter

Do include a cover letter that explains how and why the recipient will want to use the material in the press kit. In some situations, that cover letter might include a list of interesting story ideas.

Keep It Simple

Do keep your press kit as simple as possible. Include only what's necessary.

Track Your Press Kit Success

Keep track of what does and doesn't get used from your press kits. That will help you determine how to approach the media the next time you produce a press kit. Chapter 24 can help you track many components of your publicity plan.

## Chapter 13

Calling a Press Conference

Part One	
Part Two	
Part Three	
Part Four	
Part Five	

Knowing What Happens at a Press Conference

A press conference is an event at which companies or organizations announce big news. The news is typically announced by key players—company presidents or CEOs or, in the case of a product launch, an articulate individual who can best explain the product and answer questions. For most small business situations, the announcement will probably come from the president or CEO. Although venues came be innovative and fun, typically, most companies make their announcements in function rooms from a podium in front of rows of chairs. In certain situations, a single speaker is appropriate while in others—when announcing a merger or acquisition, for example—more than one speaker explains the news and its ramifications. When the speakers are finished with their remarks, which might include product demonstrations or PowerPoint presentations, reporters are invited to ask questions.

While most reporters will ask questions in front of the group, they also appreciate an opportunity to meet with the speaker one-on-one for a few minutes to develop the angle they're pursuing. To accommodate this need, the event schedule usually includes time for individual interviews, many times in a separate, private room. Reporters also receive press kits with a news release and background information; the information is delivered to those unable to attend. When all questions are answered—or before then, if you've set a time limit—the host thanks the audience for coming, and the event ends. (It is at this point that you manage requests for one-on-one interviews.)

If you're thinking about holding your first press conference, try to attend one hosted by someone else so you can see how they play out. Call a TV assignment editor, explain your situation, and ask for the name and telephone number of a person planning a press conference that week. Call that person, explain your situation again, and ask for permission to attend. (Be prepared to convince that individual that you aren't a spy for the competition, though.)

Deciding Whether a Press Conference Is Appropriate

"Maybe we should have a press conference," tumbles innocently from the lips of many business owners seeking public relations counsel. And why not?

> While most reporters will ask questions in front of the group, they also appreciate an opportunity to meet with the speaker one-on-one.

Many of the big news stories in the business pages of their daily newspaper come from announcements made at press conferences. If Microsoft announces news at a splashy press conference, why shouldn't Pluto Technology, Josie's Gift Baskets, or Acme Auto Detailing? Because small businesses don't usually generate the kind of news that warrants a Microsoft-size press conference. But there are situations when they do have news that is worthy of this kind of event. There are also times when the boss wants a press conference so badly that you have to plan one whether it's a wise choice or not. If you're considering the press conference option, you need to know when and why to host a press conference, and how to do it.

Do Hold a Press Conference in the Following Situations

Technically, you can plan a press conference any time you want, for any kind of announcement. But nobody will attend unless you're making a major announcement. So the question is, "What kind of announcement will generate media attendance at a press conference?" It needs to be big, such as an announcement that you're going to build a multimillion dollar manufacturing facility thanks to tax breaks from the county, and that you'll substantially increase employment at your company because of the new plant. Or that your company has hired a celebrity as its advertising spokesman, and that celebrity will be at the press conference to answer questions about his new role. Or that you're the lead sponsor of a sporting event that will bring impressive professional athletes to your community—and that one of those athletes will attend the press conference to help make the announcement. Or that the motivational speaker for your sales meeting is a well-known and respected sports figure who will meet with the press after he presents the sales meeting keynote speech. Or that your organization is making a substantial donation to the fundraising campaign of a high-profile nonprofit agency and that you're kicking off the campaign with the check presentation.

Don't Hold a Press Conference If . . .

When asked, "Why do you want to host a press conference?," too many frazzled employees say, "Because the boss wants one!" Sometimes a little education can go a long way—help the boss understand that many typical small business announcements do *not* warrant a press conference. Don't have a press conference if your company has:

- Signed a new contract unless it is huge and will have a remarkable impact on the local economy
- Moved to a new location that you want to show off
- Introduced a new ad campaign
- Won an award
- Hired a new president who is not already a local celebrity of sorts
- Reinvented itself with a "re-branding" campaign

As you decide whether you have something big enough for a press conference, ask yourself if your news is earth-shattering enough to draw reporters and TV cameras who are already racing around the city trying to cover "hard" news like fires, car crashes, and stabbings. Keep in mind that much of what a small business has to announce typically has a business spin to it, and TV news departments don't devote much airtime to business news.

Successful Stunt

When Pizza Hut added Buffalo-style chicken wings to its menu, company officials traveled to Buffalo, New York, to make the announcement at a press conference hosted by that city's mayor on the steps of city hall. The mayor's office cooperated because the announcement provided an opportunity for positive national exposure for a city better known for its harsh weather than its cuisine. The Pizza Hut public relations staff selected Buffalo—rather than the company's Dallas headquarters—to break the news so they could emphasize the on-site research undertaken by taste-testers to help recreate the special flavor of the original wings first sold at the city's Anchor Bar. It was a logical choice—and one that drew plenty of publicity just as the wings were being introduced to the chain's restaurants throughout the Northeast. It left a good taste in the mouths of Pizza Hut franchisees.

If you're making your announcement at a trade show, it needs to be about a major new product or technology that will significantly impact the industry or about a major alliance that also will have a substantial impact on the industry. But if you've hired a new president and want to introduce him to editors at the show, skip the press conference and schedule one-on-one meetings with them instead. Personal interviews give editors and reporters a forum for asking the kinds of in-depth and probing questions that aren't appropriate in a group situation that includes competing publications.

What If You Gave a Party and Nobody Came?

Your goal when you can't get out of planning a press conference is to make sure it's not every host's worst nightmare—a party with no guests. Press conferences for small businesses are risky. You can have a good excuse for a press conference and do everything right but still have an empty room when it's time to start. Who attended the press conference that announced a heartwarming holiday fundraiser for a much-loved camp for kids with cancer? N-o-b-o-d-y. But a press conference to announce the expansion of a shelter for battered women drew three TV stations, the daily newspaper, and a radio station. There wasn't an empty seat in the house not so long ago when the Tampa Bay Buccaneers introduced the press to their new coach—it was even broadcast live and pre-empted *General Hospital.*

Ensuring a Successful Press Conference

This section gives you two foolproof ideas and tips for holding a well-attended press conference: timing the event so that people are *available* to attend and announcing the event so that plenty of people actually *do* attend.

Time the Press Conference Carefully

Assuming you have a newsworthy event, your success can be influenced by your timing. The best time is the time that's most convenient for the media—usually midmorning and midweek. Never plan your press conference for late afternoon if you want TV coverage—the news

Time New Product Publicity with Care

There are a lot of reasons why Kimberly-Clark's innovative "Rollwipes" moist toilet paper failed to catch on in spite of widespread, national publicity. Some critics blame advertising that didn't explain what the product does. Others note that the company didn't encourage trial through free samples. And some point the finger at an important detail every business owner should keep in mind when using publicity to launch a product or line extension: The hype took place too far in advance of the actual launch—six months— and it was publicized nationally when the product was available only in a single region.

Avoid costly mistakes and lost opportunities by waiting until products are available before publicizing them. You can do all the work and have all the elements in place early— but wait until the products are in the distribution chain before releasing the news.

departments are focused on the first evening newscast then. Mid-morning offers fewer schedule conflicts than any other time of the day.

Before scheduling your event, learn what other events or announcements are planned for the day you're targeting. Don't plan your press conference for the day the mayor is going to announce his re-election campaign or for opening day at the baseball stadium. You can't avoid the conflicts of "real news"—a twelve-car pile-up on the highway or a bomb scare at a downtown office building—but by making calls to the sites that usually host big events or press conferences, by calling the local tourism and convention bureau, and by checking key Web sites, you can at least avoid competing with others hoping to make news at a press conference or a high-profile event.

If you are hosting a press conference at a trade show, work with show management to get a good time slot that doesn't compete with other companies making announcements at the show. Show management companies keep a master calendar of all show events and can provide valuable assistance with scheduling, on-site press conference room reservations, lists of media registered for the show, and so on. Early morning and lunchtime press conferences are the best attended; don't host one on the last day of the show because editors are probably gone by then. While you might be tempted—even encouraged—to host your press conference off-site at an unusual venue—don't. You want to make it easy to attend your event, and keeping it at the trade show location is the best way to do that.

"Timing" influences the food you'll serve at your event— and you will serve food. Refreshments are not only appropriate, they're expected. And they help create an air of hospitality. If you need to hold your conference at the start of the day, include breakfast. If it's at lunchtime, serve lunch. At other times, provide beverages and snacks that make sense for the time frame.

Invite More Than the Press

It's not always possible to explain why one press conference is a success and another isn't. But one thing is certain: You never know for sure if your press conference will be covered by the media until they walk in the door. If nobody shows up, and you have three speakers ready to talk to *nobody*, you have a problem. Solve that problem by making sure your event is more than a press conference—it's an announcement, a celebration, a grand opening, a whatever—anything that gives you an excuse for getting nonmedia people into the room. Invite colleagues, customers, friends of the company—anybody who will want to hear and celebrate the news your leaders want to share. Entice them with refreshments and an interesting and convenient location. Hire a professional photographer with big, imposing equipment to record the event and give the impression that it is covered by the media—even if it isn't. (You need the photos for your newsletter and Web site anyway.) When it's time to begin the press conference, the speakers will be addressing a full house willing to clap at the right time. (Seats with people in them make the event more photogenic for the TV cameras, too, even when you've got a sure thing.)

Understanding the Elements of a Press Conference

While there are all types of press conferences whose elements are influenced by the nature of the news and the event budget, all of them have certain core elements that must be included:

- A major news announcement
- A list of invitees
- An invitation sent to members of the media
- A location that is convenient to the media and appropriate for the news
- At least one speaker making the announcement
- A press kit or press materials
- Signage with your company or product logo

Announcement

When planning your press conference, start with your announcement. What kind of atmosphere do you need to communicate your message? What is the "personality" of your announcement? That will influence your location and the invitation language. Do you need props or decorations to create that atmosphere? When a manufacturer of professional and collegiate team uniforms wanted to give local sports reporters an opportunity to interview a very high-profile basketball coach in town for a meeting with company executives, they held the press conference in the company's showroom. Their team uniforms were the perfect backdrop for newspaper photos and TV news footage, and the atmosphere was relaxed. If, on the other hand, this manufacturer wanted to announce a plant closing, it would hold the press conference in a low-key, downtown hotel function room far away from plant employees.

Guest List

Determine who you want to invite, and if your announcement is celebratory, don't limit your guest list to members of the press. Invite vendors, investors, key staffers, and others who can help fill chairs and are willing to applaud. Be selective about your media guest list, too, inviting only those who might have a legitimate interest in the news you're announcing, rather than everybody in your local media database. (A TV health reporter might have interviewed you for a story before, but she might not be an appropriate choice for an announcement about a well-known brand you've acquired.)

If your press conference is at a trade show, get a list of the registered media from show management and use it as the basis of your invitation list.

> Be selective about your media guest list, inviting only those who might have a legitimate interest in the news you're announcing.

Invitation

The invitation process is determined by the nature of the announcement and how much planning time you have. With weeks to plan the event launching an exciting new product at a trade show, you can create invitations that reflect the product's personality and packaging. For a hastily called event to discuss an unexpected crisis, you'll be faxing media alerts (see Chapter 6) to key reporters or calling them, instead. Plan to make follow-up calls to reporters who didn't respond to the invitation. Be careful to tell them enough to entice them without giving away the story.

Location

With few exceptions, the press conference location must be convenient for the media. If most media outlets are based downtown, find meeting space there. If you're at a trade show, keep it on-site, rather than taking it to an interesting destination requiring a cab ride. The easier you make it, the more likely you are to get good turnout. When reserving space, keep in mind your presentation needs and ask questions that assure you that the facility can provide what's necessary.

Speaker

The press conference speaker must be your best choice possible, taking into account the announcement, speaking skills, and who is best able to answer questions that are expected. Provide this individual with a script and plenty of rehearsal. Role-play possible questions and answers. Support the speaker's announcements with a hard copy of the remarks in the form of a press kit containing an announcement release and other supporting material. Give these to reporters as they arrive; messenger them to those unable to attend.

Signage

Signage is particularly important when you expect TV coverage, because it provides important on-camera identification for your brand or company. Project your logo on a screen behind the speaker, or hang a banner with the logo behind the speaker. Put your logo on the front of the podium, too.

Details, Details, Details

Details can make the difference between success and failure. If you leave the time of the event off the invitation, reporters might not bother to call for

Press Conference Success Story

When the Medical Society of the State of New York (MSSNY) wanted to encourage state legislators to pass legislation that would limit awards for punitive damages in malpractice lawsuits, it added a series of simultaneous statewide press conferences to its publicity plan. On April 22, 2002, twenty-three highly visual events involving thousands of placard-carrying physicians focused media attention on the highest malpractice insurance premiums in the nation. The press conferences and physician rallies took place at locations ranging from hospitals to county courthouses, from Niagara Falls to Long Island. In each location, county medical societies used MSSNY-provided talking points and press materials to communicate to reporters and policymakers the importance of proposed legislation. The events generated more than sixty television, radio, newspaper, and online media stories because of the carefully thought-out and orchestrated visuals, and facts

the missing information, which means they won't attend simply because they were lacking a basic fact. Is the RSVP number on the invitation correct? Working from a checklist like the one provided here will help you make certain that your press conference is properly staffed, that all reporters have press kits, and that the AV equipment has been tested and works. Careful attention to details can make certain the boss views the event as a success, not a flop.

When the event is over, make sure you have people videotaping the newscasts of TV stations that attended, audiotaping radio station news coverage, and scanning the next day's newspaper for a story. Then leverage this coverage with all key audiences—both internal and external—so you extend the excitement of your event. Include an article with photos in your employee newsletter and upload the TV news coverage to your Web site. Use all forms of communication available to expand the reach of the press conference results. Use the press conference checklist in Appendix A.

> **Chapter 14**

Planning a
Special Event

Part One

Part Two

Part Three

Part Four

Part Five

Coming Up with Ideas for Special Events

Whether it's a toy store's Lincoln Log construction contest or a rum brand's beach snowshoe race for charity, special events can generate a lot of positive publicity for small businesses. All it takes is an attention-getting concept that's relevant to your business, careful and well-thought-out execution, and good communication with the media you want to cover the event. It's not hard, and it can be lots of fun for employees and the community. First, however, you'll have to come up with ideas for an event.

Brainstorming

What's the best way to kill the best ideas during a brainstorming session? Just use any of these phrases:

- "That will never work."
- "We tried that already."
- "We don't have the budget for that."

> A "bad" idea can generate a "good" idea. That's why you don't want to kill off *any* ideas!

The most workable ideas are often spin-offs of ideas that won't work—in other words, a "bad" idea can generate a "good" idea. That's why you don't want to kill off *any* ideas! When conducting a brainstorming session, ban all negative statements or attitudes. Write down all the ideas—even the goofiest ones. Shoot for quantity over quality—the more ideas you get up on a board or flip chart, the more they will stimulate the group's thinking. Don't toss anything out until you're done generating ideas. Only then can you introduce any negativity—and even then, it's to explore the practicality or value of each idea on the brainstorming list.

Mindmapping

Mindmapping is a nonlinear, quasi-organized brain-dumping process that helps stimulate new ideas and connections. Joyce Wycoff, author of *Mindmapping: Your Personal Guide to Exploring Creativity and Problem-Solving*, says the process involves eight steps.

1. Start the process with an open, playful attitude. (A lighter attitude makes it more fun, too.)
2. Write a word or image that symbolizes what you want to think about smack-dab in the middle of a page of paper or flip chart. It *must* be in the middle.
3. Free associate around that word. As ideas emerge, write one- or two-word descriptions of the ideas on lines branching from the central focus word. Expand outward into branches and sub-branches. Use each of these other words to stimulate other ideas.
4. Take advantage of the way your brain works by recording ideas and thoughts quickly.
5. "Break boundaries" and stimulate creativity by using larger-than-usual paper and colored markers or crayons.
6. Record everything that comes to mind, even if it is completely unrelated. You don't know what might generate another great idea.
7. If your mind slows down, draw empty lines to help generate ideas. Stand up to create energy.
8. Sometimes you see relationships and connections immediately and you can add sub-branches to a main idea. Sometimes you don't. Organization can always come later; the first requirement is to get the ideas out of your head and onto the paper.

If you've never used this technique before, start with a simple project, such as mindmapping holiday gift ideas for your spouse or a friend, before applying the technique to your publicity problem.

Special Events That Generate Publicity

There are two kinds of special events to consider when thinking in terms of generating publicity. One is the event that celebrates an occasion—a grand opening, the company's anniversary, your 1,000th customer—that you want to celebrate even if your idea doesn't garner media attention. The other type is one that is created solely to grab media attention—the city's largest Bloody Mary cocktail to promote your restaurant's Sunday brunch, a "Mr. Clean Look-Alike Contest" to introduce a house-cleaning service, a world's goofiest air guitar player competition to announce the addition of a new line of electric guitars at a music shop.

Special Occasion

It is relatively easy to turn a special occasion like an anniversary or grand opening into an event that generates publicity at the same time. For example, a fabric store celebrating its tenth anniversary can give back to the community by sponsoring a community quilt-making event that produces a unique work of art that is auctioned off to benefit a charity. A gathering of quilters to piece together the end product is a highly visual event that will appeal to TV news departments; an auction later, featuring representatives of the charity and local celebrities, can secure additional free media exposure. Plan the celebration at a time when business is slower than you'd like, and you have an event that thanks the community, helps generate traffic during a slow period, and gets you new customers who heard about your store for the first time on the news.

To begin generating ideas for your celebratory event, pull a few creative people into a room for a brainstorming session. Think in terms of concepts that are visually appealing, fun, entertaining, unusual, or clever. Review past issues of your industry's trade journals—what clever ideas have other companies in your business used? If you see something that worked in another community, adapt it to your own situation. Remember, there's no such thing as a new idea.

Stunts Staged Only for Publicity

The same thought process applies to the event that's staged just for the sake of publicity. What has worked elsewhere? Chicago got national media attention when it asked artists to paint cow statues, then placed them throughout the downtown area. A Rochester, New York, brewery has since "borrowed" the idea, bringing horses into town to help launch the brewery's rejuvenation with new owners. What's to stop you from bringing pigs, sheep, or goats to your community? Use popular media as creative fodder—what creative "stunt" have you seen in the news lately that you can bend to fit your needs? What would be fun? What would be interesting?

After you generate a list of ideas, narrow it down to those that are appropriate, do-able, and affordable. The event idea should reflect the personality of your business—or the personality you *want* it to have. A stodgy law firm celebrating fifty years with a plan to attract hipper, new media companies as clients might stage a trade show event centering around an appearance by TV's "Judge Judy," for example. Some ideas make sense but are too difficult to execute. You can probably promote your new water park with a contest to see which local media personality can scream the loudest on the scariest water ride, but bringing Shamu the Killer Whale in for a personal appearance on opening day is not realistic.

Budget makes a difference, too. Can you afford to execute your idea? Don't assume that special events require huge budgets. The biggest expense for some of the best ideas is in staff labor, not out-of-pocket costs. The beach snowshoe race mentioned previously received local and national media attention but cost the company less than $5,000.

Special Event Elements

The most successful events for generating publicity combine a number of elements. To minimize your expenses and maximize your impact, answer these questions:

Can You Create a Charity Tie-In?

The media is more likely to cover a newsworthy stunt if there's a beneficiary—it reduces the commercial sting.

Can You Involve Local Media Celebrities?

Smart event planners find a way to involve a TV anchor person, a popular radio personality, and a newspaper reporter or columnist because the personal connection often leads to publicity in each of those media outlets. Media personalities are especially useful as competition judges or contest hosts. Linking with a top personality's pet charity can make a big difference, too.

Are Good Causes Good Publicity?

Businesses often support non-profit endeavors for community relations reasons. It's a good move, especially for a company working to improve a weak public image. But some companies overextend themselves. To get the most from supporting a cause, focus on one or two causes and become committed both professionally and personally. How do you decide what cause you want to support? Make it personal. Link with a cause you are truly committed to. A co-owner of People's Pottery, a chain of stores selling American-made crafts, for example, is a breast cancer survivor who uses the stores to support breast cancer awareness campaigns and fund raisers. You can make it personal for your customers, too. What causes strike a chord with them? What are their pet charities? It will be easier for you to implement, and less like a marketing ploy, if you support a cause with a personal connection.

Is It Visual?

Without strong visual elements, you won't attract TV cameras.

Is It Newsworthy?

You can have every other element in place, but if your concept has no news value, you'll get no media attention.

Can You Extend Your Reach or Budget by Partnering with Another Company?

A radio station might offer free air time in exchange for sponsorship credit. Ask a key supplier or vendor to help underwrite the event in exchange for on-site signage.

Is It Something You Can Promote in Advance so You Have a Crowd?

As with press conferences, you'll want a built-in audience in case nobody from the press shows up.

Advance Promotion

The most successful special events are promoted in advance through a variety of means—advertising, direct mail, publicity, and e-mail, among others. If your event is open to the public and you want to draw a crowd, budget for advertising. Include information in your regular customer mailing—or do a special mailing. Make sure the event is prominently promoted on your Web site. Use all means available to get the word out so the community is informed—and excited.

Publicize the event by distributing to print media a press release that describes the event and why it's interesting or relevant. Send it to editors of "calendar of events" sections four weeks in advance. At the same time, send it to producers of morning drive-time radio shows and morning or noon TV news programs with a letter suggesting they interview you on the air about your unique event and why people will want to participate or attend. Follow up on the phone with the producers to determine their interest in an interview that you'd like to have air the week of the event. Keep in mind that a charity tie-in will make it easier for you to secure pre-event interviews because it will benefit the community while it makes the news coverage look less like a commercial.

Can You Pull It Off?

In addition to publicizing and promoting the event, you have to actually plan and execute it. Do you have the internal resources to implement your whiz-bang idea, or do you have the budget to hire an outside resource? Most publicity events require the attention of at least one sharp, energetic, detail-oriented project manager. This is the person who takes the big concept, breaks it down into next steps and activities, and either does the work to make it happen or delegates it to a good support team. Maybe it's a talented receptionist looking for a challenge or an underutilized administrative assistant anxious to prove he can do more.

If you don't have the internal resources to execute the job, look outside your organization for help. The challenge will be to find someone with the right credentials. Maybe all you need is the cousin of a friend of your accountant's who is a great project manager but currently between jobs. For

Wildly Successful Special Event

When Warner Home Video wanted to publicize the video/DVD release of its movie *Wild Wild West*, it hired Los Angeles agency Douglas, Cohn & Wolfe to generate excitement. The agency played off the film's mechanical tarantula race to rule the world by creating a live tarantula race on the Sunset Strip in West Hollywood. The publicity stunt was featured on TV news programs coast-to-coast, including *CNN Hollywood Minute*, *E! News Daily*, and news programs in markets as big as Los Angeles and Chicago and as small as Providence, Rhode Island. Let ideas like this get you thinking about the kinds of events you can host, too.

Publicity Generating Event Ideas

The most unusual event ideas will get the most media coverage; the *really* unusual ideas might generate national publicity, too. Think wacky, clever, eye-popping. Take ideas you see on national news, and apply them locally. Stage a celebrity look-alike competition—a barber shop or comedy club can present a "Three Stooges Look-Alike" contest or a record store can celebrate the release of Cher's latest album with a "Cher Look-Alike" contest. Having trouble finding good mechanics for your car repair business? Sponsor a contest to discover who has the best automotive technology skills to uncover new talent while calling attention to your interest in adding to your staff. Restaurants can collaborate to produce a Bastille Day waitstaff race involving trays with wine bottles and glasses. Get ideas by watching the last five minutes of your local news, when stations run the lighter feature stories from other parts of the country.

bigger events requiring a firm with several people, be cautious with those listed as "special events planners" in the Yellow Pages. Many don't do the types of events that generate publicity—they're more experienced planning banquets or group travel events, for example. Public relations firms are a good option, but make sure you work with one that has both special events and media relations experience. Solo public relations practitioners often charge less than larger firms, so don't overlook them.

Inviting the Media

The purpose of the event is to generate publicity, so your event to-do list should include inviting the media to the actual event (a separate action from your efforts to promote the event with the media in advance). The invitation you send to the media should be as clever as the event itself. The toy store hosting the Lincoln Log structure competition can package its invitation with logs. The invitation to the "world's largest Bloody Mary" event can be delivered with a celery stick. Wouldn't it be fun to stitch the quilting event invitation to a fabric square? Mail your media invitation so it arrives seven to ten days before the event.

As with all other publicity endeavors, work to tailor your media list so that you're sending the invitation to the right people, not to every reporter in town. For TV, send it to the assignment editors and to any on-camera reporter you know who might have a connection to your topic. If it's a sporting event, include the sports reporters. If your event benefits a charity and you know that a specific reporter has a soft spot for that charity, add that reporter to your invitation list. Your newspaper contact depends on the nature of your event, but if it is highly visual, make sure you include the photo editor as well as the appropriate section editor or reporter. Send it to the news directors at radio stations.

Follow up your clever invitation with a reminder

produced in a more traditional format, the media alert. Fax this to your list three days before the event. On the day before the event, call your entire media list to remind them about the event and determine who plans to attend. TV folks will say they won't know until the next day but that's OK—your job is to make sure it's in the folder for consideration. If it's not, fax the media alert again.

Make sure you create appropriate press materials to distribute on-site. These can include press releases, backgrounders, and photos, but what you prepare depends on the event. At a minimum, you need a press release explaining the event and its purpose for reporters covering your "news" on-site.

Execution

The best events are based on great ideas that are well-executed. And successful execution of special events requires an idea that has been tested for "do-ability," attention to detail, and lots of bodies to do the work. Do a walk-through of your concept, making certain that your execution plan makes sense. Using the Lincoln Logs building contest as an example, ask yourself if you have enough space for contestants, whether you have enough logs in stock or whether they can be ordered and delivered in time, if there's room for TV cameras (one of the main reasons for the event in the first place), whether you've allotted enough time for entrants to build something reasonable, and so on. Examine every aspect of your concept, looking for loopholes or areas that need more definition or attention. Do a dry run if necessary.

Events are about details. Are the press materials ready? Did you hire a photographer? Are all the supplies or materials ready and in place? Who's got the prizes? Do you have enough greeters and have they been prepped so they know what's going on and what to say? Who will work with the TV cameras and reporters? Who will start the event, and is that person waiting in the wings? Work from checklists (see Appendix A for a sample), and give very specific assignments to as many people as possible (recruit volunteers from your family if you have to). Let the person running the event—the project manager—oversee the entire process without worrying about instructing the photographer or making sure people register when they arrive.

Learning About Publicity on the Net

There are several excellent Web sites that offer publicity tutorials reinforcing what you're learning in this book. There are many, too, which include a mix of good information and less useful material. One site, for example, states that press releases are useless with local TV stations. This is just not true. So how do you know which publicity site has value and which doesn't? This is a case where looks count. The sites that look like advertisements and use words like "biz" and "super-powered" and "fantastic" while they literally shout at you to buy their products or services might not be as useful as those that spell out the word "business" and have a more traditionally professional appearance. Two good sites include ✍*www.publicityinsider. com* and ✍*www.publicity hound.com,* but there are many more to consider, as well.

Signage, Signage, Signage!

One of those details on your event management checklist is signage—lots of it. On-site event signage makes sure your company or brand name gets included in the media coverage of your event, even if the reporter "forgets" to mention it. News departments work hard to make sure you don't turn a news event into a commercial, particularly when there's no charity beneficiary, so they often omit references to companies and brands. Event signage helps make sure viewers know the event took place at your location, or that you sponsored it. It is an essential element for controversial products such as tobacco and beverage alcohol.

Hang banners with your name or logo in several locations so that cameras won't miss them. Have staffers wearing shirts with your logo large enough to be read during an interview. If you're sponsoring a competition or contest, have all entrants wear t-shirts or aprons with your logo or name in large type. Most of these elements can be used later in other ways, so they're a good investment.

Leveraging Your Success

When your event is over, tell more people about the fun you had with it. Put pictures and a summary on your Web site, include an article in your marketing newsletter, and send a short write-up to your trade magazines. Reprint press clippings (see Chapter 24) and send them to customers with a "just thought you'd like to know" note. Spreading the word about the fun you had with a successful event will reinforce your company's image as a progressive, innovative company.

► **Chapter 15**

Sponsoring an Event, Group, or Person

What Sponsorship Is—and What It Can Do for You

A well-chosen sponsorship can be an incredibly cost-effective way to market your company to a very specific and targeted audience. Many businesses are involved in small-scale sponsorships—Little League teams, bowling leagues, raffle donations—for community relations reasons. But an opportunity that is carefully selected because it reaches the people you want to become your customers—not because you couldn't say no to your neighbor—can add to your bottom line while costing far less than you might imagine. You can spend as little as nothing—by providing in-kind services or donated products instead—to a few thousand dollars for visibility in a local event that's a good fit for your company and its goals.

There are a number of sponsor opportunities routinely available to small businesses, including:

- Fundraising luncheons or dinners that benefit a nonprofit
- Sporting events or tournaments
- Unique or off-beat events
- Scholarships
- Local awards
- Public expos
- Conferences and specific functions within conferences (awards events, etc.)
- Festivals
- Concerts
- Cultural arts performances
- Regular meetings of local groups ranging from the Rotary and chamber of commerce to the Business & Professional Women chapter

Is a Sponsorship Right for Your Company?

Whether a sponsorship is an appropriate commitment for your company depends on a number of factors. The most important are whether:

- The opportunity fits well with your organization's goals and personality,
- The sponsorship will help you reach your target audience,
- The opportunity allows you to reach your goals, and
- It's affordable.

It's a Good Fit

"Fit" is very important. One of the most common sponsorships is one that doesn't seem to have the right fit—auto racing and beer companies. The connection between drinking and driving is so obvious that it's laughable. Avoid connections with any potential for negative backlash and spare yourself the hassle of one disgruntled individual who can turn your good intentions into something disastrous. A tanning parlor won't want to sponsor an event that benefits the American Cancer Society any more than a liquor store will want to be connected to a fundraiser for Mothers Against Drunk Driving.

But "fit" goes beyond backlash or issues of social responsibility to encompass event tone, personality, audience, and other factors. Learn as much as you can about the sponsorship opportunity to determine if there's a good match between your image and the opportunity's. If your organization is conservative, don't link with a wild concept that is guaranteed to generate publicity just so your company can be part of the excitement. Your association with an event whose image is not consistent with yours will confuse your customers and target market. But if you provide home care companions to elderly people, then by all means seek a sponsorship with an event that benefits the Alzheimer's Association. An event connected to a camp attended by kids with cancer is a great opportunity for the oncology practice that wants to continue to support the seriously ill children it treats.

> Learn as much as you can about the sponsorship opportunity to determine if there's a good match between your image and the opportunity's.

It Reaches Your Target Audience

Fit also addresses the second point, target audience. A business that provides a product to accountants, for example, won't want to sponsor the fireman's ball no matter how many times the telemarketers call. But that business might sponsor the luncheon at the American Institute of Certified Public Accountants' regional conference because it will be attended by potential customers. Similarly, a sporting goods store could be interested in sponsoring the community's annual Fourth of July Firecracker 10K race for runners or a hair salon might sponsor a charity fashion show. Too many businesses commit to sponsorships large and small for the wrong reason.

They buy into a golf tournament because the owner loves to golf, not because the company name will be seen by potential customers, or they purchase a table at a charity fundraising dinner because somebody's best friend from college is on the planning committee. Most small businesses can't afford to make sponsorship decisions based on personal preferences or relationships—they have to ask the question, "Does this have good potential for generating good will or new business with our targeted customers and prospects?"

It Helps You Reach Your Goals

The third factor is the sponsorship's ability to help you reach your goals. What do you want to get out of an event sponsorship? What makes it worthwhile for your company? If your current mission is to get people to try the new jam from your family orchard store, your sponsorship contract should allow you to give away samples. If you're working to build awareness of your company's new name or logo, then signage will be key. Are you looking for good will, or do you want to acquire names for your marketing database? Don't sign a sponsorship contract that doesn't give you what you need.

It's Affordable

Finally, can you afford to spend the amount required to make this opportunity suit your needs? Many local sponsorships allow companies to donate staff time or products instead of cash. A small spaghetti sauce manufacturer looking to generate good will with potential employees and customers, for example, can donate sauce to the PTA spaghetti dinner fundraiser, while the record store specializing in classical music can provide staff to the NPR affiliate telethon. Cash costs can range from a few hundred to a few thousand dollars for local events. Deciding whether the sponsorship is worth the expenditure is a challenge. It's usually difficult to measure the impact, so you have to make your decision based on an estimate of the number of people who will be exposed to your message, name, or logo, and what it costs you to get that exposure.

When evaluating the cost, take into account what you're getting for

Five Reasons Not to Sponsor an Event

Here are five good reasons for not sponsoring an event:

• The boss is an avid fan of the sport being sponsored,
• You want to entertain clients but can accomplish your goals just by buying tickets to the event,
• Advertising or direct mail zeroes in on your target audience more effectively,
• You can't define what you want to get from the sponsorship, or
• The event is poorly managed.

your investment. Does the cost include a banner with your company name at the sporting event? An ad in the program? The opportunity to give away product samples? Will you be included in all the publicity materials and event advertising? Are there hospitality opportunities? What are you getting for your money? What can you negotiate for?

Finding Sponsorship Opportunities

If your company has a high profile, you probably receive plenty of proposals and opportunities already. Those that drop in your lap are worth reviewing and considering, but it's more likely that you'll get a good fit by being proactive about sponsorships. Ask your customers what events they support, participate in, or find interesting. Attend events that seem like they might be a good fit for your company and observe who attends, how the events are managed, and whether the sponsors are visible. Talk to sponsors of events you're considering—have they found them worthwhile and are they well managed? Review your research on customers and prospects—what are they interested in? If you know that your customers as a group tend to be active, then investigate a sports competition such as a bike race. If your customers tend to be charity donors, then narrow your search to charity fundraisers. Do you sell to a highbrow clientele? Then don't wait for the opera to call you—call them first! Contact the chamber of commerce for its list of opportunities; do a Web search for other local options.

Postpone Your Decision

Consider delaying your sponsorship commitment—particularly if you're considering a low-level package—until planners are closer to the event date and hungrier for funds. You can often negotiate a bigger package for a lower financial commitment when event planners are near the end of the sponsor solicitation process and are more interested in reaching financial goals than in what they're giving away for the money. Use your negotiating skills to help them meet their financial needs while they help you achieve your marketing goals. Don't be shy about putting together a creative sponsorship package either—you won't know what you can secure unless you ask.

As you explore sponsorship opportunities, keep in mind two things. First, don't let yourself be limited to what appears on the event's list of sponsor packages. In other words, you'll rarely find a sponsor option that says "in-kind donations," but you can be certain that organizers are happy to consider any product or service that will save them money. Similarly, while the list of event sponsorship opportunities might detail what you get for $5,000, $2,500, and $1,000, make an offer for $500 if that's what you have to spend. If the $1,000 package includes a table for ten and a ¼-page program ad at the annual awards dinner, ask organizers to consider giving you a full-page ad and two dinner tickets for $500, even though that option isn't on the list.

Three Questions to Ask Before Signing a Contract

Whether you're donating time, products, or dollars, you'll want the terms of your sponsorship in writing. Here are three questions to ask the event organizers before signing the contract:

Do you have category exclusivity? This is a bigger issue for some companies than for others. If it's important to you, ask *before* you sign. And if you have exclusivity, get it in writing.

What are the specific terms of your agreement? Make no assumptions, regardless of conversations. Spell everything out.

How is the event being marketed? If it is being underpromoted, you'll want to know that in advance so you can budget for promotion of your own.

Don't limit your questions to the organizers. Quiz past sponsors, too. Did they get what they paid for? Would they do it again, and why or why not? Were the organizers difficult or easy to work with? Were they responsive to your calls and requests? Was it more work than expected, and if so, why? Did it give them opportunities to make new contacts they could potentially convert to customers? Also determine the newsworthiness of the event. How much media coverage has it received in the past? And speaking of media, do the organizers usually have a media sponsor connected to the event? If your customers don't listen to the radio, but each year the event has a radio station as sponsor, is it a good choice for you? The more information you can get about a sponsorship opportunity ahead of time, the better able you'll be to get the most from it.

Maximizing Sponsorship Impact

Too many businesses fail to get the most possible from their sponsorship dollars. Don't just sign the check and walk away. Wring every bit of value you can from your sponsorship! Here are a few ways to make sure your sponsorship doesn't go unnoticed.

Get Involved

Jump in with both feet. Join the planning committee. Volunteer on-site and connect with potential customers or clients.

Make Sure Your Company's Name Is Big and Bold

Review all event promotional materials before production to make certain your company is identified properly.

An Uncanny Event Idea

When Foodlink, a western New York food bank that aggressively reclaims usable food, wanted to increase food donations while stimulating community participation, it created the "Cans Festival," a special event with outstanding publicity value. Foodlink invited community organizations, businesses, and schools to use nonperishable food items to create sculptures for display at a local mall. Each group had to use at least 700 items as sculpture building blocks. The items, which were donated to Foodlink after the festival, could be obtained through food drives, purchases, or donations. One year, the annual festival raised 30,000 pounds of food used to feed the area's hungry. It also raised awareness of the group's mission through TV and newspaper publicity.

Leverage Your Mailing List

Use the sponsorship to build a mailing list. Are you sponsoring the library's summer reading program by providing coupons for free ice cream cones at your ice cream shop? Require children to write their name and address on the back of the coupons as part of the redemption process. If you're sponsoring a fundraising luncheon, ask the organizers to provide you with a copy of the attendee list, with addresses.

Follow Up with More Promotion

Continue to generate good will from your sponsorship— even months later—by writing about it in your marketing newsletter, your Web site, and your e-zine. Include all sponsorships in your company description in your brochures and Web sites.

Keep Seeking Promotional Opportunities

Look for holes in the event's execution and offer to fill them with options that meet *your* needs. Do organizers need more staff on-site? Bring your staff wearing shirts with *your* logo. Or offer to provide *all* staffers with event shirts that include your logo!

Promote the Sponsorship

While an organizer usually has a promotion plan for sponsored events, that plan is designed to promote the event itself, not to secure maximum exposure for the long list of sponsors. Event promotion is geared toward generating attendance, so the name of the event takes center stage—along with the naming sponsor ("The Coca-Cola Golf Classic"). So who promotes your connection to the event? You do.

At a minimum, make certain that your contract gives you

the right to review all event promotional materials, from ads and brochures to press releases. Only you can know for sure if your company is identified properly or whether your new logo—not the old one—is used in ads. Do more than that, though. Consider these options:

- Send out your own press release announcing your sponsorship.
- Give reporters storylines they won't get from the event organizers. A business reporter will be interested in your perspective on how to make sponsorship decisions or why high-profile events could not happen without all levels of sponsorships (including yours).
- Make sure your sponsorship activities include doing something eye-catching at the event, and tell the media about it. If you're passing out apple juice samples at a festival, dress your samplers in giant apple costumes and make sure the TV stations know about it before they arrive. And tell them where to find you on-site.
- Add a tagline to your current advertising—"Village Hardware is a proud sponsor of the Toys for Tots campaign."
- Stage a tie-in event at your facility and promote it with the local media through press releases.
- Partner with other sponsors to send a mailing about the event to your combined marketing list, encouraging your customers and prospects to attend.
- Write about your sponsorship weeks in advance in your marketing newsletter. Tell readers why the sponsorship is important to your company.
- Give the sponsorship a place on your Web site and link to the event site. (Make sure the event site links to yours, too!)
- Distribute event literature at your facility. Add it to bills and other mailings.
- Hire a professional photographer to shoot good, newspaper-quality photos chronicling your on-site activities and submit them digitally to local newspapers that same day.

Each year, Starbucks sponsors a Holiday Angels toy drive at its locations coast-to-coast, but it doesn't rely on the beneficiary of the campaign, the Salvation Army, to let people know where they can donate gifts for

Do Some Good

When Manhattan law firm Stroock & Stroock & Lavan "adopted" Engine Co. 4, Ladder 15, which lost fourteen firefighters in the collapse of the Twin Towers, it didn't do so to get publicity. The firm wanted to help by providing free services. But it got big publicity—a major feature in the *Wall Street Journal*, a powerful news outlet among the city's business community. So if the firm wasn't telling reporters about its work, how did the *Journal* find out about it? The lawyers' pro-bono work was described by the Association of Trial Lawyers of America, which was communicating its plan to provide free legal aid to all victims and surviving family members seeking damages from the Victim Compensation Fund. It was a good story all around. But it leads to that question: If you're doing something good, do you undermine your image by promoting your work to the press? Generally, the answer is "yes." It's like anything else in life—what goes around, comes around.

needy children. Starbucks stores send out their own press releases announcing the drive and follow up later, closer to Christmas, with releases reporting how many gifts were donated. It's how the stores generate maximum awareness of the campaign while helping to generate good will in communities where the company does business.

Should You Create Your Own Sponsored Event?

Many companies prefer to create an event that they own because it gives them more control over how it is executed and promoted while it lets them maximize the company's sponsor benefits. STA-BIL, a product used in lawnmower gasoline to keep it from deteriorating during storage, created and owns the STA-BIL National Lawn Mower Racing Series, an incredibly appealing publicity concept. Its motto? "We turned a weekend chore into a competitive sport!" In addition to generating publicity year after year—publicity that included a front page story in the *New York Times* in 2000—the series is also televised. See a press release for STA-BIL's proprietary national lawnmower race competition in Chapter 8.

Event ownership is an option for a small business with a big idea, one that will zero in on the target audience while generating widespread publicity. Should you do it? Do you have the staff and budget to execute your concept on your own, or should you partner with an event organizer? As soon as you partner with an outside company, your out-of-pocket expenses increase dramatically. If this is an appealing concept, explore ways to underwrite the event through subsponsorships sold to noncompetitive businesses targeting the same audience. If you have a really great idea for an event you can repeat year after year, a savvy event organization will figure out how to make it a win-win for you and them, so don't be afraid to explore the possibilities.

> **Chapter 16**

Becoming Opportunistic

PART FOUR   SEEKING OUT WAYS TO FURTHER YOUR PUBLICITY OPPORTUNITIES

■ CHAPTER 16 Becoming Opportunistic ■ CHAPTER 17 Using Tools for Opportunistic Publicity ■ CHAPTER 18 Getting Interviewed ■ CHAPTER 19 Preparing for an Interview ■ CHAPTER 20 Becoming a Public Speaker

Calendar Creativity

Charlotte Libov, an expert on women and heart disease, created National Women's Heart Health Day" to call attention to heart disease as the top killer of American women. Each year, Libov distributes press releases positioning February 1 as an opportunity for the media to promote heart health in women by focusing attention on risk factors for heart disease in females and what they can do to reduce their risk. A heart patient, author, and professional speaker, Libov also uses Women's Heart Health Day to generate speaking engagements that allow her to educate large groups of women about their heart health risks. By being proactive and creating a special day for her specific cause, Libov generates publicity for her topic rather than waiting for reporters to discover the topic—and her. Read one of Libov's press releases on Women's Heart Health Day in Chapter 8.

What Does "Opportunistic" Mean?

If you're really serious about using publicity to boost business or sales, you'll want to become opportunistic. This means that you'll look beyond the more obvious publicity opportunities—a product introduction or a new facility—and be more aggressive about getting your company's name in the news. It's easy to do, but you will have to be tuned in to the national and local media and you will need to react quickly when you spot a publicity opportunity for your company. In some cases, all you'll need to do is make a telephone call to be opportunistic. But usually, you will need to be alert to trends, current news stories, and even themes on prime-time television dramas.

Being opportunistic is about being proactive rather than reactive. It's about calling a reporter when you know something about a hot national news topic rather than waiting for the reporter to find you when he's looking for the local angle to that national story. It's about being alert to trends, and taking advantage of them. It's about becoming a resource to the media relations department at your trade association. It's about having the appropriate tools on hand when an opportunity presents itself. It's about positioning yourself or your company as the expert—and experts are always prepared.

The Opportunistic Expert's Tool Kit

Before you can become opportunistic, you need to have your tool kit in place. This is a slim package of information that contains your narrative biography, a color head shot, a company fact sheet, and press clippings. Produce several sets of these documents, keep one set near the fax machine, and have the material available in electronic form for e-mailing too. You'll want to make it available in the format that works best for reporters.

A Narrative Biography

A narrative biography is not the same thing as a resume or curriculum vitae. It is a few paragraphs of text that summarize your professional accomplishments. It is written with a "third person" voice in a nonacademic style that is free of industry buzzwords. If you have expertise in several topics, you might consider writing several bios, each one emphasizing a different strength or topic. Here's an example that emphasizes the expert's work with women's health and nutrition:

Susan Calvert Finn, PhD, RD, FADA

Susan Calvert Finn, PhD, RD, FADA, one of the country's leading authorities on women's health and nutrition, helps women dramatically improve their long-term health by showing them how to make informed nutritional choices. Dr. Finn provides women with the knowledge that they need to eat healthfully and maintain their energy and well-being at any age. She brings to her presentations a message of hope and confidence embraced by women coast-to-coast.

The author of *The American Dietetic Association Guide to Women's Nutrition for Healthy Living*, Dr. Finn is a past president of the ADA and chief architect of its Nutrition and Health Campaign for Women. Dr. Finn was recently one of a prestigious group of health care leaders who convened for the National Institutes of Health's "Women's Health Strategies for the 21st Century." She has participated in more than 500 radio and television interviews, including appearances on network programs such as *The Today Show* and *Good Morning America*. Currently director of nutrition and health care services at Ross Products Division, Abbott Laboratories, in Columbus, Ohio, Dr. Finn has received numerous awards for her accomplishments.

Color Head Shot

Your tool kit includes a color head shot taken by a professional photographer. You want to use color because it gives publications more options—they can always get a black and white print from a color portrait, but they can't get color from a black and white photo. Have it available as prints and as an electronic JPEG file that can be e-mailed or distributed on a floppy disk. If you have a Web site, post it there, as well, so it's always accessible to editors who can copy it off your site immediately and eliminate the delay of phone tag or e-mail requests.

Company Fact Sheet

The company fact sheet is a list of bulleted points that explains key points about your business. Whether you're a sole proprietor consultant or a manufacturer with 76 employees, you need to provide the press with a snapshot of your business so they can put your expertise in some kind of context. Include a one-sentence description of what your company does, your location, number of employees, a list of products, etc.—any fact that will help a reporter get a sense of what you do and the size of your operation. If the company has won any awards or been honored, include that information.

Press Clippings

Complete your tool kit with press clippings—copies of articles that feature you or your business, or articles you have written. Clippings tell a reporter or producer more about your expertise while they reassure him or her that this won't be your first interview. The more media experience you have, the more likely you are to get more interviews. Beyond that, though, clippings or article reprints suggest an "expert" status that you don't have if you don't have clippings. How can you be an expert if nobody has interviewed you before? We all know that the "experts" are the first people to be called when it's time to learn more about a topic. Even if a reporter doesn't read your clippings, they say something about your worth as a media resource.

"For Your Files"

Being opportunistic means sending your tool kit to local reporters so they've got information about you on file. Include a brief cover note that

What's Your Position?

Position papers, often used in press kits or posted on Web sites, state your company's "position" on an issue of public interest. They are useful background documents designed to both influence and inform relevant audiences, including employees, customers, and the press. They are most useful to those businesses or organizations lobbying to effect change or to keep change from occurring. If a position paper will help explain your company's stand on an issue or topic, remember to keep it fact-based or you will lose credibility. Start your position paper with a brief summary of the issue's history. Offer the opposing viewpoint on the topic, then state your company's position clearly using objective evidence or statistics that support your claims. If appropriate, offer solutions to the problem. While your objective is to make a persuasive argument, be careful to remain factual and unemotional.

says, "Please keep this information on file for when you need an expert for interviews on . . ." and include the topics you are qualified to discuss. They will be happy to keep your material on file because, contrary to what you might think or have been told by people who dislike the press, reporters are always looking for more sources to interview. And they won't know you're an excellent resource unless you tell them—so do so.

Becoming Part of the Headline News

Always watch for unexpected, unplanned ways to keep your name in the news in the following ways.

Offer a Different Angle on a Current News Story

Perhaps the headline news this morning was about a house fire made extra tragic because a lack of smoke alarms led to lost lives. If you sell smoke alarms—even if you sell 500 other products, too—get on the phone with the assignment editors at the local TV stations and offer to do an interview about where to place smoke alarms in the house and how often to change batteries. Come armed with statistics—how many lives are saved annually because of home smoke alarms? How many more could be saved if more homes had alarms? Or, was the fire caused by an electrical problem and you're an electrician? Again, get on the phone and offer to go on camera to discuss the most common causes of electrical fires in homes, and what can be done to prevent them. And make sure you're wearing a shirt or jacket with your company name on it when you're interviewed, too, for that extra exposure.

Offer a Local Angle on a National Story

Did the early evening network news bring a story you can comment on? Offer to do so! If you're a security consultant and you hear a story about a baby being kidnapped in a public location, or a rash of pickpockets in downtown Los Angeles, or an unusual robbery in St. Louis, offer to do an interview with local TV stations about kidnapping/pickpocket/theft prevention. In other words, as soon as you see, read, or hear a news story that makes you begin to comment with your own expertise, share your comments with the local media, not your spouse! Train yourself to tune in to the news, then react with a phone call. Keep the assignment editor phone numbers in your home address book, too, because they aren't in the phone book.

Offer a Local Angle on a Prime-Time Television Drama

Today's TV shows are creating drama by incorporating real-life issues and tragedies into their storylines, making them increasingly relevant to viewers while offering nonprofit organizations, in particular, great publicity opportunities. The shows about police departments and lawyers, with stories "ripped from today's headlines," are just as useful as the medical dramas that incorporate public health messages. (Television has a powerful impact on health care—research shows that 70 percent of Americans get their medical information from TV.)

Determine which shows tend to include stories you can use as launch pads for interviews, and monitor what's coming up by reading program descriptions in *TV Guide*, on network Web sites, and by watching previews. If you see one that is relevant to your mission, call the assignment editor at that network's local news affiliate and discuss whether the station wants to play off the show's theme with a local follow-up story that would air on the 10 P.M. or 11 P.M. news after the show.

NBC's *ER* covers so many public health issues that a TV station, a medical school, a foundation, and the show's producers have teamed to create "Following ER," a 90-second health news segment that tells viewers how to prevent the type of accident or disease portrayed in the weekly television drama. In fact, many of the local network affiliates, and NBC's, in particular, schedule their weekly medical and health news reports to air immediately after the popular medical dramas. These shows, and the networks' efforts to leverage their impact on the local level, provide ongoing opportunities for local nonprofit agencies, medical and health care professionals, hospitals, and others. Shows built around lawyers and the police cover a wider range of topics that offer additional follow-up publicity opportunities for those who are alert to them.

Be Available

If reporters are interested in working with you when you call, they might ask you to fax your bio and fact sheet, or they might schedule an interview immediately. Rearrange your schedule if you have to. You've given them another angle on a news story and if they can't fulfill it with an interview with you, they might interview your competitor. Have your materials ready to send, and have your calendar in front of you to take advantage of the opportunity you've been smart enough to create.

> If reporters are interested in working with you, they might schedule an interview immediately. Rearrange your schedule if you have to.

Call Yourself an Expert

The best way to get people to start calling you an expert is to do it yourself. Once you have a few appropriate credentials to your credit—a bylined article or two, a few interviews, perhaps an award from your local trade association chapter—start referring to yourself in your media materials as an "expert." Start small—identify yourself as "a local expert"—because you're not "a national expert" until you've been interviewed several times by the national media in your industry. And note that language says "a" local expert, not "the" local expert. There's always room for more than one

Opportunistic Publicity Success Story

When a retired Catholic priest began talking to literary agents about representing his autobiography, a book that advocates for optional celibacy for priests, he learned that his book proposal could be enhanced by evidence that he had media interview experience. At the same time, news broke of a Boston priest accused of pedophilia. Suddenly, journalists all over the country were looking for experts who could comment on this problem, which appeared to be happening in other parishes as well. The priest took advantage of the headlines, and his ability to comment on them, by faxing his short narrative biography to the local television stations. He included a cover note that explained that while he couldn't address pedophilia, he could talk about the role of celibacy in the problems of the church. He now has the material he needs to show publishers that there is media interest in his topic.

expert in any community, and you alienate fewer peers when you put your expert label into a more realistic context.

Support your "expert" status claim by being active in your trade association's local chapter as a leader and by always being open to learning more about your industry or trade. Experts have not only mastered the craft—they are tuned in to what's new, different, or innovative in the field and can be counted on to be knowledgeable and current on the topic.

Trend Spotting

Trend spotting is another way to be opportunistic and keep your company in front of the media. What are the trends in your industry? Can you translate them into a local news story that you offer to your newspaper or TV station? Or, do you see a local industry trend that you can turn into a story idea for a national trade or consumer magazine? Maybe you're a restaurateur who has noticed a gradual increase in the number of take-out orders. Turn that into a trend story—"Are people eating at home more—but cooking less?" for your local food section. Pitch the food editor on the idea, include national statistics on the "trend" from the National Restaurant Association or your state restaurant association along with names of a few other (noncompeting) local restaurants the editor can call for a good story.

A building contractor might see an uptick in requests for certain home design elements—perhaps new homeowners are abandoning the separate living room/family room concept and opting for a "great room" design instead. A quick call or letter to the home-building trade magazines to inquire about whether there's interest in a story about this "trend" could lead to an interview in a key publication. Chances are, the trade magazine editors are on top of trends you're seeing on the local level. But if everything's in alignment, your name and contact information will go to the writer who is starting to find people to interview about that trend, and you'll score a big publicity hit by sharing what you've seen as a trend spotter. (That same story can be pitched to the local newspaper's home or real estate section, too.)

Make Friends with Your Trade Association

In addition to generating news coverage for their industries and its constituents, the public relations departments of trade associations field inquiries from reporters looking for association members to interview for articles. By keeping your association's public relations department informed about your own media relations work, you put yourself in a position to be in the public relations department's list of resources for national journalists. Consider doing the following, too:

Find out who talks to the media at your association, and add their names to your marketing mailing list so they're informed about your innovative activities.

Call them regularly to find out what story angles they're having success with on the national level, and try to duplicate that success on the local level.

Ask to be added to their press release distribution list so you can forward those releases with a personal note to your local media.

Keep a file for all survey, research, or statistical information released to members by your association. You'll be able to use their efforts the way they want you to—to help build your business in your own community.

Create a Marketing Newsletter

A well-considered, thoughtful newsletter that markets your business in a way that serves others can generate just as much publicity as a year's worth of press kits. There are two secrets to the success of small business marketing newsletters: First, they must feature useful, how-to information that showcases your expertise rather than "Hey, we're great!" material. Second, your distribution list should include the media.

Use a simple three-column, two-page format that you can photocopy inexpensively in the office or at Kinko's. Devote the space on the first page to a "service" article that tells readers how to do something better, faster, or for less money, or that offers tips or advice that will be useful in their work. Use the back page for short news items describing new projects or announcing new employees. Avoid being overly self-promotional or self-congratulatory. Instead, focus on providing information that will be useful to your readers while showcasing your company's expertise. Publish this at least quarterly, and mail it to customers, prospects, and your media list. You will enhance your reputation with customers, you will warm up your prospects because they will feel they have come to know you, you will establish yourself as an expert because of the useful information, and some of the media outlets on your list will begin using your newsletter as a source of story ideas—and interview you for the resulting articles. The cost to you? Copying and postage. It's well worth it. To learn more about how to create a newsletter that promotes your business, get a copy of Elaine Floyd's *Marketing with Newsletters*, available from Paper Direct and book retailers. According to Floyd, people like to read about interesting subjects telling them how to make money or save time that are presented in short articles with good visual elements and simple designs in an organized way. People also like bullet lists, calendars, and special offers.

➤ **Chapter 17**

Using Tools for Opportunistic Publicity

Moving Forward with High-Profile Publicity Tactics

Are you really serious about maintaining a higher profile for your company? There are many print and Internet resources that can help you be more proactive in identifying media interview opportunities. Other resources can help you position yourself (or your boss) as an expert, then take advantage of that expert status. Use the resources outlined in this chapter to add turbo chargers to your proactive publicity endeavors.

Editorial Calendars

An editorial calendar is a tool that helps advertisers link their ads to relevant themes or magazine content while it helps publicity-seekers find opportunities for interviews or other editorial contributions. (Business and consumer magazines do not usually publish editorial calendars.) These calendars are essential opportunistic publicity tools because they let you review a trade magazine's planned content for the next twelve months and identify articles you can either write yourself or contribute to through an interview. See a sample editorial calendar worksheet in Appendix A.

Surf the Web for Editorial Calendars

Editorial calendars are free and easy to obtain. Most magazines with Web sites publish them online—look for an icon for "editorial calendar" or "advertising." If you can't find what you need online, call the magazine's advertising department and ask them to either fax it to you or to mail a media kit with an editorial calendar. Then, review the calendar for topics you can contribute to. Monthly magazines work at least three months in advance, so you need to contact them well before then to be included in a specific issue. If there's an opportunity for your company in the September issue, make your first contact with the publication in early April. (Looking to get into a weekly publication? They work a few weeks in advance.) Call the editor, state briefly that you would like to contribute to the article, and ask for the name of the writer. If the editor hasn't assigned a writer yet and is looking for someone from the industry to write the article, then by all means volunteer! (Read more about article writing in Chapter 10.) If it's been assigned to a writer, call that person and briefly explain how you might contribute. Then send appropriate background information. If there's a place for your information or expertise, the writer will schedule a telephone interview.

Create a Grid to Track Deadlines

If you're targeting several publications with opportunities in many issues, create a grid that helps you stay on top of the deadlines. For each opportunity, list the publication, the article, the deadline, the editor or writer, and that person's phone number. Design it so the first deadline is at the top of the grid and the last is at the bottom. Incorporate this information into your tickler system so you make inquiry calls on a timely basis and do everything possible to be included in all of the articles.

Printed and Electronic Media Relations Newsletters

This is where you start spending money to be opportunistic, but if you get one solid placement as a result of a lead from a media relations newsletter (and you probably will), your subscription has more than paid for itself. Most of the newsletters allow free trial subscriptions that will let you determine the usefulness of the publication for your company before you commit to a hefty subscription fee.

Partyline

One of the oldest publications is the weekly two-page *Partyline* newsletter, available via e-mail or U.S. mail. *Partyline* focuses on providing short, one-paragraph summaries of

Let Your Web Site Create News

Do you have an interactive Web site? If you do, use it to create story ideas and angles. If you don't, consider making it interactive so you can mine it for its publicity value. Online surveys, trends you can uncover through postings to message boards, customer feedback information, and information requests can all be used to uncover publicity ideas and to help you find people who reporters might want to interview on the topics you identify. Let's say you're an executive recruiter and you ask corporate clients to complete an online survey about executive compensation. You can turn those survey responses into a press release that announces the results in a newsworthy way. And, if your survey asked respondents to tell you if they would be willing to be interviewed about their answers, then you've also got people you can call and quote in your press release, or refer reporters to for interviews.

immediate or general editorial needs or media profiles for all forms of media outlets. It's especially useful for helping subscribers stay on top of new outlets or staff changes. Here's a typical *Partyline* listing—each issue contains two pages of listings similar to this one:

> "*Health Care's Most Wired Magazine* is being launched by Health Forum. It will go to 37,000 CEOs, CIOs, and information technology strategy team members in hospitals and health systems and will contain case studies featuring success stories of executives recognized as the leaders of the Most Wired organizations in health care, according to the annual Hospitals & Health Networks Most Wired survey. The new publication will illustrate the use of existing technology to solve strategic problems in hospitals and in the health care system, and will be a breakthrough magazine inspiring and building on the successes achieved by the top 100 hospitals in the H&HN Most Wired annual survey. Suggestions go to the editor, Bill Santamour, Health Forum AHA, 1 N. Franklin, 28 fl., Chicago, IL 60606, (312) 893-6834; Fax: (312) 422-4600."

Because *Partyline* is published weekly, its leads are fresh and timely. View two sample issues and subscribe for $200 at *www.partylinepublishing.com,* call 212-755-3487, or e-mail *info@partylinepublishing.com.*

Infocom Group

Infocom Group publishes several useful newsletters, including *Bulldog Reporter, Media Relations Insider,* and *Lifestyle Media Relations Reporter. Bulldog Reporter* ($349), published every other week in both Eastern and Western editions, emphasizes business media contact updates and "intelligence on how to successfully place stories." *Media Relations Insider* ($319), on the other hand, combines general media news and information with articles on how to achieve success with media relations assignments. *Lifestyle Media Relations Reporter* ($349) is the consumer media version of the *Bulldog Reporter,* combining short personnel updates with longer, in-depth media outlet profiles. Order trial subscriptions for all three online at *www.infocomgroup.com* or by calling 800-959-1059.

Media Relations Report

Media Relations Report ($347), published biweekly by Ragan Communications, offers information on business and consumer journalists along with how-to articles and success profiles. It's a good mix of content that is especially useful for people who are thirsty for more information about how to work with the press. For more information and a free trial subscription, visit ✎ *www.ragan.com* or call 800-878-5331.

ProfNet

One of the most useful but most expensive tools is ProfNet, a daily string of specific media interview requests delivered via e-mail. Founded originally as a way to link reporters with university resources—hence the title—ProfNet was later acquired by PR Newswire, a press release distribution service, and expanded to include a wider range of inquiries that can be responded to by a wider range of publicity seekers. Journalists representing a broad spectrum of print, electronic, and Web-based media outlets send their specific requests to the editors at ProfNet, who then distribute the "postings" to the thousands of e-mail subscribers. Readers respond via e-mail to those that are relevant to their businesses. The price of a one-year ProfNet subscription, which also allows the subscriber to contribute profiles to

Your Electronic Press Room

It's not enough to upload your press materials to your Web site. In order for them to be easily accessible to those who need them—journalists—segregate them in a separate area identified appropriately as a "press center," "press room," or "for journalists," and make sure there's an icon for that section on every page of your site. Also include an index on the "press room" page that lists the titles of all press materials and indicates whether they are press releases, fact sheets, backgrounders, illustrations, or photos. Link the index titles to the documents. Finally, make sure every document includes the date it was released and a contact name, phone number, and e-mail address for reporters who need more information.

ProfNet's online experts' database for reporters, ranges from $500 for a nonprofit to $2,400 for a public relations firm. Visit the Web site at ✑ *www.profnet.com* for more information and a free trial subscription.

Printed and Electronic Directories of Experts

Becoming an expert is just a matter of calling yourself one—then backing up your claim by showing that you know what you're talking about.

Advertise in the *Yearbook*

First, call yourself an expert by advertising in the *Yearbook of Experts, Authorities, & Spokespersons,* one of the most credible expert resources for journalists. Ad costs for the annual directory vary by size but include a listing in the online database with a link to your Web site. Go to ✑ *www.year book.com* to order an information package or call 202-333-4904. The prestigious National Press Club in Washington, DC, also offers *a News Source Directory* that lists experts at ✑ *http://npc.press.org/newssources/ index.shtml.* A 100-word directory listing costs $460; display advertising is more expensive.

Donate Your Expertise

Learn from the experiences of one marketing consultant who received a book contract after an editor with a major publisher read several of the consultant's postings on an Internet bulletin board and decided she was a knowledgeable source of information for an upcoming title looking for an author. As this consultant discovered, one of the best ways to promote your business or service is to share your advice freely on Internet bulletin boards, in chat rooms, through e-zines, and on your own Web site. "Show, don't tell," that you know your stuff. Reporters are like other information seekers—they wade through information on the Internet to find out who really knows what they're talking about—and who's really just talking. Start by showing what you know in an informative, nonpromotional way on your own Web site. Then reach out for other opportunities.

Use Online Expert Directories

Web sites specializing in linking talk show producers and journalists with experts include the National Talk Show Registry. This site connects either people with interesting stories to tell or credentialed experts with television talk show producers. Apply to the online directory at ✍ *www.talk showregistry.com* for just $32; you will be asked to submit a description of no more than 400 words of what you're qualified to discuss on television. Note that this site is not limited to "experts"—it's also a resource for people who are compelled to share their personal story (think *Jerry Springer* guests) with a national TV audience. Another Web-based resource is ✍ *www.authorsandexperts.com,* which positions itself as a resource for authors and experts seeking media interviews and speaking engagements. A six-month listing costs $125; twelve months is $198. The database is searchable by anyone. Before signing up, query a few members about whether they got their money's worth.

Become an "Ask the Expert" Volunteer

Consider signing up with the "ask the experts" Web sites, too, to answer questions on your area of expertise. Sites such as ✍ *www.experts.com,* ✍ *www.expertcentral.com,* ✍ *www.exp.com,* ✍ *www.askme.com,* and ✍ *www.all experts.com* allow people to enhance their credentials by answering questions on a specific topic via e-mail or telephone. Some require experts to volunteer their time, while others have payment-for-advice systems in place. Regardless, if you become affiliated with any of them, send a press release to your local print and trade publications to let them know that you are sharing your knowledge with the world as an "expert"!

Tips for Authors, Speakers, and Experts

The media lead service ProfNet is an excellent resource for any individual seeking local and national publicity opportunities. Each reporter inquiry in the ProfNet system includes a 100-word description of the reporter's needs and the type of resource he or she is looking for, the name of the media outlet, and an e-mail address for the reporter. PR guru Dan Janal has partnered with the service to offer a customized, affordable media lead service for experts, authors, and speakers. Through his "PR Leads" service, Janal interviews individuals at length to understand their key topics, then sends them only those media inquiries that are specific to their expertise. Janal also provides subscribers with tips on how to respond effectively to reporters' requests for interview sources. This personal service costs $495 per year; for more information, visit ✍ *www. prleads.com/index.html.*

TV News Magazines and You

Good news! Your public relations firm has secured an interview for you with a reporter from primetime television news magazine *Dateline NBC*. How exciting is *that*? What a great opportunity for you and your revolutionary new product, the one you're convinced will help thousands of people lose cellulite in ten days or less! Or *is* it an exciting showcase for your brand? Exposure on programs like *Primetime Live, 60 Minutes,* and *20/20* could be great for sales of your product—or it could be devastating.

Unlike the staff of your local noon news program, producers of these high-profile shows are less interested in "news" and more interested in drama, controversy, and entertainment. This means you should proceed with caution when dealing with them since they often produce segments with a predetermined agenda designed to reach a conclusion that doesn't match yours.

Looking to Appear on Radio or TV?

If you're promoting a book, a consumer product, or an issue relevant to a consumer audience, then don't overlook *Radio-TV Interview Report: The Magazine Producers Read to Find Guests* (*RTIR*). While it describes itself as a trade publication, *RTIR* is actually a collection of advertisements purchased by authors, speakers, and other experts. It is published three times a month and mailed to more than 4,000 radio/TV producers across the United States and Canada. Each issue lists 100 to 150 authors and other spokespeople available for telephone and in-studio interviews; issues are often compiled around a theme.

RTIR is without a doubt one of the most cost-effective ways to generate broadcast media interviews—a half-page ad run one time costs $497; many advertisers purchase a discounted three half-page ad run, which costs $978. *RTIR* staff-written ads will get your phone ringing if you truly do have something interesting to talk about on radio or television. Visit ✍ *www.rtir.com* for more information; call 800-553-8002, ext. 408, for a media kit that includes a sample issue plus a booklet with tips for getting talk show publicity.

Crashing the Crowd at *The Today Show*

It's getting harder and harder to find somebody without something to promote in the crowd gathered outside NBC's *Today Show* studio every morning. If you're considering heading to the plaza at 30 Rockefeller Center, here are a few guidelines: First, make it worth your while even if you don't get on camera by passing out product samples and coupons. Second, make sure you're visually appealing to the cameras—if you're promoting a candy bar, dress up as a candy bar. Finally, bring a gift for the hosts and give it a nonprofit connection that reflects the hosts' interests. (And don't forget to practice your biggest on-camera smile.)

> ► **Chapter 18**

Getting Interviewed

<var>
</var>

Part One

Part Two

Part Three

Part Four

Part Five

PART FOUR   SEEKING OUT WAYS TO FURTHER YOUR PUBLICITY OPPORTUNITIES

■ CHAPTER 16 Becoming Opportunistic ■ CHAPTER 17 Using Tools for Opportunistic Publicity ■ CHAPTER 18 Getting Interviewed ■ CHAPTER 19 Preparing for an Interview ■ CHAPTER 20 Becoming a Public Speaker

Deciding Whether Interviews Are for You

One publicist tells a story about a client who hired her to get him interviewed by the press. Period. There did not have to be a business connection to any of the interviews. There just had to be interviews, and plenty of them. Fortunately, this entrepreneur had a colorful background (including prison time for a white-collar crime) and plenty of opinions. Both made the publicist's job easier.

But you might be a more typical business owner, someone who would prefer to get publicity without doing interviews, someone who isn't interested in publicity that doesn't link directly to your business. You *can* get publicity without doing interviews. Short news items are often generated by well-written, well-thought-out press releases that answer all of a reporter's questions, making an interview unnecessary. And if your target publications are trade magazines, you can write bylined articles or case histories. But when helping time-strapped business owners set publicity priorities, publicists encourage them to try to secure interviews on their topic of expertise, rather than writing and placing bylined articles, because interviews take less of their time.

It also saves money for those working with an outside public relations firm or writer because article researching and writing is time-consuming—and you're charged for that time. The downside of being quoted in an article, rather than being the writer, though, is that you do not dominate or control the article, its tone, or its content. In addition, when you are interviewed, there's a good chance your competition will be interviewed, too (you'd never let that happen in an article you write yourself!). On the other hand, an article that quotes you has the same image-building and marketing value as a bylined article. And if the audience you're targeting reads and watches consumer rather than trade media, interviews are essential (see Chapter 2 for a better understanding of consumer and trade media publicity opportunities).

This chapter helps you see how easy it is to secure the interview that will help establish you as an expert or position your company as a leader, while Chapter 19 shares tips for the next step—the interview itself. These two chapters go hand-in-hand—you can't do the interview without making the pitch, but you don't want to pitch the interview until you've prepared for it.

The Pitcher's Toolbox

You pitch an interview in the same way you pitch an article (see Chapter 10)—by phone, e-mail, fax, or regular mail. The most important tool, the one that is essential regardless of the media outlet you're targeting, is the pitch letter. Even if you begin the process with a telephone pitch, you will still need to follow up with a letter that summarizes your idea in greater detail. As discussed in Chapter 9, your pitch letter will need to catch the journalist's attention, describe the story or segment idea, and convince the reader that the story can't be pursued without an interview with you. Make it clear in your pitch letter that you're not only trying to sell the reporter or producer on the story idea, but you're also trying to sell him on an interview with *you*. After outlining the idea, include a paragraph that says, "Please consider interviewing me for the article as part of your research. I am particularly qualified to discuss this topic because (insert your credentials here)." While your credentials should relate to your job, include media interview experience if you have it. Tell the reporter how to reach you by including your phone number and e-mail address in the body of your letter and under your signature.

Lining Up Your Information

What information do you have that supports the idea you're pitching? It might be a press release, a trade magazine article, or your narrative biography. Attach that to your pitch letter. After learning that a writer was looking for women to interview for a local business magazine article on women who changed careers after they turned fifty, a publicist sent a short e-mail pitch with his client's bio. He noted that his client left a corporate job in her early fifties to launch a company in a new (for her) field; the bio explained more about his client's previous work and her new career path. The client got an interview that resulted in prominent placement in the article.

Simultaneous Pitching

Should you pitch your story idea to two journalists at the same media outlet, even if they work in separate departments (lifestyle versus business, for example)? No. It puts the journalists in an embarrassing situation, and that's a good way to make sure they never cover your company's news again. Wait until one rejects your idea before you pitch it to another section (and even then, make sure you use a different angle, one that's appropriate for that section). Similarly, if you've done an interview with one reporter and a colleague from that same outlet calls for an interview, too, tell the second reporter that you've already done an interview and name the first reporter. The second reporter will be grateful for the "heads up" and will reward you later for not capitalizing on the opportunity to double-dip.

Tip Sheets Can Help

If your article or segment idea is how-to oriented, attach a tip sheet release you've prepared that showcases your excellent ideas on the subject. When we pitched the national cable *Home and Family Show* on a segment about how to get a good gift from the man in your life during the holiday season, we included a tip sheet offering gift-getting suggestions (read the release in Chapter 8) and a press release summarizing the findings from our "Worst Gift from a Man Contest." The resulting interview two weeks before Christmas provided an opportunity for helping viewers while also providing another guest, actor George Segal, with gift-giving advice for his new wife.

Including Additional Resources

Busy reporters and producers love it when you help them do their jobs, so when it's appropriate, include a list of additional resources for the story idea. Put yourself in the reporter's shoes—if you were researching this topic, what individuals or organizations would you need to talk to? Where could you get background information on the subject? For example, if you run a pain clinic and want to encourage your newspaper to interview you and write an article about pain management, consider including among your supporting attachments a list of other resources, including Web sites and national organizations, that the reporter can contact for information or interviews. Sometimes it takes a little work to compile these resources, but it's worth it if it helps you sell the story (and it will!).

In summary, your tools will include a pitch letter, supporting information, and when possible, a list of additional resources.

Seven Pointers for Telephone Pitches

Many public relations people start the process with a telephone pitch—it saves time if the idea is rejected, but it also helps the "pitchers" refine the idea and improve the pitch for use elsewhere. Here are a few tips for your phone pitches.

Make the Call

Make the call, even though it's hard to do or you don't like doing it. When you sell the idea and secure an interview, you will be very pleased.

Summarize Your Idea

View the telephone pitch as a sales call. Summarize your idea in no more than two sentences and say, "Does it sound like something you might be interested in?" If he is, offer to send a detailed letter and background information immediately.

Practice, Practice, Practice

Practice what you will say before you make the call. Say your pitch out loud before calling. It's okay to use a rough script if that makes it easier for you, but don't sound like you're reading from one.

Start with the Least Important Outlet

If you're pitching several media outlets, warm up by calling the least important one first. That way, if you make a mistake or stumble, it won't be with your most important media target.

Track Feedback

Pay attention to feedback on these calls. It can help you pitch them again on another idea, or it can help you improve your current pitch.

Never Argue Your Point

Do not argue with an editor, reporter, or producer. If your contact says, "Thanks, but it's not right for us," accept that, *even if you know he's wrong*. Proving to him that he's wrong won't make him change his mind. He'll only remember you as the person who knows he made a mistake. Accept "no" graciously, and hope you'll get a more favorable response with your next idea.

Following Up

Apply the rules in this section to follow-up calls, too, after you've sent a letter and supporting material. These people are generally considerate, and if they're not interested, they'll tell you so. If they say they'd like you to resend the material, do so. It's a very good sign.

If you sent your pitch and supporting materials via e-mail, you can follow up via e-mail, too. It's less intrusive and more convenient for the reporter, and sometimes more comfortable for you. Many professionals use a combination of both. They like e-mail because it's relatively painless for everybody, but they also like the enhanced personal connection and relationship building that comes with voice-to-voice conversation. While we're on the subject of following up, accept failure after three follow-up inquiries get you no response. Then it's time to take a hint.

Print versus Broadcast Media

Print media reporters need you to know what you're talking about. But radio and television interviewers need you to entertain listeners and viewers with your wit, animated personality, and, oh-by-the-way, some knowledge of the subject. That means that for broadcast media outlets, telephone pitching is essential—this is how they decide if your voice and personality are appropriate for their shows.

You can be evaluated for your suitability as a radio guest easily over the telephone. A producer will ask you a few questions about your topic, and listen carefully not only to *what* you're saying, but *how* you're saying it, as well. You need to sound enthusiastic and have vocal variety—a monotone style is deadly. You also can secure a local TV interview with good materials and a solid pre-interview with a host or producer over the telephone. But national television is different. Whether you're pitching a talk show on ABC, NBC, or CBS, a nationally syndicated show, or a cable program, you need to prove that you can be an engaging, articulate, and entertaining guest before you can get booked. Producers at *Good Morning America*, for example, do not want guests who act like mothers caught stealing their children's Halloween candy when the camera is on them.

Try this experiment: Watch *The Today Show* during the week, and watch *Weekend Today* on Saturday and Sunday. Pay attention to the public-ity-type guests—the book authors, the restaurant chefs, the professional ath-letes promoting a cause—rather than the breaking news-type guests (the mother who gave birth to triplets named Katie, Matt, and Al; the passenger on a plane that made a successful crash landing; the hero who pulled a family of four from a burning building). You'll see that the weekend shows, with lower ratings, use the less-experienced publicity guests. These are the people who speak more softly, are not very animated, and use too many words to answer questions. Clearly, they know their stuff and there's a rea-son to have them on the show, but they're just not good enough to appear on the show on a weekday, when more people are watching.

Secure your weekday slot by proving to producers that you are a great guest. You must submit, on request, a videotape of previous television inter-views. That's why those who aspire to national TV exposure need to get booked on a few local shows for the practice . . . and for the videotape. Then, when pitching a national talk show, state that you will provide a videotape of previous interviews upon request. (This always gives you a reason for that important follow-up call—you can say you're calling to see if they would like you to send your videotape.)

Annie Jennings of Annie Jennings PR, which specializes in placing guests on radio and TV shows, has developed a specialized approach to generating broadcast interviews. Using a combination of print advertising and press release techniques, Jennings captures broadcast media attention in a document that highlights controversy, hones in on segment ideas, offers tips and advice, and features suggested questions. "This style works well for busy producers who want to see several segment ideas at a glance," Jennings notes, adding that the more traditional methods and tools are still required for print media interviews.

> Those who aspire to national TV exposure need to get booked on a few local shows for the practice.

Media Deadlines

Be aware of and sensitive to media deadlines. When calling a journalist, try to avoid deadline times and ask if it's a good time to talk. They always answer honestly. Here are *guidelines* for deadlines, but use them as guidelines, not hard and fast rules. And, when a media representative tells you about the out-let's deadlines, as in, "Wednesdays are usually not good days for us because

What Journalists Look for in Sources

Why should a journalist interview you—or anyone from your company—for an article or news segment? What credentials do you need? Whether you're pitching a weekly newspaper or a daytime talk show, you absolutely need to be a credible information source. No reporter wants to rely on information from an individual who is discredited later. It makes both the journalist and the media outlet look bad. So how do you prove you're a good source of information about the topic you want to discuss? How long have you worked in the industry or in your area of expertise? Are you a member of the appropriate trade association? Do you have a leadership position in the local or national chapter? Have you won awards or been honored? If a credible source has suggested that a reporter call you for more information, that can do more for you than the best bio your mother could ever write about you.

we're putting the weekly paper to bed then," make a note in your media database and check that note before you call again.

Daily Newspaper

When following up with the media, the best time to call a daily newspaper that is delivered in the morning is late morning or early afternoon. Late afternoon is the worst time to call a morning paper. The opposite schedule applies for a paper delivered in the afternoon—the best time to reach a reporter or editor there is late in the afternoon.

Deadlines also relate to when you want your news to appear in print or on the air. Contact a daily newspaper with your news three to four weeks before you'd like to see it in print. A reporter needs at least three weeks to sell an editor on the feature you're proposing and to line up and execute the necessary interviews with you and others.

Weekly Newspapers and Monthly Magazines

The best time to call a weekly newspaper reporter depends on its publication schedule, which varies from market to market. In general, the worst time to call is two days before publication date, so if your paper hits the newsstands on Thursday, then Tuesday is the worst date to contact a reporter. The best day is the day before publication date, when reporters are starting work on the next week's assignments. Again, if your newspaper comes out on Thursday, you'll get your most receptive audience on Wednesday.

Contact a weekly newspaper four weeks before you'd like the publicity. If you need your article idea to appear in a magazine in a specific month, then send your material to the monthly magazine at least four months ahead of time. Magazines are published anywhere from one to three months ahead of time (three is more typical), so pitch your idea early to make sure you get into the issue that's best for you.

The Future of Magazines

Will magazines go completely digital? Some publications are taking a step in that direction by partnering with Zinio, a company that creates and delivers electronic versions of print magazines. The company's process produces magazines that mimic the look and feel of an actual publication, complete with ads, photos, and other graphics, along with interactive and multimedia elements. Readers also can use navigation, search, and annotation tools. But do people really want to read their magazines on computer screens? Judging by Zinio's early magazine partners, technofolks do. Initial magazine offerings include *PC Magazine*, *Technology Review*, and *eWEEK*. So if your target audience is techno-savvy, try to get placement in a print publication that is also distributed digitally. But many people—perhaps in your audience—still like to hold an actual magazine in hand while reading it. And because of them, print will never be dead.

Local TV News

For local TV news broadcasts, your timing depends on the timing of the newscast you're targeting. Some markets offer early morning news programs, some air news shows at noon, and most have early evening and late evening broadcasts. If you're targeting the 6 P.M. news broadcast, for example, don't call before 10 A.M. because assignment editors are in news planning meetings. And everyone's busy putting the newscast together late in the afternoon, so unless you have an incredibly hot, breaking news story, don't call then. Contact local radio and television news departments one week in advance for a news interview. For a talk show interview, send your materials four weeks before your ideal date.

National Television

National television talk show deadlines vary from show to show. Some book one week ahead, others book two months ahead. Call the show you're targeting and ask how far ahead they're booking guests. For seasonal opportunities, like back to school or Valentine's Day segment ideas, contact them six weeks in advance. Deadlines for e-zines depend on publication

Recording the Details

Recording details of your contacts with the press will help you better understand the individual preferences of the media you're targeting. For example, using this "record everything" approach has alerted one publicist to the patterns of an editor at *Fortune Small Business*. The editor reads the e-mail pitches, but doesn't respond to the publicist's follow-up notes and phone calls unless she's interested. Then, the publicist might get a phone call from a writer assigned to the idea outlined in the pitch letter. Observing and recording these preferences reminds the publicist six months from now that she can continue to pitch the editor with her ideas, and if she likes them, the publicist will get a call. If not, she will accept the silence and move on.

frequency; deadlines for Web sites are ongoing. Inquire with both for specifics.

Radio News and Talk Radio

The only rule that applies for radio news is don't call just before or during a newscast. It works the same way for radio talk show programming. The deadlines and availability of producers are influenced by the time the show airs. It's usually easiest to catch morning show producers in the one-hour window following the end of the morning show. If the show runs from 6 A.M. to 10 A.M., call between 10 A.M. and 11 A.M. to catch the producer.

Media Preferences

By now, you should have some kind of database or contact management software in place that allows you to track all of your media contacts, even if all you've done is mail a press release. It can be something as simple and easy-to-use as a table in Word for Windows, or it can be a file in ACT! or other contact management software. Update this database every time you make contact with anyone in the media. Use it to log the number of times you've sent e-mails or left voice-mail messages. Use it to record a summary of telephone conversations or e-mail messages.

Use that database of media preferences to record other bits of information that help you better understand or assist that reporter, editor, or producer. If she's mentioned she's working on a series on a topic that doesn't relate to your industry, but you see an interesting article about that topic in a magazine you suspect she doesn't read, then fax her a copy of the article with a note. Use that database of information and preferences to build positive media relationships that will help you secure the interviews you need to move your business forward.

> Chapter 19

Preparing for an Interview

PART FOUR   SEEKING OUT WAYS TO FURTHER YOUR PUBLICITY OPPORTUNITIES

■ CHAPTER 16 Becoming Opportunistic   ■ CHAPTER 17 Using Tools for Opportunistic Publicity   ■ CHAPTER 18
Getting Interviewed   ■ CHAPTER 19 Preparing for an Interview   ■ CHAPTER 20 Becoming a Public Speaker

General Interview Tips

Most businesspeople dread interviews as much as teenagers dread being seen in public with their parents. Most are afraid of the unknown—what will reporters ask?—or worry that they might not have the answers. Don't worry. Interviews get easier with experience. It's like anything else you've done that was frightening or difficult at first, whether it was public speaking or getting rid of that comb-over and admitting you're bald. The more interviews you do, the easier they become. Preparation makes a huge difference, too, so don't use what you learned in Chapter 18 to secure an interview until you read on and learn how to prepare for one!

There are a number of guidelines to keep in mind during all media interviews:

- Research the media outlet before the interview so you have an idea of the material it uses and how you can provide that kind of material during your interview.
- Stand up when doing telephone interviews, particularly for radio. Your voice will have more energy and you'll be more animated.
- Connect with your host and the audience during radio interviews by using the host's name during your conversation.
- If you don't have an answer to a question, say so. If it's an answer you should have, offer to get back to the reporter with the information after the interview. If it's within somebody else's area of expertise, give the reporter a name and telephone number to call for the information.
- If you make a mistake during a taped interview, ask for a "do-over." In most cases, your interviewers want you to look good, because that makes them look good.
- Speak in a friendly, conversational tone.
- Keep responses brief, but not too brief. "Yes" or "no" answers are deadly for interviewers hoping to entertain viewers.
- Politely correct misperceptions or inaccuracies presented by someone else as fact.
- Remember to use "flag" phrases, such as "the most important thing

to remember is," to call attention to your messages.

- Don't say anything you wouldn't want to see in print or on the 6 P.M. news.

Developing Your Message

What is the ultimate, bottom-line message you want to communicate in this interview? It is crucial to be clear on this, or your interview could be a waste of time—you might not get your point across (especially if you're not even certain what your point *is*), but worse, you might not say anything worth using in the article. The best way to make sure you aren't disappointed with the outcome is to prepare by developing your message(s).

Identify Just Three Messages

Spend time identifying *no more than three messages* to make in an interview. Develop these points by examining why you want to talk to the reporter—what do you need the article or interview to do for your business? Is it sell a product? Then your message can center on what makes your product different or better than its competition, or what makes your product useful to readers, and so on. If your objective is to educate people about an issue, then write down the three things you want them to learn about that topic. This message is called a "headline."

If you're the owner of a pricey, high-quality clothing store being interviewed for an article on fall fashions, your headlines should address the topic but also promote your store as a source of the latest fall fashions. So one of your headlines might be that "shoppers in today's economy have discovered that it pays to spend a little more for quality apparel because it lasts longer and doesn't go out of style as quickly." Another headline might relate directly to your current inventory—"If you buy only one new item this fall, make

Off the Record

"Off the record" means you are providing background information that can't be quoted or attributed to you as the source. When you do this, you're trusting the reporter to do just that—keep those specific comments "off the record." But can you really trust the reporter to do this? Because you can't, never go off the record in an interview. That way, you will have no regrets, and the journalist won't be put in the position to burn any bridges. And while you're censoring yourself, remember that when doing an interview in front of microphones, always, always, *always* assume the microphones are "live." George W. Bush learned that lesson the hard way during his presidential campaign when he described a *New York Times* reporter in an . . . er . . . unflattering way in front of a mike that was still on. If you don't want comments to be heard or used, don't speak them.

Someone Like You on a Big Talk Show?

In the movie *Someone Like You,* a national television talk show producer played by Ashley Judd uses a pseudonym to moonlight as a favorite columnist for a men's magazine. Her popularity earns Judd a spot as a guest on her own TV show, but we don't see the real behind-the-scenes "booking" process that's involved. In reality, it can move quite quickly. When a producer is interested in the segment or concept you've pitched, she calls you to talk about it. Sometimes she has questions about it, sometimes she wants to bounce ideas off you. Once she has an idea she thinks is solid, it's discussed in a staff meeting much like those featured in the movie. If the idea is accepted, she calls you to do a "pre-interview." Take notes during your pre-interview call— you'll probably be asked these same questions during your on-camera interview.

it a brown blazer." If you're a pain clinic director, one of your headlines might be, "If your health care provider cannot manage your pain, change providers until you find one who can," or, "In cases where pain management is especially difficult, you might need a pain specialist."

Find Out What Your Competition Is Saying

Your message development does not need to be driven completely by your company's needs. To stand out in an article based on interviews with others—including your competitors—you need to deliver a message that both suits your needs and offers something the others won't be providing. Research the topic ahead of time to learn what other potential interviewees might have said in previous interviews, or go to their Web site to study how their companies are positioned and, hence, what they might say. For an article on how and why to re-landscape your home, you, as a landscape architect, might observe that others likely to be interviewed will probably emphasize what's most popular in local landscaping, or how much a homeowner should expect to spend. You might differentiate yourself in the interview—and gain credibility with the audience, as well—by focusing on how landscaping enhances a home's marketability, since the landscaping is one of the first things a potential buyer sees when visiting a home that's for sale.

Uncover Supporting Material

Once you've identified no more than three headlines, you must uncover supporting material for your statements. This is the information that brings your message to life, the information that makes your message memorable. You offer this supporting information with your message point. Let's go back to the pricey fashion retailer who wants to communicate that expensive clothing is worth the price. She can support, or back this up, in a number of ways. One of them might be through an anecdote, which is an excellent way of helping people understand the message. In this case, an anecdote supporting the headline that says expensive clothing lasts longer might be, "Just last week one of my customers told me she's still wearing the black wool dress coat she bought from Le Chic Shop five years ago, and she still gets compliments when she wears it!"

Statistics and research also are good supporting information. When citing them, be prepared to provide a reporter with information on the source or a copy of the research so the reporter can verify the information. Personal stories also provide memorable support to message headlines while giving you credibility, as well. As readers or viewers, we are more likely to believe you when you support your assertions with experiences from your own life. If you're being interviewed by a trade magazine on how to improve hiring practices, we're going to believe you know what you're talking about if you tell us a story about the time you made a bad decision—and what you learned from it.

Delivering Your Message

It's important to limit yourself to three message points in an interview. In fact, even if you're the foremost authority on the subject, limit your observations to the three relevant message points that will do the most good for your company. Make your most important point first, and conclude with the least important. During shorter interviews, you might be challenged to work all three points into the interview, but during longer interviews, take advantage of the opportunity to repeat your messages so they are remembered. Repetition is important. Give a print reporter a couple of times to hear your messages so they stand out in his or her notes. Give your listeners or viewers the same opportunity through repetition.

Use Short, Plain Sentences

When doing interviews, use short sentences and plain, simple language that is free of acronyms and industry buzzwords. (If you must use buzzwords, even in a trade magazine interview, take a moment to explain them. Just because a writer works for a magazine doesn't mean the writer

Vivid Word Picture

During an interview on physician-assisted suicide, a physician who specialized in pain management explained to the network TV reporter that "Dr. Kervorkian's idea of pain management is death." Her observation was pithy, yet it painted a vivid picture with just eight words. Did this language just come to mind during this interview? Probably not. The physician might have worked with a media trainer to identify the most memorable sound bites to use for such an important occasion. You can develop this language skill, too, by listening for sound bites in the news media, and by studying newspaper articles to see what kinds of comments make it into quotation marks. Focus on the morning news programs like *Good Morning America*. They're good sources of sound bites because so many of the guests on these shows have received professional media training, which often includes sound bite development and practice.

is thoroughly familiar with the industry's unique language.) Armchair observations of television interviews and cocktail party conversation reveal that people in the health care profession, education, and the military are particularly guilty of using exclusive language that the average listener won't understand. And while some interviewers are smart enough to pause and say, "Wait—what's an MRE?," many more are uncomfortable admitting their own ignorance on the air and will not ask for clarification. Don't risk alienating your audience by using language that excludes them from the conversation.

Talk in Sound Bites

Learn to talk in "sound bites." A sound bite, according to a *Smithsonian Magazine* article, is "a device used . . . to reduce complex issues to simple formulas in order to sway public opinion." It's a way of expressing your message with vivid, colorful, or memorable language so that your quote will be used on the newscast or in the article. It's a technique for making what you have to say sound more interesting than what your competitor, opponent, or detractor has to say. Politicians are prolific users of sound bites. Mark Twain was a master of the sound bite. On education, he said, "I have never let my schooling interfere with my education." On relationships, he said, "Familiarity breeds contempt—and children." As a reporter, how could you not quote Mark Twain?

Using sound bite language comes naturally to some people, who are always quotable. They use catchy phrases or analogies that make their point easier to understand in the same way that others are natural athletes. These gifted communicators are hard-wired to speak in a way that engages us quickly. For most of us, though, speaking in a way that captures the interest of others—especially when there's competition to be heard—is a challenge.

The best example of a sound bite in recent history is Connie Chung's interview of Gary Condit in August 2001. Condit, the California Congressman involved with missing intern Chandra Levy, offered his lengthy sound bite so many times during the interview that it became fodder for Jay Leno, David Letterman, and other public wiseguys. By the end of the *Primetime Live* interview, we all knew it by heart: "I've been married for 34 years, I've not been a perfect man, and I've made my share of mistakes. But out of respect for my family, and out of a specific request from the Levy family, I think it's best that I not get into those details about Chandra Levy." It's a sound bite gone bad.

Condit used this response to questions he didn't want to answer. But a bigger problem for most businesspeople in interviews will be finding opportunities to use your message points when the interviewer doesn't ask you the "right" questions. Here's what to do: Answer the question that's asked, and use it as an opportunity to "bridge" to the point you want to make. A reporter might ask the pricey clothing retailer mentioned earlier, "Because your store isn't at the mall, isn't it less convenient for our readers to shop there?" and the retailer can respond, "Actually, our customers tell us that our location is *more* convenient for them because they can get in and out of the store quickly without fighting crowds and walking long distances through a huge mall parking lot. They also tell us that because our garments last so long, they have to shop less often for new apparel, which is very convenient for them because it saves them time."

Flag Message Points

Call attention to your message points by flagging them with phrases such as, "The important thing to remember here is . . ." or "What people are overlooking about this issue is . . ." or "The key point is . . . ." This is crucial in a short or confrontational broadcast interview, when you want to bring the attention back to *your* messages, not the interviewer's. If you don't flag your messages, especially in a longer print media interview, they might get lost in the reporter's notes. Help the viewer, the listener, and the reporter by reminding them of what really matters—from your perspective.

Another way to make sure your message gets across is at the end of the interview, when a reporter asks, "Is there anything else you'd like to add that we haven't discussed?" This is typical, and it presents you with the opportunity to either work in the message that you forgot to offer before, or to repeat your most important message point so it hits home. If the reporter doesn't ask you this "anything else?" question, and there's time for you to add something, don't hesitate to say, "Before we end our conversation, I'd just like to add that the most important point here is . . . "

Practice Makes Perfect

Once you have developed your message points and created sound bites, practice your interviewing skills through role playing. Give your media materials to a colleague or friend, and ask that person to be a reporter and interview you for an article. Ask the person to take notes, too. Pay close attention to the questions this person asks—they're probably similar to those you'll get from a real reporter. Note, too, when the reporter has to ask you for clarification because you've used a phrase or language that she doesn't understand—you won't want to make that mistake with a real reporter. Require your friend to ask a few tough, antagonistic questions, too, so that you're not caught off guard by a real reporter with an axe to grind.

As best you can, have these practice sessions mimic real ones in terms of length of time, too. If you're shooting for newspaper exposure, take fifteen minutes. Radio interviews conducted over the phone typically take three to ten minutes, depending on the program. TV reporters interviewing you in-studio will give you three to five minutes, but if you're interviewed on the spot at an event or news happening, your interview might involve three questions in less than three minutes.

After a round of questions, use your pseudo-reporter's notes to evaluate your answers. Which ones were great? Which were vague or unclear? Which need more thought? Did you present your messages? Are there any areas where you need to do more research so you're not caught off guard? (If you don't have an answer to a question, it's okay to say so.) Discuss how you might change your answers or use different language to make your points.

Practice, practice, practice. The more experience you have with pretend interviews, the easier the real ones will be.

> Once you have developed your message points and created sound bites, practice your interviewing skills through role playing.

Interviewing on Television

Television interviews are high-energy situations that provide instant feedback. Unlike radio, magazine, and newspaper interviews done over the phone, TV interviews offer nonverbal cues that guide your answers. If you see that you're not striking a chord immediately, you can shift gears quickly and use another approach until you connect. The downside, though, is that TV interviews are so short. They're like a wedding—the whole thing is over before you've had a chance to enjoy it! The other downside to the short time frame for TV interviews is that as guests, we have to be very focused on our messages, often grasping at opportunities to bridge from the question asked to the answer we want to present. It underscores the importance of memorizing your message points and of practicing your answers, because the more you practice, the more you remember.

Study the Show

You'll be more comfortable during your television interview if you study the show beforehand. How long do interviews last? What kinds of questions do they ask? What do the hosts and guests typically wear? Are you interviewed by one person, or two? Do other guests have an opportunity to comment on your subject? The more you know about what to expect, the more in control of your own interview you will be. Ask questions when the producer is booking you for an interview, too. You have a right to know what to expect. Producers don't like surprises, either, so most talk shows will do a pre-interview with you a day or two in advance. A producer will ask you the kinds of questions you can expect the on-air interviewer to ask. This allows both you and the show to be well-prepared for your appearance.

Pay Attention to How You Speak

In addition to focusing on what you need to say, you must pay more attention to how you say it, too. TV cameras sap your energy. This is key. They drain you, so you have to compensate by being more animated than usual. Prove this to yourself by asking someone to videotape you being interviewed by a friend in your normal style. Then repeat the process and be more lively and animated. You'll see the difference on tape immediately—the second version, while it might have felt phony or silly, will look more like the real you.

Here are a few tricks for staying alert and appearing animated during a TV interview.

Don't Get Too Comfortable

Remain physically less comfortable by sitting on the edge of the chair. This allows you to sit straight and remained focused. Do not lean back and get comfortable—this will drain your energy even more.

Use Your Hands When You Talk

You do this naturally when you're enthusiastic about a subject, but when we appear on camera, most of us grip the arms of our chair, making our hands unavailable for gesturing. Free them up by placing them in your lap, and use them naturally when you talk.

Smile As Often As Possible

Nobody wants to watch a sourpuss being interviewed. A smile is much more captivating.

Ignore the Camera

That's right: Ignore the camera and maintain eye contact with the interviewer. The only time you look at the camera is when you're taking questions from a caller. In those situations, ask the interviewer or producer ahead of time where to look when you're listening to callers' questions.

Practice, Practice, Practice

Have your practice interviews videotaped so you can see what works, and what doesn't. Then continue to practice what works. As noted already, the more experience you have, the more successful you'll be in the actual interview.

Using a Media Trainer

If you are extremely uneasy with any kind of interview—print or broadcast—then consider hiring a professional media trainer to prepare you. Good media trainers are worth it. You'll have no trouble finding a good trainer if you live in a major market such as New York, Chicago, or Los Angeles. In smaller communities, you'll have to look harder. You can use the Yellow Pages to find one or ask for a referral from a public relations firm or a media-savvy friend, but also consider asking a popular local TV reporter to work with you as a consultant. Who knows better how to ask questions than someone who does it for a living in your backyard? Avoid any conflict of interest by approaching someone you will not be pitching your story to. Ask the reporter to help you understand the kinds of questions to expect and how to answer them, to videotape your interviews, and to evaluate your responses.

> If you are extremely uneasy with any kind of interview, consider hiring a professional media trainer to prepare you.

Dressing the Part

How do you dress for in-person interviews? It depends. If it's a meeting with a reporter without cameras, then it's acceptable—and appropriate—to wear whatever you wear to work. If a camera is involved, whether it's for a still photograph or a videotaped interview, you should dress so that viewers aren't distracted by your clothing.

For still photographs for a newspaper or magazine, and assuming the photo is business-related, dress as you would normally on the job, but in a minimalist way. Women should not use this opportunity to make a fashion statement. They should also not overdress, wearing apparel they wouldn't normally wear to work. Imagine seeing a newspaper picture of the owner of the local bakery wearing a suit. If she never wears a suit in the bakery, she shouldn't wear one for the photographer just to "look more professional." She looks more professional, and says more about her business, if she's wearing the apparel of a baker.

Here are other tips to keep in mind.

Getting Radio Publicity

If all you want is radio publicity, you'll want a copy of Alex Carroll's *Radio Publicity Manual*, a how-to guide for securing and conducting radio interviews, available for purchase in the traditional format or as an e-book at *www.radio publicity.com*. Veteran radio talk show guest Carroll is the author of a few other books, including *Speeding Excuses That Work*, which he sells via the radio publicity he generates for his publishing business. To receive a free copy of his radio tips e-zine, submit your e-mail address in the window that pops up when you leave his Web site.

Carroll tells people that there are four ways to get radio publicity: hire a public relations firm, buy a listing in a guest resource publication, mass mail (or fax or e-mail) your show idea to producers, or call the producers yourself and pitch your show idea directly.

Watch the show and study other guests: If you're going to be on television, study what others are wearing on that show, particularly the host and hostess. If it's appropriate, try to mimic them.

Be comfortable: Wear something that makes you feel good about yourself. This is very important. If you feel confident in what you're wearing, you'll be less distracted and more focused on your messages. If that means wearing a favorite navy blazer, then do so. If it means splurging on a new outfit, then do that, too, because it will be worth it if it gives you confidence.

Don't wear a suit on camera if you never wear one in real life. You won't feel comfortable and it won't ring true.

Stick to plain, conservative clothes: Avoid busy patterns—checks, stripes, plaids, etc. They're distracting. We want to notice you, not your wardrobe. Dressing conservatively in brown, navy blue, or gray, especially for men, is always safe.

Avoid white but wear red: Avoid white. It causes camera flares and reflects on your face in a way that drains you of color. Wear blue or off-white shirts under men's jackets or another solid-colored shirt or sweater when not wearing a jacket. The objective is to avoid white and keep it simple. Do try, however, to wear something with red, which adds warmth to your complexion on camera.

Avoid accessories: Avoid accessories that distract, including large or unusual jewelry. Somebody should have given Hillary Clinton that advice before she appeared on *The Today Show* wearing a suit accessorized with a cardigan sweater tied around her neck like a scarf. What woman knows what Clinton said during that interview? Viewers were distracted by the peculiar idea of using a sweater as a scarf.

Wear your normal "uniform": Do wear what's appropriate for the reason you're on camera. If you work at the zoo and you're talking about the new primate addition, wear your zoo clothes, not office fare.

➤ **Chapter 20**

Becoming a Public Speaker

PART FOUR   SEEKING OUT WAYS TO FURTHER YOUR PUBLICITY OPPORTUNITIES

■ CHAPTER 16 Becoming Opportunistic ■ CHAPTER 17 Using Tools for Opportunistic Publicity ■ CHAPTER 18
Getting Interviewed ■ CHAPTER 19 Preparing for an Interview ■ CHAPTER 20 Becoming a Public Speaker

Examining the Business Benefits of Public Speaking

Want to get people talking about your business? Talk to them first—give a speech. Physicians in a private pediatrics practice in Atlanta use breast-feeding workshops presented by their patient education coordinator as a marketing tool that entices patients to the practice. A coach who helps patients communicate better with their health care providers gives educational speeches to a wide range of community groups. What do you know that will help others live or work better? Share it in a speech and see how you can expand your network from the platform.

If you were looking for a publicist, you'd probably give serious thought to hiring one you heard speak with knowledge and authority at a chamber of commerce meeting, wouldn't you? What accounting firm would you hire—the one who sent you a brochure as part of a mass mailing, or the one that was represented by a speaker at the Kiwanis luncheon? There are countless business benefits to public speaking, including the opportunity to position yourself or your company as an expert in its field. And while you're doing that, you can use your speaking engagements to generate publicity for your business, spreading the word even farther.

Public speaking allows you to connect with an audience of potential customers in a way that nothing else can. It's an opportunity to give away information that showcases your expertise while, at the same time, you leave audiences wanting more information that only you can provide. You don't even have to be a fabulous speaker! As long as you make a presentation that is useful or informative, inspirational, or motivational without putting people to sleep after a carbo-loaded pasta entrée, you'll find that you are on your way to becoming your community's expert on your favorite topic.

Select Several Topics

Begin your adventure as an occasional public speaker by selecting several topics that serve your business purposes. This is easier for consultants and authors to do than it is for manufacturers or retailers, but it can be done by anyone, because everyone's got something interesting to say. Get inspiration by checking out topic titles of professional speakers at their Web sites. Review the calendar of events of your newspaper business sections—what are the popular topics? Don't limit yourself to your company's specific expertise as you explore possibilities. The owner of a sign company might talk about "Seven surefire marketing techniques" or "Six ways to destroy your business" as easily as he presents "Five ways to make sure your store sign gets noticed." Let your business experiences—good and bad—influence your thinking, too. Keep in mind the interests of the groups most likely to be interested in inviting you to speak. The local chapter of the National Association of Women Business Owners will be interested in hearing from a woman business owner, but the topic that's appropriate for that group might not be the same topic that the women's club at a country club might want to hear from the same speaker.

Develop a List of Groups to Contact

Once you have a few topic ideas in mind, start thinking about groups to speak to. You will be aware of some already—at the top of your list should be groups you belong to. The newspaper calendar of events will give you others, as will your library, which might have a directory that you can photocopy of local clubs and groups. An interior decorator might identify groups of business owners interested in learning how to incorporate feng shui into their office décor, or women's social groups for a program on how to do the same at home. The owner of a local Midas Muffler shop who aspires to speak at the annual meeting of franchisees might want to practice his presentation locally before a group of retailers. A pediatric dentist who wants to educate parents about the importance of dental care at a young age might target PTAs or the Welcome Wagon Club.

Workshops Can Lead to Increased Income

There are a number of ways to use public presentations to boost your business. You can charge for your time, you can speak for free hoping to generate new clients or to sell products, or you can do a combination of both. Two sole proprietors who provide similar consulting services to different markets did the latter when they teamed to present a series of half-day workshops through the chamber of commerce business training program. Pooling their knowledge and resources, they created one four-hour program that they presented on three occasions to participants who paid a reasonable registration fee. In addition to making a profit on the registration fees and from the small bookstore they set up in the back of the classroom, the entrepreneurs earned significantly more from their program when several workshop participants hired the presenters later as consultants for their companies.

Write Your Own Speaker Introduction

Perhaps you've been in the workforce for longer than you care to admit. Can you distill your career down to four sentences that summarize the most important information? Would you trust somebody you barely know to do this for you? And would you still trust this person to select the most important information to use when introducing you as a speaker? That's too much of a burden to put on anyone who knows you only through your speaker marketing materials and a few phone calls, so do everyone a favor by writing your own speaker introduction, one that is customized for each unique speaking occasion. Include brief information on why your topic is important or relevant to the group and why you are the best person to present this information. Conclude with a sentence that summarizes what you'll be talking about and one that welcomes you to the podium.

Call Your Target Groups

Call your list of targeted groups to get the name and mailing address of program committee chairs or meeting planners. Send each a letter asking to be considered as a speaker for a future meeting. Include your topic title along with a description of how and why it is relevant to their audience. Don't send a generic form letter that forces the recipient to think about whether you'd be a good choice. Be specific about why you think each group's members will want to hear your speech. Reassure the meeting planner that your remarks will be customized to meet the needs of the audience—that they will reflect your solid understanding of their needs. State what's in it for them—will your presentation help them do their jobs quicker, smarter, or better? Will it make their personal lives easier, more meaningful, more comfortable?

Follow Up

Later, follow up on the phone to determine interest and answer questions. One of the first will be, "Do you charge to speak?" Until you've given many speeches, your answer should be "no." Most local groups don't have a budget for speakers, so if you charge a fee, you'll lose the opportunity to speak. Secondly, you shouldn't be paid to speak until you're really good—and not just in your opinion. The evaluation forms should say so, too. While some local groups will ask for references from other groups you've spoken to, most won't. Most realize that local speakers hone their presentation skills in business presentations—they don't expect them to be the next Tony Robbins. Have your calendar ready when you phone so you can review dates, and be prepared to e-mail a short description of your presentation and a one-paragraph bio that will be used in the meeting announcement.

Preparing Your Speech

After you've booked your first engagement, start working on that speech! Begin by listing the three main points you want to make—and limit it to no more than three points. Build your content around these points. Don't include any information or story that doesn't support these (no more than) three points. Outline your thoughts in the same way you'd outline a magazine article, but use this tried-and-true formula for speechmaking: Tell them what you're going to say, say it, then tell them what you said. Along the way, use stories or anecdotes to illustrate your points. People like listening to stories, and they make your key points more memorable. Use humor carefully—what's funny to you and me might not be funny to someone else—because humor is very subjective.

Do not script out your entire presentation. The worst speeches are those read word for word from a script. You know your topic well enough to follow an outline on note cards or on overhead transparencies. (Lots of us like to work from PowerPoint on laptops, but most local function rooms are not equipped with the proper—and expensive—projection equipment needed for this format.) The trick to working from an outline, rather than a complete script, is rehearsal.

Ten Tips for Successful Public Speaking

When it comes to public speaking, there is no substitute for practice, practice, practice. Only by practicing can you both hear and refine the stories you'll tell *and* learn your own material so well that all you'll need to speak from is notes.

Feeling some nervousness before giving a speech is natural and healthy. It shows you care about doing well. But too much nervousness can be detrimental. Here are tips on how you can control your nervousness and make effective, memorable presentations from Toastmasters International (✍ *www.toastmasters.org*):

Know the room. Be familiar with the place in which you will speak. Arrive early, walk around the speaking area and practice using the microphone and any visual aids.

Know the audience. Greet some of the audience as they arrive. It's easier to speak to a group of friends than to a group of strangers.

Know your material. If you're not familiar with your material or are uncomfortable with it, your nervousness will increase. Practice your speech and revise it if necessary.

Relax. Ease tension by doing exercises.

Visualize yourself giving your speech. Imagine yourself speaking, your voice loud, clear, and assured. When you visualize yourself as successful, you will be successful.

Realize that people want you to succeed. Audiences want you to be interesting, stimulating, informative, and entertaining. They don't want you to fail.

Don't apologize. If you mention your nervousness or apologize for any problems you think you have with your speech, you may be calling the audience's attention to something they hadn't noticed.

Concentrate on the message—not the medium. Focus your attention away from your own anxieties, and outwardly toward your message and your audience. Your nervousness will dissipate.

Turn nervousness into positive energy. Harness your nervous energy and transform it into vitality and enthusiasm.

Gain experience. Experience builds confidence, which is the key to effective speaking. A Toastmasters club can provide the experience you need.

Join a local Toastmasters International club (*www.toastmasters.org*) to practice your presentation, learn more about how to speak like a pro, and get feedback from your peers. (Each club has its own personality, so visit several before making a decision about which one to join.) If you have more than a passing interest in using public speaking to help promote and expand your business, consider attending one of the regional or national conferences hosted by the National Speakers Association (NSA). These events are packed with how-to sessions designed to help everyone from beginners to pros refine the craft. Many cities have local NSA chapters, too.

To find out if there's one near you that will let you attend meetings as a nonmember, go to ✍ *www.nsaspeaker.org*.

Keynote or Workshop?

As you uncover speaking opportunities, you will probably find that there are two needs—one is for breakfast, luncheon, or dinner presentations called "keynotes" and the other is for longer, interactive, instructional programs called workshops or breakout sessions. Does your topic lend itself to both formats? If it does, then by all means capitalize on this flexibility and develop two presentations to market. Many local professional organizations hold annual one-day professional development programs that will consider your topic—if it's relevant—for either a keynote or workshop timeslot. (Conference keynotes differ from monthly meeting keynotes in that they tend to be more motivational and inspirational in content.) In addition, local conference planners are happy to consider one speaker who can do both—inspire the group with an uplifting opening program and present a workshop on a different topic, as well.

Promote Your Appearances

When you have been successful securing local speaking engagements, promote your appearances to as many key audiences as possible. First find out what the meeting planner will do—for example, in addition to mailing a meeting notice to the club's mailing list, does he send a press release to the local media? If so, ask to review the release, and make any changes necessary to describe you or your company accurately. If the group doesn't plan to send a press release, write and distribute one yourself with your head-and-shoulders photo. This is a simple announcement release that states when and where you are speaking, what you are speaking about, and why it will be of interest to readers. Include information

Checklist of Speaker Materials

You accept a public speaking invitation because it serves a business purpose. Make sure you get the most out of the opportunity by controlling what is said about you and your business when the organization announces or promotes your presentation. Begin by providing the event planner or meeting organizer with a description of your presentation and a very short narrative bio to use in the meeting announcement. (Most organizers are busy people who welcome the extra help.) This approach eliminates misunderstandings about the content of your presentation—and leads to fewer disappointed audience members—and you will be certain that the meeting notice includes the biographical information that does *you* the most good. Do they plan to write a newsletter article to promote your appearance? Offer to write that, too.

on how people can register to attend, and conclude with a one-paragraph description of your business. Send it to the calendar editor of the appropriate section of the newspaper at least three weeks before the event.

Get Permission to Invite the Press

Get your meeting planner's permission to invite the press to your presentation. Then, the week before your speaking engagement, send a copy of that announcement release to the appropriate newspaper reporter and to TV assignment editors with a cover letter that invites them to attend your presentation and write an article. Spell out what you will be saying that will be of interest to readers and viewers, particularly if your comments are "how-to" oriented. Follow up with these individuals to determine interest; if even one says a representative is planning to attend, then notify your meeting planner that a reporter might be there to provide valuable publicity for the group. Most organizations welcome this kind of exposure that attracts new members.

Send a Release After the Event

After your presentation, send another press release that summarizes your remarks to the print media on your mailing list. While this approach is less likely to generate publicity, it does communicate to reporters that you have expertise in a particular area, and this communication will help them think of you six months later when they're looking for an expert on that subject to interview.

Offer, too, to help generate attendance at the event by providing the meeting planner with mailing labels for people in your contact marketing database that you think might be interested in attending. If they are reluctant to expand their mailing list, ask for extra copies of the meeting notice and do the mailing yourself.

Add the Event to Your Mailings

Remember to add information about your speaking engagement in any upcoming marketing mailings such as an e-zine or printed newsletter, and

Speaker Evaluations

The best speakers generate the most news stories when they speak, so if public speaking is part of your publicity plan, you'll want to make the effort to be the best speaker you can be. Speaker evaluation forms can help. They provide valuable feedback on your presentation skills and style as well as your content. Listeners will tell you if your material is useful—or useless—and if your visuals were clear or your handouts helped. But a word of caution: When you receive your evaluation forms, throw out the best one and the worst one. The best evaluation was probably written by one of your friends while the worst one was completed by somebody who's *never* happy. Focus instead on those in the middle. These forms are the most accurate reflection of what you did the best and how you might improve.

to include information on the company Web site, with a link to the group's Web site, too. Your goal is to make sure as many people as possible know that you'll be speaking on your topic of expertise—whether or not they attend the session is less important than knowing about it. And, if the host organization runs a news article about your presentation in its member newsletter, ask for permission to reprint it in your marketing newsletter and on your Web site, too.

Get Evaluations

Finally, ask the meeting planners to send you copies of the evaluation forms so you can learn what people like and don't like about your presentations. Use this information to continually improve your performance until the reviews are overwhelmingly positive and contain less constructive criticism.

The Next Level: Trade Shows and Industry Conferences

With experience, confidence, and feedback from several local presentations to your credit, step up to the next level by exploring opportunities to speak at regional or national trade shows and conferences attended by your customers and prospects. Do this for image-building purposes as well as for any other reasons, including the possibility of meeting potential clients.

This takes advance planning. While local meeting planners sometimes recruit speakers as little as two months in advance, national groups usually begin identifying potential speakers more than a year before the conference date. Many turn to their membership base first, so you should do the same—make your first targets those groups you belong to. You will have an advantage over proposed speakers who are not members. Most, but not all, mail a "call for proposals" to members. It indicates what they're looking for from speakers and a deadline for submission of proposals. Many national organizations post this information on their Web sites, too. Call the association and request the information if it's not online. When completing the proposal forms, resist the temptation to just cut and paste from a proposal submitted to another group. Customize it, because whether or not your workshop concept is accepted will depend on the planning committee's sense that your program will be relevant and tailored to the needs of its membership. Prove that it will be.

Market Yourself as a Speaker

Give yourself an advantage on the regional and national level by including professional-looking marketing literature about your work as a speaker. The most common marketing tool for speakers, the "one sheet," is easy and inexpensive to produce. It's a one-page sheet that includes your topic title, a program description, information on how your program will help audiences, positive comments about your speeches from members of past audiences (usually pulled from evaluation forms), and your photo. The sheet is faxable; if produced as a Word document or saved as a PDF file, it can be e-mailed, too. Because it's a commonly used tool among professional speakers, it says to meeting planners that you've "done this before," making you a lower-risk speaker than somebody who has good content but less public speaking experience. (Use it with local opportunities, too.)

Some meeting planners like to see letters of reference for speakers, so make a habit of asking for them after you speak to groups. Photocopy them and include copies with future requests for information. As you become more experienced—and more in demand—you might find a need for a professionally produced demo videotape. This is a standard tool for professional speakers but is not usually required for local presentation bookings.

Get the Word Out

Once you're booked as a speaker at a regional or national event, send an announcement press release and a head-and-shoulders photo to your local and trade media. This, too, is a simple announcement release that states when and where you are speaking, what you are speaking about, and why it will be of interest to readers. For trade magazines, include information on how people can register to attend. Omit that paragraph for local releases, but for both, conclude with a one-paragraph description of your business. Will people who read about your upcoming speaking engagement in your hometown *Racine Business Journal* want to attend? No, but they *will* be impressed. Speaking at any event outside your backyard is an accomplishment, so don't hesitate to crow about it.

Use your announcement release to generate an interview with a newspaper or magazine reporter in the community where the event will be held. Send the release with a cover letter that suggests an interview and explains why readers will be interested in your remarks. Be sure to play up your credentials, since many reporters are more impressed by out-of-town experts. Follow up on the phone to determine interest and to schedule an on-site or telephone interview.

This presents another opportunity for you to make sure your customers and prospects know about your increasing stature as an industry expert. If the local business section runs a short item from your press release, photocopy it and send it to your marketing mailing list with a "thought you'd be interested" note. Add a short item about it to your marketing newsletter or e-zine, and put it on your Web site, too. Through this process, you might learn of customers who plan to attend the event, and you can arrange to have dinner with them or otherwise network on-site.

Turn your presentations into bylined articles you place in publications read by your audiences, too. Tape record one of your practice sessions and have it transcribed. Then edit it so it fits a specific publication's format, and send it to the editor with an author credit at the end that includes a short reference to your work as a speaker on that topic. When it appears in print,

> Once you're booked as a speaker at a regional or national event, send an announcement press release.

purchase reprints, distribute them to your mailing list, and include them in your marketing folder—both for your main business *and* your speaking career.

Turning Participants into Leads

Every public speaking engagement, whether it's local or national, has the potential for generating sales leads. Be aggressive about maximizing that potential. At a bare minimum, make sure your handouts have your name, company name, address, phone and fax numbers, your e-mail address, and your Web site URL. Have you written a book or published a booklet that you sell? Most groups will let you sell them at the back of the room after you speak. Do you consult? Offer a free one-hour session to attendees. If you sell products or services, offer a special, time-limited discount to audience members. Give them a tangible reason for contacting you later. But don't wait for the phone to ring. Ask the meeting planner for a list of attendees so you can mail that special offer to them as a reminder. (Not all groups will want to release that information, but some will, and you won't know unless you ask.) Or get names and addresses by collecting business cards from audience members for a raffle prize drawing.

At the same time, be careful about not appearing overly commercial in your efforts to get the most from your speaking engagements. Meeting planners and audiences are sensitive to speakers who are more in touch with their own needs than those of the audience. They don't like blatant sales plugs, but they will embrace a speaker who is clearly before them to help them do their jobs or live their lives better—not to sell their products or services. You can get the most out of each opportunity without being offensive or annoying.

► Chapter 21

Creating Your Publicity Plan

PART FIVE   CREATING AND EXECUTING YOUR PUBLICITY PLAN

■ CHAPTER 21 Creating Your Publicity Plan ■ CHAPTER 22 Sample Publicity Plans ■ CHAPTER 23 Using an Agency or Putting Your Plan to Work on Your Own ■ CHAPTER 24 Tracking Results and Measuring the Impact of Your Plan ■ CHAPTER 25 Putting What You've Read into Practice

Putting Your Plan Together

Now it's time to use the tools in this book to create your company's publicity plan. It's a simple document that will take you only a few hours to create, but it's a valuable document because you will use it to generate the free media exposure that will help your business grow. And as you execute your publicity plan, you might decide to make changes based on your experiences with the press or with specific publicity tools or tactics. In fact, you should plan to make changes. Load up on tactics that are working; eliminate those that aren't yielding results. At the same time, remember that not everything you try will work the first time. With publicity, persistence is often the key, not a change in tactics.

Most small-business publicity plans are written in a format that combines prose with bulleted points. The prose allows you to explain complicated situations while the bullets make it easier to list "things to do" in a way that makes them easy to understand and act upon. Publicity plans usually contain most or all of these elements: a situation or overview, a review of audiences being targeted by the publicity effort, goals, objectives, strategies, tactics, a budget, and a timeline. Using all of these elements in your first publicity plan forces you to ask the right questions as you develop your plan. It also makes it easier for colleagues to understand why you've selected specific tactics or strategies to execute.

Lurk at a Meeting of PR People

Learn more about publicity and meet people who do the work by attending monthly meetings of your city's Public Relations Society of America chapter (a few larger cities have Publicity Clubs, too). Find your local chapter online at *www.prsa.org*, then contact the group to be added to the meeting mailing list. Not all of the meetings will interest you, but in the course of the year there are certain to be a few that will both educate you and offer potential networking opportunities, particularly if you're considering hiring an agency to develop or help execute your publicity plan. You'll probably even get some free PR advice from the pros at your lunch table, too, just by sharing information about the challenges your company is facing.

Situation/Overview

Start your publicity plan with a description of your problem or situation. What is motivating you to seek publicity? Spell it out so that everyone on your team understands your view of the situation—and can make corrections if necessary. Write as much, or as little, as necessary to communicate the situation, and do so in a paragraph format. Here's an example:

"While Company XYZ continues to grow on the strength of its work and the reputations of its partners and staff, the company operates in the shadow of its only significant competitor—Company PDQ. This larger company dominates at trade shows, in the trade press, and among clients with $1 million+ programs.

To counter this, XYZ needs to look bigger than it is. The company also needs more visibility among key audiences so prospects and clients understand its competitive advantages, which include program customization designed to meet the client's needs, hands-on attention from XYZ's owners, and proprietary program software.

This is difficult to do without a structured public relations effort. At the same time, there is not a great amount of marketing money to spend on a public relations initiative, especially considering there are two arms to XYZ's business—collegiate athletics and recreation.

The following recommended public relations strategies and tactics make the most of the funds available to tell the XYZ story."

Audiences

Next, use bullets to list your target audiences for the publicity campaign (see Chapter 3 for more information on audiences). There may be one audience, there may be several. Or, while your company might target several audiences, perhaps your publicity plan targets just one. List only the

Putting Everyone on the Same Page

Always include a descriptive situation/overview in your publicity plan, even if you think everybody on the team already knows what's going on. Putting it in writing eliminates confusion and misperceptions, especially in small businesses, where situations can change quickly and the changes aren't always communicated. It gives you an opportunity to say, "This is how I see the problem. Do you agree?" Seeing the company's situation in writing helps managers identify areas of confusion or provides the impetus for a long-overdue conversation about what really *is* going on in the company. A correct situation description provides validation—which is always reassuring—while an incorrect summary prevents the agony of moving in the wrong direction with an incorrect message or vision.

Publicity Training Opportunities

Think you (or someone on your staff?) would benefit from an intensive publicity training experience? Several organizations offer workshops that help individuals of all skill levels learn the basics and more. Two public relations newsletter publishers, Infocom Group and Ragan Communications, offer intense sessions with excellent speakers who are generally public relations veterans. Infocom Group's yearly media relations conference (✐ *www.infocomgroup.com*) is packed with how-to sessions and includes a high-technology PR forum for those with that specialized interest. Ragan Communications (*www2.ragan.com*) also offers an annual media relations conference built around "tracks" that allow participants to zero in on the workshops that are most useful to them. The industry's trade association, the Public Relations Society of America (✐ *www.prsa.org*), also offers media relations workshops.

audiences you're targeting with your publicity program, and be as specific as possible with your language. If you want to reach "married women with no children and a household income greater than $50,000," say so. The more focused you are, the more likely you are to reach the right audience efficiently.

Goals and Objectives

Chapter 3 defines and gives examples of both goals and objectives. This section is a brief refresher.

Goals

A goal is a broad statement of direction that is determined by the needs of your organization. This is the big picture view. What do you want to achieve with your publicity campaign? This is your goal. You might want to raise your profile. Achieve expert status. Begin selling products to a new audience. Update or change your image. These are goals. They are specific and provide direction but are not measurable. Without goals, you can't create objectives, strategies, or tactics, all of which must answer this question: "Will this help us reach our stated goals?"

Objectives

Objectives are measurable targets set within a specific time frame. While goals tell you where you want to go, objectives tell you how to get there. Even more specifically, objectives should detail what is expected, who will do the work, the deadline for the work, and how you will know the objective has been achieved. Objectives are particularly useful for the people executing the plan because they will know what is expected of them, when it's expected, and what they'll have to achieve to be considered successful.

Strategy and Tactics

Strategy and tactics are the nuts and bolts of your plan, explaining exactly *how* you plan to achieve your goals and objectives.

Strategy

What, exactly, is your strategy for getting publicity for your company? Put it in a bulleted point or two. Your strategy might be to mine your company's intellectual property for trade magazine articles. It might be to leverage your relationship with the daily newspaper's business section editor, who lives across the street from you. Or, it might be to build your entire plan around a series of press releases because that's what your organization is best-suited to handle. Your publicity plan strategy will reflect your big picture thinking and set the stage for your selection of tactics.

Tactics

These are the "meat and potatoes" of your plan. The tactics are the *things* you're going to do to get publicity. They've been described in great detail in previous chapters—they're press releases, bylined articles, press kits, special events, and so on. Tactics are the tangibles. And the tactics you select are those that will help you achieve your goals. To select the right tactics, go back to your goals and ask yourself, "What do I need to do to make this happen?" If your goal is to position yourself as an expert, consider a mix of tactics that includes tip sheets, bylined articles, media interviews, a press kit, and public speaking. If your goal is to use repositioning to begin selling an existing product to a new audience, then consider sponsorships, news releases, tip sheets, and a press kit for starters. Review your tactical options—the actual things you will do to generate publicity—and select those that meet your needs and your budget.

As you write the tactics, think in terms of specific activities, such as "Write a New Year's resolution tip sheet providing advice on how to organize your office for greater efficiency and productivity," or "Invite the newspaper food editor to lunch to determine how the company might be able to help her provide additional editorial coverage of our industry."

Budget

Create a list of tactics you believe will work, then pull out the calculator to determine which or how many of them you can afford. If your budget is limited, select those you believe will have the most impact for the least amount of money. When calculating cost, take into account the cost of using an outside consultant if necessary (a consultant will provide you with an estimate for specific assignments) and relevant expenses for your list of tactics. These can range from postage to photography fees to sponsorship costs. Be as complete as possible when estimating the cost of your campaign so there will be no surprises six months later, and require your outside vendors or consultants to be equally specific.

> Create a list of tactics you believe will work, then pull out the calculator to determine which or how many of them you can afford.

Timeline

A timeline is an excellent time management tool for everyone working on the project. Use it to help you manage the tasks and tactics included in your plan. If you want your bylined article to appear in the June issue of a magazine, for example, then note both your start date—at least December—and your targeted publication date on your timeline. If you plan to mail one press release a month, let your timeline reflect not only that schedule, but when you need to start writing each release. If your plan includes developing a grid for editorial opportunities in trade magazines, include the development process in the timeline. Then, once that grid is completed, update the timeline by adding the magazine opportunity deadlines to the timeline so you can use it to keep you on track as your work progresses.

Sample Publicity Plan

This sample publicity plan was developed by marketing communications firm Cindy Lee Associates. For more samples, see Chapter 22.

Research Findings

A review of the company's business plan (submitted by Jon Forward), Internet review of the stated competition, personal discussion with the principal client contact, and interviews with current clients were conducted as research for PR plan development. The following were found to be of significant relevance to the development of the public relations program.

Market Segments
E-commerce, information, and interactive: Interactive is fastest growing.

Marketplace Situation
- The market has expanded rapidly in the past several years.
- Growth is expected to continue at a strong pace for the foreseeable future.
- Rise in lack of knowledgeable designers, a lack of systems for identity development, and limited ways of qualifying the success of identity efforts.
- Trends are to create new Internet presence; develop improved presence; develop new markets and sources of income through the Internet.
- Most common sales method employed by firms are examples of past successes, referrals, and own Web presence.
- In a review of Web sites of the four primary competitors, all have and showcase design knowledge. Two of the competitors stress the ability to design promotions that "extend brands." One, Navistream, seems to focus more heavily on the technology aspect than on the design elements. The most similar competitor in services and positioning is Forward Branding and Identity, which stresses interactive, latest thinking, and adapting identities across all categories.

Opportunities
Unfulfilled need for brand identity and interactive/Web design featuring good processes, cutting-edge graphic design, and an understandable information structure. In addition, appeal of a new, more focused and systematic approach that more directly addresses customer needs.

Current Situation of XYZ Design
Positioning: XYZ Design provides the most professionally designed solutions available today. Its highly customized solutions are created for

customers with particularly demanding or specific requirements.

The company addresses the need for strategic identity and interactive design that works on numerous levels. It does so by creating innovative, cutting-edge designs that take into consideration more than just how they look but also how they support the brand identity, marketing focus, and how the user/viewer/customer interacts with them.

The company's strategy is described as providing innovative and cutting-edge techniques to all aspects of running the business.

Distinguishing Characteristics

- Focus on supporting innovative companies that want to create an identity that works through graphic design, advertising, packaging, PR programs, and particularly the Web.
- Systematic process that includes documented information-gathering process, comprehensive competitive study, and action plan.
- Proprietary template of necessary elements for strong brand ID.
- Twenty-one- to ninety-day completion time for projects.

Recent Projects

- MPX, Inc.—ID and Web
- Dr. Kazdan & Associates—ID
- Soliton Associates—Web site

Current Client Perceptions

In the research phase of this program, two clients of XYZ Design (as Jon Forward) were interviewed. Current client perception, based upon these two conversations, is that Jon has an ability to understand the client's needs and the "big picture" and reflects that in his work. The design is not derived from the artist's desire to insert his own personality or opinion, but rather from true client need and expressed want.

- "Jon understands the intent of the communication and can design graphics to reflect that."
- "Jon provides big bang for the buck and creative thinking; he can think outside the box."

Neither client has used Jon for interactive/Web work, but has used his services for catalogs, sell sheets, logos, naming, and packaging. In those capacities, his design skills are considered to be very strong, "top notch."

Two potential perception problems were discovered in conversations with both clients.

- XYZ Design is not known for having technical expertise for hi-tech, "lots of bells and whistles" work. XYZ would be passed up for other firms that are more established and well-known in that arena because the young agency is seen as being in the start-up phase when it comes to technology. When resources and time are weighed, XYZ does not come on strong in the ability to get this kind of work done efficiently.
- As a small company, XYZ presents a lack of formal processes that makes it harder to work with them as a corporate client with a requirement to produce formal paperwork (i.e., estimates in advance and timely billing).

Problem Statement

XYZ Design is a relatively new business in Rochester. Although its owner/creative director has extensive design experience and an impressive portfolio, the company as an entity cannot boast many brand and interactive programs. Awareness of the company's existence as well as its service offerings and expertise needs to be developed and/or increased among primary target audiences.

Target Audiences

Primary Audiences (Prioritized)
- New, start-up high-tech companies
- Ad agencies to obtain specialized branding work by contract
- Older companies with established brand and Web presence
- Older companies with an established brand but no Web presence

Secondary Audiences

- Media
- Local newspapers
- Trade magazines (including vertical/high-tech)
- Industry newsletters
- Employees

Goals

- To introduce XYZ Design and its focus on identity and interactive design
- To inform potential customers of previously completed projects
- To obtain hits to new Web site

Objectives

- To increase name recognition of the company by X percent among all target audiences within one year
- To increase awareness of XYZ Design's services/expertise by X percent among the two top priority audiences within six months
- For (#) of audience members called to recall at least two projects previously completed by XYZ
- To obtain (#) hits to the company's Web site by the end of the first six months
- To increase clientele by X percent at the end of one year

Planning

Key messages are as follows:

- XYZ Design brings a fresh new approach to branding and interactive to the Rochester market by learning from the more than twenty-five years of experience of its principals.
- XYZ Design is a leader in the development of innovative and integrated branding solutions.
- XYZ provides highly customized solutions for customers with

particularly demanding or specific requirements.
- The company has the necessary technical expertise (multi-platform experience).

To develop a viable PR plan for XYZ Design, a Strengths-Weaknesses-Opportunities-Threats (SWOT) approach was taken to summarize the company's situation and develop a plan to best fit that situation. Each element of SWOT was looked at in regard to XYZ Design, and the approach decided upon was to develop a plan that best builds on the company's strengths and the opportunities that exist in its external environment (an SO strategy).

Strategies

Strategy I Tactics
Prepare logistical groundwork for public relations activities.

- Development of targeted media lists for local media and horizontal trade (design) media
- Development of a press kit with background information about XYZ Design's services and distinguishing features. Include photos of the principals as well as camera-ready graphics

Strategy II Tactics
Use special promotion and media relations to demonstrate that XYZ Design creates innovative branding solutions that pique interest and work across several platforms (logos, Web, interactive).

- "XYZ Storm" in Rochester: Start with twenty anonymous novelty deliveries to key agency and secondary corporate target audiences. Include ribbon or card with teaser such as "Coming soon . . ." or "XYZ Coming Soon to Ignite the Power of Your Business."
- Targeted XYZs: package and limit deliveries to twenty more focused potential client groups. This targeted element of the program will be hand-delivered to communication/Web directors at high-tech corporations (tier one).
- Packaging: Helium balloon anchored by bag of XYZs; balloon rises

when box is opened. Pitch letter and CD-ROM or company CD business card included.

- XYZ e-mails: innovative e-mail referral campaign using associates/past clients to send a pre-designed e-mail to a large potential customer base. If technically possible, the e-mail should contain XYZ design elements and be easy to forward "chain letter" style. Also include a link to the company's new Web site. E-mail will also be used as the follow-up to the anonymous XYZ deliveries.
- Feature article pitch: pitch exclusive feature article to RBJ/D&C about unique campaign and the new company's approach to extending brands.
- Distribute follow-up release in press kit explaining the XYZ promotion and its goal.

Strategy III Tactics

Educate target consumer markets about the importance of developing and extending a brand through use of powerful design.

- Create speech, "Igniting the Power of Design," which can be used at a variety of venues.
- Speaking engagements/seminars: "Igniting the Power of Design" speech. Obtain speaking engagements before key audience groups for Jon. Potential groups: Small Business Association; Rochester Women's Network; chamber of commerce; Lennox Technology Center residents, ITEC 2001, etc.
- Pitch radio interviews locally.
- Seek out opportunity for participation on panels to discuss branding/design.
- Seminars/training workshops: Hold training workshops or seminars to present the latest in interactive technology to employees. When applicable, invite members of client organizations in for the free seminar as well (e.g., Webmaster of a client organization to be included in seminar about new interactive Web software).
- Client newsletter: Provide news of latest in technology, approaches, studies about branding, identity, packaging, promotion, and Web. This is also a good platform for distribution of case study articles

that are not guaranteed to be picked up by the media. Given that XYZ Design must continually emphasize its Web/interactive expertise, this newsletter can be distributed either by e-mail or printed on the Web as a showcase piece using the latest design techniques.

- Voice-mail recording: record a voice-mail or on-hold message that discusses the capabilities of XYZ Design and the importance of "Igniting the Power of Design." This could be similar to a radio ad in its creativity and message.
- New office open house: Invite current and potential clients to an open house to showcase the new office and exhibits of past projects completed. Serve hot/spicy hors d'oeuvres and drinks in red glasses/cups in keeping with the name of the theme.
- Press release to announce opening of new office and expanded capabilities it provides (client meeting space, opportunity to host training seminars for employees, etc.).
- Case studies: Send press releases that detail the cases of particular clients. These case studies would show the capabilities XYZ has and how it served a particular client in a particular industry. These can then be distributed/pitched to the client organization's local press and/or the Rochester media, if different. Optimum timing would be every other month.
- XYZ releases: releases about awards, board appointments, new employees/employee accolades, etc. when available and necessary. Try for every other month.

Strategy IV Tactics

Utilize a community relations program that positions XYZ Design as an industry leader and innovator.

- Young Artists Shadow Day: program in collaboration with RCSD/ Edison Tech to bring several art students to the studio for a shadowing morning or day. The students would get a mini-lesson in branding and integrating design into all elements and then lunch with Jon, XYZ staff, and some VIPs (political, school system, industry).
- Distribute press release positioning XYZ as an innovator and leader

How to Handle Bad News

What would you do if a malfunction at your plant polluted the environment, or if one of your employees was arrested after shooting his wife in a convenience store, or if there was a major fire in one of your offices? What's the best way to handle bad news when you're dealing with the press? First, be honest and direct. Second, be honest and direct. Third, be honest and direct. Fourth, do not hide. The worst thing you can do in a crisis or other bad situation is to say, "no comment." Regardless of the situation, "no comment" makes you look guilty of something. Fifth, be available to answer questions. Don't speculate. "Guesses," observations, and conjecture can be misinterpreted as facts that might haunt you later.

in comprehensive branding that is educating tomorrow's businesspeople and designers about the importance of incorporating branding across all platforms.

- Award judging: look for opportunities to sit on judging panels for industry awards. This works toward credibility of expertise.

Strategy V Tactics

Use successes in the Rochester market to conduct media relations in additional market(s).

- Develop national media lists for business publications as well as vertical trade publications. Also develop list of radio stations nationally that present an opportunity for phone interviews and Web-based publications that accept news from outside sources.
- Revisit any horizontal trade publications that expressed interest in case studies or would have required change in XYZ Design, its income, or client base, etc. to consider writing an article.
- Write and pitch case studies for vertical market publications in the three strongest client industries. By focusing a case study on a client's industry, it shows others in the same or similar industries what you could do for them.
- Research and pitch speaking engagements at larger venues (e.g., national trade shows, keynote speeches at client industry conferences, etc.).
- Pitch radio show interviews (national).
- Send case studies or other releases to national news media/horizontal trade publications when applicable.

Evaluation

Evaluation of the public relations program will be conducted quarterly via client meetings, analysis of press clippings, and interviews with client prospects. Additionally, Cindy Lee Associates will continually seek feedback from XYZ Design via e-mail and personal contact with Jon Forward. The PR Program will be amended at any time during its course if warranted by evaluative measures.

Create Your Publicity Plan

Combine the information in this chapter with the samples in Chapter 22 to begin shaping your own useful document. You'll see that while different organizations use different formats, they generally include most of the elements outlined in this chapter. The worksheet in Appendix A outlines one popular format. Customize it so that it works for your organization.

► Chapter 22

Sample Publicity Plans

Using Sample Plans

The three sample publicity plans in this chapter demonstrate how different—in content and in length—publicity plans can be. Using the information in Chapter 21 and the examples here, you can create your own publicity plan in no time.

Sample from a Technical Writing Firm

This sample publicity plan was developed by marketing communications firm Cindy Lee Associates for a technical writing company.

Current Situation/Problem Statement

SoftSource, Inc. is an established business in the Rochester marketplace, having been working with Rochester-based clients for seven years. However, due to the nature of its work (ghostwriting and creating for clients), it is not as well known as it could be. Awareness of the company's existence, strengths, and track record as well as a brand ID needs to be developed to generate new sales leads and to increase business among existing clients who may not be aware of the company's breadth of services.

To accomplish this, the company's principals have already discussed a spin-off brand name to target the health care market, a growing segment of wireless/handheld technology users. CareForge, Inc., the new company, will be considered in the ensuing plan.

Client Positioning

According to the client, the current position of SoftSource is that it is a Rochester-based engineering firm that does technical work.

Target Audiences

- Business managers outside of the IT/IS departments at local companies (general business)
- IT/IS managers—to develop more opportunities

- Health care management—25–45-year-old decision makers; mostly educated, male IT people or procurement. This includes Medical Record Departments in hospitals and the like.

Plan Goal

To "grow business along any point of the spectrum" of SoftSource's service offerings and to generate "more work within the health care channel."

Objectives

- To increase name recognition of the company within the Rochester marketplace
- To increase awareness of SoftSource's services/expertise among existing clients
- To generate awareness of the new company, CareForge
- To position CareForge as: "A realistic, honest medical information systems provider that can integrate and develop health care systems. They are experts in document movement."
- To create sales leads within either or both segments

SWOT Analysis: Strengths, Weaknesses, Opportunities, Threats

Strengths
- Broad expertise and experience
- Paul is a health care expert
- Client list includes Xerox and J&J (tried and tested with big-name clients)
- Can prototype developed products in own facility

Weaknesses
- Ambiguity: "Who are you and what do you do?" This can be answered many different ways depending upon who asks. This results in lack of one core identity or "brand."
- Inability to cite client list and projects by name in most cases; lack of "bragging rights" for testimonial and credibility.

- Stigma that exists between IT label and engineering label—can't take on either name without potentially alienating the other.

Opportunities
- Growing health care market
- Increasing wireless/mobile demand and usage, particularly in the health care segment
- Clients looking to meet HIPAA requirements; the most seemingly compliant products will get the sale

Threats
- More established health care-specific information technology providers exist.
- Competition has more user-friendly or obvious names.
- Competition is more strongly branded.

Upon conducting research into the current state of news generated about and by health care service providers and their products (see Appendix A), it has been decided that it would be to SoftSource's best advantage to take on a combination Strengths/Weaknesses and Strengths/Opportunities strategy. In essence, this means that the PR plan will be focused on emphasizing the company's strengths to both counter its weaknesses and take advantage of opportunities in the marketplace.

Planning

Strategy I Tactics
Prepare logistical groundwork for public relations activities:

- Development of brand identities for both SoftSource and CareForge.
- Create key message points to be used in all company communication to external audiences.
- Development of a press kit with background information about both companies. This would include case studies reworked for PR purposes, profiles of the companies' principals, photos of same, announcement release for CareForge and other relevant material.

- Development of targeted media lists for local media and national audience trade (health care) media. Note that national general news media list(s) will be created as necessary.
- Research editorial opportunities within trade publications for the year 2002 and beginning of 2003.
- Identify industry analysts, consultants, and advocates to include in press distribution lists.

Strategy II Tactics

Use latest company news to reintroduce company and background successes:

- Introduction of CareForge to both the local media marketplace and the relevant national media (health care and some national news). This would be done via press kit mailing, follow-up calls, and interview pitching. Within announcement of CareForge, we would elaborate on the parent company's history and experience.
- Direct-mail pieces: send letters or e-mails announcing CareForge to existing clients and to health care management in Rochester with whom the company currently has a relationship.

Strategy III Tactics

Development of HIPAA expertise.

- Create a HIPAA expert at CareForge via research, seminars, or any other means necessary to get "up to speed" on the subject.
- Include this person's experience, education, and any other compelling HIPAA statistics in all press materials directed at health care segment.
- Research potential alliance with HIPAA expert, C. Peter Waegemann, and/or the Medical Records Institute, Newton, Massachusetts. (Waegemann helped develop the American Society for Testing and Materials' Committee E-31 on Healthcare Informatics and was instrumental in promoting voluntary standardization within the health care industry. He contributed to progress on standards for electronic patient records and medical documentation formats as well as several proposals for digital signatures now involved in HIPAA.)

- If alliance formed, announcement of this alliance would be developed and carried out in the national marketplace.

Strategy IV Tactics

Use ongoing company news to develop and maintain awareness among audiences and to educate them as to its abilities.

- Rework some of the existing case studies into press releases announcing project completion. These could also be sent to vertical trade publications within the markets of the client—security, health care, and human resources.
- Write new case studies as projects are completed and distribute these as press releases to relevant news and trade media.
- Announcement of Nokia phone dictation device upon completion and/or partnership with company that will distribute it. This would include the development of a fact sheet of its features and a press release as well as trade show support via interview pitching.
- Announcement of blood analyzer prototype completion for J&J or development of case study of this product with client name removed if permission not available to use name.
- Writing and distribution of press releases announcing new hires, board appointments, awards, memberships, and new product/service offerings as they happen.
- Development and distribution of press releases or pitch letters (or placement of pitch phone calls) to take advantage of any opportunities identified in editorial calendar research. This would then also include follow-through to work with reporters to complete the story.
- Include all relevant collateral material on the company's Web site.

Strategy V Tactics

Utilize HIPAA expertise to make CareForge appear the most knowledgeable on the subject and therefore the only company clients would be comfortable working with or buying from.

- Write a standard speech or talk that can be given at trade shows, conferences, etc. expressing the importance and difficulty of HIPAA compliance in light of new technology proposed for use by doctors.

- Research and pitch speaking engagements to present this speech. Such possibilities might include AHIMA or ITECH shows and conferences by professional associations of health care medical records people.
- Present company spokesperson as hot interview prospect to health care and IT/IS trade media.

Strategy VI Tactics

Trade show support (HIMSS, ITECH, AHIMA): For those trade shows that SoftSource/CareForge participates in, pitch media booth interview and supply attendees with supporting press kits/materials.

Strategy VII Tactics

Utilize a community relations program that positions SoftSource as an industry leader and innovator within the Rochester market.

- Seek out and obtain any possible guest teaching opportunities within BOCES, RIT, Edison Technical School, or other relevant local institutions.
- Distribute press release positioning SoftSource as an innovator and leader in (X) that is educating students to make tomorrow's innovations even more dynamic.
- Either create and hold workshops for invited IT/IS people highlighting the latest in software development or electronics technology or provide minimal number of hours of free consultation on a particular topic. This would show that SoftSource is current with the technology necessary to provide clients with the best solutions possible, and would reinforce the impression that the company is a resource and partner in business.

Newsletter Option Tactic

Use direct communication to educate target audience about areas where SoftSource/CareForge could help their business. Write and distribute a quarterly newsletter with latest news on available technology, software, languages, etc. of relevance; case studies of completed projects; advancements in the mobile and/or wireless fields; employee profiles; technician's how-to columns, etc. Use of this strategy and tactic would be dependent upon whether or not the client can generate enough news quarterly for this publication.

Evaluation

Evaluation of the public relations program will be conducted quarterly via client meetings, analysis of press clippings, and interviews with client prospects. Additionally, Cindy Lee Associates will continually seek feedback from SoftSource/CareForge via e-mail and phone contact and any other necessary meetings. The PR program will be amended at any time during the course of the year if warranted by evaluative measures.

Billing

Hourly Rate: $XX

The first four months are considered the "launch months" for this one-year PR plan. The first four months will be very labor intensive while the foundation is laid for ongoing public relations efforts. It is during these months that a brand will be developed; media and analyst lists will be generated; editorial opportunities will be identified; messages will be developed; and a press kit will be researched and written. It is expected that the CareForge announcement will take place during this time as well. Key media will also be contacted during this phase to begin to establish necessary rapport and to determine other opportunities that may exist. In this process, it may become necessary to write and distribute other materials or to coordinate interviews for any immediate-need opportunities that are discovered.

During the remaining months, five through twelve, it is difficult to determine exact activity patterns. At this time, efforts will be focused on maintaining coverage of the company and its products/services and seeking proactive opportunities. Although it is my hope and intent to carry out most tactics outlined in the plan, many depend upon the client's project schedule (to publicize completed projects and write case studies) and the news generated by the company, as well as logistical feasibility. It is more difficult to estimate the number of hours needed each month to perform these tasks, especially as it is part of the scope of the plan to continually research and respond to opportunities that arise both within the media and the marketplace.

Retainer Format

Given this, I recommend the following revolving retainer format: For the first four months, it can be anticipated that thirty hours of work will be conducted on SoftSource's behalf each month. Therefore, a retainer of $X,XXX would be billed at the beginning of each month to cover work for that month. This includes hours spent working on projects, administration, and a clipping service that will start in the third month or upon distribution of the first release.

Starting at month five, when it is difficult to determine how many hours will be utilized, a nominal retainer of $X,XXX will be billed. The retainer will cover the anticipated administrative fees and the clipping service as well as be credited toward approved project costs. Any additional fees incurred that month above the retainer amount will be billed at the end of the month (added to the next month's retainer). Conversely, if a month is "light" and fees are less than those anticipated, the coverage will be credited to the next month's bill. During these last months, a project estimate will be issued at the beginning of the month outlining what major projects are anticipated and what the estimated cost is. At this point, the client will be able to either approve the estimates or express the desire to alter that month's project schedule to suit the budget.

Separate Costs

Activity and/or costs budgeted separately would include:

- Postage
- Phone/fax costs
- Photography, reprints, subscriptions
- Newsletter design, development, and printing or other major projects
- Out-of-pocket expenses incurred by Cindy Lee Associates

Estimates for these items will be submitted to the client for prior approval as necessary.

Clipping Service

A clipping service is a necessary component of the plan both from a strategic standpoint and an evaluative one. The press clipping service provides us with clips of articles that appear in any publication within the scope of our contract. For national coverage, the contract includes all national news publications as well as trade publications of our choosing (in this case, the health care information and management pubs). We would, therefore, receive copies of articles that appear in Rochester papers as well as those obtained in magazines such as *Health Data Management* and *Healthcare Informatics*. By gathering these clips, we can determine what worked and what didn't, who picked up what pitches and releases, and what subjects were of most interest to those who included the company in their reporting. Strategically, we can then refocus our efforts to better target our pitches. As an evaluative measure, looking at the number of clips, content, publications they appeared in, and readership, we can determine if the plan as implemented appears to be working or if we need to refocus our efforts to better reach the media. Clips are also beneficial as reprints for sales materials and in press kits, if prominent enough.

Cost of the clipping service is $287/month for national and trade coverage (included in retainers and not "bumped").

Sample from a Book

This sample publicity plan comes from *The ADA Guide to Women's Nutrition for Healthy Living*.

Communications Goal

Use publicity and public speaking to heighten awareness of women's nutrition/health issues through the media and via book sales.

Communications Objectives

- Supplement publisher's book launch
- Maintain ongoing book publicity program months after launch
- Leverage existing speaking engagements and travel schedule
- Generate additional speaking engagements; make maximum use of trip to each market

Communications Tactics

Stage 1—Launch: November–January

- Write press kit on book and author (pitch/cover letter, announcement release, author bio, fact sheet with interesting "did you knows?" from book, two- to three-page Q&A); distribute to health reporters at lifestyle sections of daily newspapers in top 100 markets plus syndicated columnists. Follow up on telephone with selected publications TBD to encourage interviews, usage of press kit materials, etc.

- Place ad in *Radio/TV Interview Reports*, a publication of ads for authors and others on the talk show circuit (there is no editorial material). This biweekly magazine is read by national TV talk show and local radio program producers nationwide; it is a cost-effective shortcut for reaching these key media people. I expect this to generate mostly radio phone interviews.

- Send press kit to print, radio, and TV outlets in Columbus, Dayton, Cincinnati, Cleveland, and Chicago; follow up to schedule telephone or in-person interviews with Sue Finn. Angle: Local/hometown expert writes important book.

Stage 2—Add Speaking to the Mix and Keep Publicity Flowing: January–May

- Generate ongoing publicity for book (crucial for sales and speaking leads/"celebrity status") by distributing monthly press releases from book material, pitching article ideas to health and women's publications, and being opportunistic about what's making headlines. For example, as we monitor breaking women's health news, we will continually contact appropriate media outlets on a timely basis to offer Dr. Finn as an expert source to comment on current news topics (recent news about the recall of diet pills would be a wonderful time to pitch a women's nutrition expert to *Dateline NBC*, *PrimeTime Live*, etc.).

- Develop package of materials positioning Dr. Finn as speaker on women's nutrition or health topics. Package to include cover/pitch letter, professionally designed speaker "one sheet" (standard speaker's marketing tool that combines information about speaker's topics with testimonials, a brief bio, and photos of speaker and book on one page that can be faxed), letters of praise from meeting planners, newspaper clippings/article reprints, book.

- Use package to pitch Dr. Finn to allied health professional groups (e.g., nurses), women's health centers, and women's health conferences as expert speaker; capitalize on "bookings" by coordinating in-market media interviews and book signings.
- Coordinate media interviews and book signings with Dr. Finn's existing travel opportunities.

Stage 3—Expand Markets, Keep Publicity Flowing: June–October

- Expand speaking markets to include annual meetings of national women's associations, such as Women in Construction, Women in Publishing, etc. and contacting speakers' bureaus (bureaus may require demo videotape).
- Distribute monthly press materials and pitch Dr. Finn as expert.

Sample from a Band

This sample publicity plan for a band was developed by Christopher Knab, a music business consultant with FourFront Media & Music, ✍ *www.4front music.com.*

Objectives

Prototype is a four-piece alternative funk band from Seattle, Washington. Their sound is reminiscent of Pavement, with a healthy dose of funky rhythms thrown in for good measure. Their simple yet beat-based songs have attracted an enthusiastic audience to date. Together since 1991, Kip Stanford (lead vocals), John Tremmer (lead and rhythm guitar), Ron Malcolm (bass), and Judy Winter (drums) have released two 45s and two cassette tapes on their own, before signing to Dental Records in January 1996. Their debut CD release, *Calling It a Day*, will be released on January 17, 1997. The first single off the CD will be the song "Deadly Accurate," which will be aimed at college radio at first, with an independently produced video available on a limited basis.

The publicity campaign's objective is to build upon the strong alternative print support the band received from their previous releases, with added concentration on expanding into some national music trades and consumer magazines. We will position Prototype as intelligent and politically concerned Generation X-ers. Their unique propensity for meshing funky rhythms with driving melodies around social and political issues will make writers and editors in newspapers, magazines, and fanzines stand up and take notice of this issue-oriented band. The songwriting team of Kip Stanford and John Tremmer will be made available to the print media and select college/alternative stations for interviews, in conjunction with their touring schedule.

The publicity campaign will support any and all promotion and marketing plans from Dental Records, and monitor all activities in radio and retail, as well as closely track attendance at live shows, to take full advantage of any developing newsworthy events that may develop.

Summary of Radio, Sales, and Live Show Plans

Radio

The song "Deadly Accurate" will be made available to college radio on January 10. Promotional concentration will remain with noncommercial college stations for the first month. Based on the successes achieved at this level, commercial alternative rock stations (KISW, KNDD, etc.) will be approached next. If all goes well with those stations, Active Rock and Hard Rock stations will be targeted for adds quickly. Note: The video of "Deadly Accurate" is an independently produced video that will be sent only to select cable access stations in the Northwest. There is a commitment from Dental Records to fund a more professional video, should successful airplay demand it.

Sales

Distribution for the CD will be through the independent network of I.N.D.I.E. with concentration on select mom-and-pop alternative music stores, as well as the chains, and any crossover retailers that can be brought on board. Posters and blank covers of the CD will be made available to the stores. Promotions such as in-store visits and in-store concerts will be set up through arrangements by the Artist Development department of Dental Records and the band's management, coordinated through their touring schedule.

Live Shows

A Northwest tour will kick off on January 24 in Seattle (opening for Soundgarden), with stops along the Washington leg of the tour in Spokane, and the tri-cities. Other stops on the tour will include college campus venues throughout eastern Washington, as well as Oregon, Idaho, and Montana. As developments break, the band is prepared to continue touring across the country as inroads are made in radio airplay, and through the publicity generated from the following plan.

Publicity Plan

The press kit for Prototype will consist of a promo copy of *Calling It a Day*, a bio, fact sheet, photo, and press clippings highlighting the positive feedback from the band's previous 45s and tapes, as well as live concert reviews. The campaign will build on the successes the band has already had, taking full advantage of their favorable reviews in such Northwest publications as *The Rocket*, *The UW Daily*, *Pandemonium*, the *Seattle Times*, and *Seattle Weekly*. Commitments for reviews from these publications have already been secured and will be a priority in launching the publicity campaign. Advance CDs will be sent to these publications on December 6.

Level One Targets: Upon Release
- Album reviews and features in regional publications to appear upon release: *The Rocket*, *The UW Daily*, *Pandemonium*, the *Seattle Times*, and *Seattle Weekly*
- Album reviews and features in national alternative magazines to break upon release: *Alternative Press*, *RayGun*, *Magnet*, *Seconds*, etc.
- Album reviews and features in national and regional fanzines: *Flipside*, *Village Noize*, *Puncture*, *Cake*, *Fizz*
- Album reviews in daily newspapers, weeklies, influential regionals, plus college radio interviews in Seattle (KCMU) and Bellingham (KUGS)
- Trade reviews and features: *CMJ*, *Virtually Alternative*, *Next*, *Hits*
- Album reviews and features in national consumer press: *Spin*, *Pulse*, *Hub?*, *CD Review*, *Addicted the Noise* (on the Internet)

Level Two Targets: Upon Touring

- Get press to live shows in every city and town they play
- Tour coverage in daily newspapers, weeklies, regionals, and college press
- Album reviews in consumer press: *Spin, Rolling Stone, Musician*, etc.
- Additional radio interviews on college and commercial alternative stations

Preliminary Publicity Timeline

Day	Date	Event
Fri	12/6	Advance promo copies at *The Rocket, UW Daily, Pandemonium, Seattle Times,* and *Seattle Weekly*
Mon	12/9	Arrange interviews on KCMU, Seattle, and KUGS, Bellingham
Fri	12/13	Deadline for completing database of print/broadcast mailing list
Fri	1/10	Single sent to college radio
Fri	1/17	*Calling It a Day* CD release day
Mon	1/20	Album mention in *UW Daily/ Seattle Times*
Tues	1/21	Album mention in *Seattle Weekly*
Thur	1/24	Tour begins in Seattle
Thur	1/24	Album mention in *CMJ/Hits*
Tue	1/28	Album mention in *The Rocket* and *Pandemonium*
Tue	1/27	Album mention in Spokane and tri-city daily papers
Mon	2/2	Album mention in *Cake* and *Fizz*
Fri	2/6	Album mention in *Flipside* and *Village Noize*
Wed	2/15	Album mention in *Spin*
Wed	2/15	Album mention in *Virtually Alternative*
Fri	2/17	Album mention in *Next*
Fri	2/24	Album mention in *Magnet*
Mon	2/27	Interview on KUGS, Bellingham
Mon	2/27	Interview on KCMU, Seattle
Tue	2/28	Feature story in *The Rocket*

Public Relations

Due to the fact that Prototype's lyrical content is concerned with political and social issues of our times, it is imperative that its image of concerned "political rockers" be maintained at all times. Emphasis should be placed on their involvement with anti-censorship issues in particular. Backgrounders will be available to all broadcast and print media contacts highlighting the key issues that current legislation in Washington state and in Washington, DC, are concerned with. Any and all opportunities to discuss in print or on the radio the anti censorship stand that the band has taken should be explored thoroughly.

A concerted effort will be made to present the band in all "Rock The Vote" campaigns to help get its fans registered to vote in November.

After five years of laying down a foundation of independent, political thinking through their music, Prototype is poised to seize the moment with their new CD *Calling It a Day*.

The Publicity Department of Dental Records is ready to meet the challenge of breaking the band through a detailed and organized print and broadcast publicity campaign geared at working its existing fan base into a national audience for its music.

> Chapter 23

Using an Agency or Putting Your Plan to Work on Your Own

Part One

Part Two

Part Three

Part Four

Part Five

Executing Your Plan

A publicity plan is more than a description of what you want publicity to do for your company. It's the blueprint for making things happen. It tells you what needs to be done, when it needs to be done, and who's going to do it. It's not something you tuck into a file drawer and forget about. It's a tool that you use regularly to move your business forward, so keep it among your active file folders and refer to it often. You don't want to miss any steps in the execution of your carefully thought-out plan.

Who Does the Work In-House?

Begin your execution by reviewing the list of tactics. Did you assign names to them? If you did, are those assignments realistic and do-able? If you didn't, now's the time to do it. This is also the time to be hard-nosed about the skills and availability of the people you've assigned to execute those tactics so you can determine if you need to retain outside assistance. Use this quick review of the skills needed for typical publicity assignments to guide you.

Look for the Best Memo Writer

Who writes the most concise, easiest-to-read memos and reports? That's the person to write your press releases, tip sheets, press kit materials, articles, columns, and pitch letters. If your best writer doesn't happen to be your best marketer or salesperson, team the writer with an employee who has a solid understanding of how to position your company or products. One can provide the ideas, angles, or facts while the other produces the prose. (This also is how you proceed when working with an outside consultant who has the writing skills but not the knowledge of your company.)

Choose Someone Who Likes Talking to Strangers

Give the job of pitching or following up on story ideas over the phone to the employee who is most comfortable talking to strangers on the phone. This is *not* a job for a telephone novice. It's a job for someone who isn't intimidated by the brusque voice of a busy reporter who needs your pitcher to get to the point quickly. It's a job for somebody who can summarize the idea in two sentences, say it clearly, listen closely, and shift gears to reposition—and repitch—the idea, all in about two minutes. While this might describe your favorite salesperson, this is usually not a good assignment for a salesperson. Salespeople are good at not taking "no" for an answer, but editors, reporters, and producers are just as good at hanging up on people who don't accept "no" the first time—and never accepting calls or material from them again.

Search for Clerical Skills

You will also need someone with clerical skills to set up, maintain, and update your media database and manage press release distribution. Whether you send your releases via U.S. mail or e-mail, somebody with good technical skills needs to merge files to create mailing labels or manipulate your e-mail software for a mass mailing.

Look for Organizational Skills and Obsession Over Details

Planning a press conference or special event? Give those tasks to your most organized, detail-obsessed person, because both events are for somebody who likes to make things happen. They are very task- and detail-oriented processes but, at the same time, require someone who can maintain a vision of the expected end result. Turn a sponsorship over to someone who's good at marketing because you want that responsibility managed by someone who has a good grasp of the company's positioning and target audiences.

Use Two People for Speaking Opportunities

If you're going after speaking opportunities that you can publicize, then you might enlist two people—someone to

What About Interns?

College interns studying public relations, journalism, or communications are inexpensive resources when you need assistance executing your company's publicity plan. Whether they're truly useful, though, depends on how much they've learned so far and whether you're in a good position to both guide and educate them as they do your publicity work. Before securing an intern, ask the coordinator at the college for references so you can talk to employers who have used public relations interns from that school. Their experiences might guide you in the intern selection process. Do ask the coordinator for several students to interview for your open position, and conduct the interviews in the same way you would for a permanent new hire. You're looking for someone who is bright, highly motivated, doesn't mind hard work, and knows when to ask questions. You want somebody who isn't afraid to stuff press kits as long as they're learning from the experience.

identify and secure the slots on the platform, and someone else to make the presentations. Sometimes one person can do both, sometimes not. If the speaker is the CEO or senior executive, you don't want her identifying and booking her own presentations if you can avoid it.

Hiring an Agency

What if your plan is too ambitious to execute internally? Or, what if it's a simple plan, but not one you can manage internally with current resources? A successful publicity campaign needs the involvement of someone with good communication skills, so if that doesn't describe anyone on your staff of computer experts, then it's wise to go outside for help. It's not unusual for small companies to hire outside publicists in the same way that they retain the services of accountants or law firms.

Determine How Much Help You Need

Can a sole proprietor handle your assignment, or do you need a larger firm because of the nature or volume of the work? You don't want to be the smallest fish in the big pond served by the largest agency in town, but you also don't want to link up with a group that's too small to meet your needs. Fees make a difference, too. Sole proprietors typically have lower

Avoiding Advertising Agencies

A word of caution about agencies: Your first choice is a public relations firm that has publicity and media relations experience. Whenever possible, start your search with straight public relations firms. If your options are limited to agencies that provide both advertising and public relations capabilities, be alert to pressure from them to change your publicity plan so it includes an advertising component. Don't even talk to an advertising agency that has no in-house public relations capability. That firm will have to hire a freelancer to do the work, so you might as well find that freelancer and save money by hiring him or her directly.

overhead than larger firms, and can charge slightly lower rates for work that can be as good as or better than the big guys. Sole proprietors in the public relations business also tend to be experienced pros who don't need much hand-holding, whereas with large agencies, your work will be done by junior staffers who will require a fair amount of both agency and client supervision. If your project is too big for a one-person shop, a sole proprietor can contract with freelancers to do your work. Small and mid-sized firms are a good option, too. They employ a blend of less expensive junior talent and more experienced pros who often work side-by-side with the others.

Ask for Referrals from Colleagues and Friends

You find a good publicist in the same way you find a good accountant or attorney—you ask people you know to refer you to a good firm. (You don't sit down with the Yellow Pages and start calling agencies alphabetically. Any PR agency can get a Yellow Pages listing, but only good firms are recommended by multiple sources.) Ask the owners of businesses you see in the news a lot. Ask your business owner friends who they have used or have heard good things about. Contact editors of media outlets you're targeting (trade magazines, the appropriate newspaper section editor or beat reporter, the local TV station assignment editors, and so on), and ask them to recommend a few individuals or firms who consistently provide high quality, usable material and information.

Call the Public Relations Society of America

If checking in with your peers doesn't yield enough, call the president of the local chapter of the Public Relations Society of America (go to *www.prsa.org/leadership/chapterpres.html* for a list) and ask for the names of appropriate local members who might be able to help you. You can also search the Internet for agency Web sites, but this approach is only slightly more enlightening than a Yellow Pages review, since there is no referral from a trusted source involved. Internet searches are more useful if you are not limiting yourself to working with a local agency. If, instead, you are more interested in a firm with experience in your industry than you are in where they are located, then an Internet search combined with conversations with trade magazine editors could be fruitful.

Call the Firms on Your List

Once you have a list of three to four firms or individuals, call them. Briefly describe your business and your publicity needs and ask if they would be interested in working with you. If they are, send a briefing letter to each that outlines your situation and describes the information you need from them. Include a description of your company and the situation that requires outside assistance, identify the audiences you want them to reach on your behalf, state the objectives of your publicity assignment, and provide a budget range. This background information will help shape their response to you. Ask them to provide you with, in return, a letter that describes the firm's general background, its experience in your industry or with your communications situation, the professional experience of its staff, a current client list, and its fee structure. Some might direct you to their Web site for this information, but this is not what you're looking for any more than mailing you a brochure is an acceptable substitute for a personal letter. You don't want to take the time to search for the information you need. You want them to write a letter that specifically addresses your needs and questions—let them do the work, not you.

Evaluate Each Agency

While you wait for their letters, develop a grid that allows you to evaluate each agency according to your own priorities. Use the following list to determine which qualities are important to your organization (plus any other qualities) to develop an evaluation grid. Include a column that ranks those qualities in order of importance to your company on a scale of one to five. When you meet with each agency, rank it, too, on a scale of one to five in a separate column. Then compare the columns. Which agency comes closest to your expectations?

- Media relations experience
- Writing skills

- In-person communication skills
- Knowledge of your industry
- Whether it was referred to you by more than one source
- Your impression of its ability to meet deadlines
- Creativity
- Chemistry with your group
- Internet capabilities (if relevant)
- Reputation

Look for Credentials

Once you receive the agency letters, review and compare them. Who has the best credentials? Which agency attached relevant case histories or samples of its work? Which one seems the most enthusiastic about the possibility of working with your company? Who seems to have the right combination of skills, experience, and resources to handle your assignment? Use these letters and supporting material to weed out any that don't seem to be a good fit. Move ahead with the remaining firms by scheduling a capabilities presentation, perhaps your first face-to-face meeting with each group.

Meet with Each Agency

Set aside a two-day period to meet with each agency in two-hour time blocks. Ask each firm to be prepared to present its capabilities, to listen to your presentation about your company and its specific publicity needs, and to ask and answer questions.

Ask the agency to bring to the meeting the individual or individuals who will be working on your account if you assign it to them. This is important. You want there to be good chemistry between you and your staff and the agency personnel you'll be working with, and the only way you can determine that ahead of time is by meeting the individuals. In addition, an agency is only as good as the talent of the individuals it employs. It's not enough for the firm to say, "Trust us. We'll give you one of our best people." Their idea of "best" might not match yours. You want to be certain that you've had an opportunity to at least get the impression that the person assigned to your project is smart, creative, responsive, and experienced.

> Set aside a two-day period to meet with each agency in two-hour time blocks. Ask each firm to be prepared to present its capabilities.

If an agency tells you that it won't decide who will work on your account until it's been retained, or that it will hire somebody after it gets your business, then make the contract contingent upon a successful meeting between you and the person assigned to you. This is the only way you can be certain that you won't be working with someone with questionable ability or that you just plain don't like.

During the agency meetings, work to get a sense of the intelligence of the people present as well as their understanding of your industry and their own profession. Notice if they ask good questions. In addition, determine how comfortable they are executing your publicity plan. If they don't want to just "execute"—if they want to have a hand in the plan development, is that because they can truly improve what you've created, or is it because they prefer to execute their own plans? Some groups are comfortable handling the execution, but others prefer to control the creative process, too. Most often, small businesses prefer working with agencies who approach the process as partners.

Evaluate Again

Immediately after you've completed all meetings, use your filled-in grid to help you select the best firm. Call the agency you've selected to move the process forward, but call the agencies you didn't hire, too, and tell them why you selected another firm. Meet with the agency you're hiring to go over your needs and plans in greater depth, to discuss how they will execute the assignment, and to review what they will charge for their services. (Remember, you shared your budget in your briefing letter, so there shouldn't be any surprises at this point. If there were questions about whether your budget was realistic, they should have been raised at the capabilities presentation.) Produce a detailed letter of agreement that spells out what each group is responsible for providing or creating, payment terms, and procedures for canceling the contract.

> Meet with the agency you're hiring to go over your needs and plans in greater depth.

Public Relations Agency Fees

Public relations agencies base their budgets on an estimated number of hours for the assignment, on a retainer basis, or on a project basis. If your agency works on a hourly rate basis, charging you for time spent on the project each month, protect yourself from financial surprises by making sure there's a ceiling on the amount they can charge for the assignment. Bad estimates should be the agency's problem, not yours.

Monthly Retainers versus Project Fees

Under the monthly retainer format, the agency estimates what it will cost to do the job, then divides that total by the number of months required. You are charged the same amount each month, no matter how much or how little time the agency spends on the project. While this often generates a "what have you done for me lately" mentality among clients, many prefer this approach because they know in advance what the next month's work will cost them and can manage cash flow accordingly.

With a project fee, which is based on an estimate of the amount of work involved, the agency typically charges one-third of the fee up front to begin the work, bills the second third midway through, and bills the final third upon completion. This works best with short-term projects that aren't expected to expand or otherwise deviate from the original assignment.

Agencies also bill their out-of-pocket expenses, including postage and copying, overnight delivery, photography, printing, and so on. Some mark up these expenses, but many don't. Make sure you know how your agency handles expenses.

Staying Within Budget

Budget problems happen when you're wildly successful, shift gears dramatically, make mistakes, or estimate badly. Perhaps you've planned a press breakfast at a trade show and budgeted for twelve reporters but have twenty-five RSVPs. While your accountant might suggest that you stick to your estimate and tell thirteen of those people that the event has reached capacity and they cannot attend, you don't want to do that. Alienating even one reporter negates the value of entertaining the other twelve. You have to live with your success and learn from the experience for your next endeavor, even if it means maxing out your credit card.

Budget problems can result from bad direction or supervision of an

Pay-for-Placement PR Firms

It's not the norm, but some public relations firms work on a "pay for placement" basis, charging the client for successes, not failures. Theoretically, it's a way to share the risk—if the firm isn't successful, you haven't spent much. Fees are typically based on the type of media, the market size, and the type of coverage your story receives. An appearance on *Oprah,* for example, will cost you more than an appearance on *Noon News* on Channel 7 in Hometownville. You can be a highly profitable client for this type of agency because a high-profile, high-paying placement takes the same amount of time to secure as a low-paying placement at a media outlet in your backyard.

Before signing with one of these firms, do your homework. Talk to others who have used these types of services; make sure the firm you're investigating has a track record with the type of story you have to tell.

outside vendor or agency, too. If you've changed your public relations agency's assignment in a way that requires them to spend more time on the project, you will have to find the money to pay for that time. Or, if the text provided to the sign maker for the special events banner has a typographical error, and all the signs include that error, you have to pay for more signs or not use signs at all. Sometimes, you underestimate because you've never done this before. When that happens, and there is no extra money to be found, you might have to remove elements from your program and execute them the following year during a new budget cycle. Regardless of the cause, keeping good records of expenses from the beginning will help you learn how much to budget for future programs. With good financial record keeping, there is no reason that any organization should repeat a budget crisis.

What You Can Expect from an Agency

Realistic expectations are important to a good client/agency relationship; put yours on the table up front and see how they compare with the agency's. Expect your agency to provide quality work, meet deadlines, report its activities and accomplishments in a written document every month, and meet the objectives of your publicity plans. Your agency should always be a step ahead of you—not the other way around. If you find that you're calling often to check on the status of the press release or another program element instead of being nagged to provide the information for the press release, then take a step back and examine the relationship. Your agency should be making it easy for you to meet your goals, not making it harder. It should be operating in a responsible, independent manner, with continual input and guidance from you, but without constant hand-holding.

On the other hand, it's up to you to provide the agency with all the information, material, and support it needs to get the job done. If you are continually inaccessible or find it difficult to invest the time needed to share necessary information, then be prepared for the agency to re-evaluate its relationship with *you*. The agency-client relationship works best only when both parties are open and available.

Staying Alert, Shifting Gears

With or without an agency partner in the execution process, it's important to monitor the progress of your publicity plan on an ongoing basis. Evaluate what's working—and why—and what isn't working—and why not. Do more of what's working; examine more closely what isn't working. Some businesses are frustrated when editors don't pounce on their article ideas right away, or when their first few press releases don't get used. It could be that the article ideas weren't good, or that the press releases had no news in them. But it could also mean that the article ideas were good but were already used by that publication, or that they're being pitched to the wrong media outlet. Publicity requires great persistence, so you could be doing

Sign Up for Publicity Tips

Several organizations that provide public relations products or services offer people like us free newsletters with publicity tips and advice. Even if publicity isn't a big part of your job, you'd be wise to sign up for these e-zines because they will remind you on a regular basis that you need to work constantly and consistently to get and keep your company's name in the news. Here are some of the most useful and credible:

- *PR Tips* from ✐ *www.enewsrelease.com*
- *Bulldog Reporter's Pitching Success* available online only at ✐ *www.infocomgroup.com/Webzine/pitchingsuccess.html*
- *Journalists Speak Out on PR* at ✐ *www.infocomgroup.com*
- *PR Do's and Don'ts Newsletter* from ✐ *www.prleads.com*
- *The Publicity Hound's Tips of the Week* from ✐ *www.publicityhound.com* (includes bonus freebie, the booklet *89 Reasons to Send a News Release*)
- *ExpertPR* from ✐ *www.mediamap.com*

everything right but just not getting the results you want quite yet. Before removing any piece from your program, try to get an objective opinion on what you've done so far from someone with some publicity experience. Offer to buy an hour of the individual's time to review your materials to see if you're on target, or if tweaking them would improve your success rate. Even the best publicists bounce ideas and materials off each other, so don't discard any of your ideas without getting a second opinion.

Similarly, if you've distributed three tips sheets in six months and each one has been used by key media outlets, then produce more of them—try six in the next six months. Then consider combining the best of your tips into an article that you pitch to a newspaper or magazine.

Listen to the feedback you get from the media, too. If you pitch an idea over the phone and it's rejected, the reporter will usually offer a reason. If you get the same reason repeatedly—including "it's not right for us"—then study the publication again to determine why it's not right and to figure out what *would* be right. The solution might be to take your original idea to a more appropriate outlet. Work to build on your successes, and minimize your failures.

► **Chapter 24**

Tracking Results and Measuring the Impact of Your Plan

Part One

Part Two

Part Three

Part Four

Part Five

PART FIVE CREATING AND EXECUTING YOUR PUBLICITY PLAN

■ CHAPTER 21 Creating Your Publicity Plan ■ CHAPTER 22 Sample Publicity Plans ■ CHAPTER 23 Using an Agency or Putting Your Plan to Work on Your Own ■ CHAPTER 24 Tracking Results and Measuring the Impact of Your Plan ■ CHAPTER 25 Putting What You've Read into Practice

Knowing Why You Need to Track Your Plan

Whether your publicity campaign is national and involves multiple press release mailings to a large media database or is local and focused on one-on-one contacts with specialized reporters, you want to monitor and record the outcome of your efforts. In addition to justifying the expenditure, tracking results helps you better understand what techniques were particularly effective—or ineffective—at generating media exposure. Tracking also is essential if you're introducing a new product in regional markets and want to make sure retailers have enough product in stock to respond to the demand generated by media exposure. It's also necessary to track your results if you want to determine whether publicity played a role in generating inquiries or an increase in sales.

Creating Systems to Track Results

Publicity tracking systems can be as simple or as complicated as needed for your marketing and sales purposes, but they should be computerized and custom-designed for each publicity situation. The tracking system for

Consultant Uses Publicity Successfully

Bob Phibbs, a Long Beach, California, marketing consultant who calls himself the "The Retail Doctor," uses publicity to promote his consulting services, speaking topics, and book, *You Can Compete*. "Good publicity gets me on different people's radar screen," he explains. "I was recently hired to give a speech in Indiana because of an article someone read about me two years ago," he adds. Phibbs says his ongoing publicity (see some of it at ✍ *www.retaildoc.com*) also builds credibility, helps communicate his message about how smaller businesses can compete with giants, sells books, and generates new consulting clients. A feature article about his book that originated in a local daily newspaper and was syndicated to other newspapers coast to coast gave him a national audience for the advice he offers in media interviews. "The national exposure helps me become more recognized, which is especially important for a speaker," he notes.

Target Media	Podunk Gazette	WXYZ-TV	WCBA-AM
Tactic	Tip sheet, "Six ways to pay less income tax"	Tip sheet, "Six ways to pay less income tax"	Tip sheet, "Six ways to pay less income tax"
Date Distributed	February 4	February 4	February 4
Outcome	Used in "news briefings" column of business page	Did in-studio interview on 6:30 A.M. news broadcast	Not interested
Date of Outcome	February 11	Aired March 1	Follow-up phone call February 18
Next Steps	Send thank-you note to editor	Send thank-you note to assignment editor	None

the publicity component of a special event, for example, will be less complicated than one used to monitor the success of a national new product rollout supported by an intense publicity campaign. At a minimum, any tracking system should include the publicity tactic (press release, press kit, pitch letter, and so on), the date it was employed, the media outlets targeted with the tactic, and a dated status or outcome. You want to be able to spot patterns—does one newspaper use your releases or tip sheets consistently within two weeks while another one uses maybe every other release within a month? An example of that simple chart appears above.

This same format can apply to tracking reports for larger mailings, too. If you've done the mailing in-house, your mailing list is probably in a database format. Add fields to that database that allow you to log the follow-up activities and results along with next steps. Next steps can range from changing the name of the person you've been mailing to because that person has suggested a more appropriate individual to removing the outlet from "tip sheet" mailings because your contact said the outlet never uses that type of material. If you discover that your media contact is hungry for more information like the material you've provided, your next step might be to take the reporter to lunch to discuss additional article ideas. Recording that information in a format that is usable to you will allow you to capture and act on trends, patterns, and changes.

Some publicity situations are more complicated—which makes tracking results even more important. A book author who has secured an interview in a daily newspaper article that will mention the book will want to make certain that books are in stores in that community. Or, if you know an influential e-zine is about to mention your widget with a link to the order form on your Web site, you'll want to make sure your Web ordering process is glitch free and that you have widgets in the warehouse. Tracking the media response helps you prepare for the response of the consumers of that media. Make sure that your system is in place and that the person who receives your company's publicity feedback knows what to do with it.

Understanding Clippings and Clipping Services

In addition to establishing a system that lets you determine how your material is being used, you need a process in place for getting copies of all clippings resulting from your publicity campaign. You'll use those clippings in marketing efforts, but you'll also want to evaluate them for their effectiveness at communicating your key messages. In addition, comparing what appears in a magazine or newspaper with what you submitted is a good way to learn how to improve your writing. Were all your superlatives ("best," "fastest," "most exquisite") missing from the newspaper description? Make sure they're missing from your next press release, too.

Clipping reports take different forms.

Local Media

If your campaign is focused on local media, it will be easy for you to monitor newspapers and local magazines for news items and articles that quote you or a company employee. Get a more than one copy of each clipping, keeping one in your project file. Neatly clip the other copy and use a glue stick or spray-on adhesive to mount the clipping on a piece of plain white paper on which you've typed at the top the publication name and clipping date. Add it to your clipping file so it's readily available for future marketing efforts.

National or Targeted Media

When your campaign is broad, national, or targets publications you don't subscribe to or have easy access to, consider hiring a clipping service. A clipping service charges you to monitor the print media for news about your company. Typically, national services charge a monthly "reading" fee of around $275 and a $1.55 per-page clip fee. One of these services, Bacon's Information, includes in its monthly fee a "NetClips" service that monitors Web sites that include substantial news coverage and provides clips from those outlets, too. There are also less expensive regional clipping services. Before hiring a clipping service, however, check to see how much of the clipping you can do with your own resources, including online at publication Web sites.

The best known clipping services are Bacon's Information, (✑ *www.baconsinfo.com*), Burrelle's Information Services (✑ *www.burrelles.com*), and Luce Press Clippings (✑ *www.lucepress.com*). All of these long-time businesses are well-respected. An Internet search can help you find local press clipping services.

Working with a Clipping Service

When selecting a clipping service, look for one that is experienced in the type of monitoring you're looking for. Don't hire a regional service, for example, if you need clippings from trade magazines. Similarly, if you need weekly newspapers monitored, make sure the service reads a large number of weekly newspapers and doesn't treat them as inconsequential. If you've never used a clipping service before, don't get locked into an annual contract until you've tried the service for at least three months and can compare costs with results. Most reputable services are willing to give you a trial agreement without a contract.

Here are a few tips for getting the maximum number of relevant clippings once you've selected a service.

Finding Your Placements

Suppose you send a tip-sheet news release to the top fifty newspapers in the country and want to find out if any of them used it. A quick way to find out is through NewsLibrary online at ✑ *www.newslibrary.com.* NewsLibrary lets you search many daily newspapers for keywords or names; if what you're searching for has appeared, you receive a citation and the opportunity to pay a small fee to retrieve the complete article. Sometimes you can avoid paying the fee by using the NewsLibrary search to identify where your item has appeared, then going directly to the newspaper's Web site to find and print the article for free. But not all newspaper Web sites include all of the printed paper's content, and some of those that do still charge you a fee to access older articles. Even so, the per-clip fee is still far less than costs associated with a monthly clipping service.

Be Specific

Be very specific in your clipping instructions. List the company, product, and people names you want monitored, along with other key words. Also provide similar names that you *don't* want monitored so you reduce errors. Champion Products, for example, is easily confused with Champion Paper, which can generate clippings for the wrong company.

Be as specific as possible about the media outlets you want monitored. If you are looking for clippings in the top 100 daily newspapers, but are not interested in trade press coverage, say so—it will eliminate fees for trade media clippings you have no interest in receiving.

Monitor Quality

If you receive "bad" clippings, return them to the service immediately with an explanation of why they're wrong, and ask for a credit. This kind of feedback will help reduce future errors.

Keep the Service Informed

Add the clipping service to your press release distribution list so service readers have a better sense of what to watch for. If you expect publicity in a particular publication or group of publications, alert the service to watch for it.

Set a Deadline

Review clipping delivery options. Typically, you will receive clippings a few weeks after publication. If you need them sooner than that, discuss this with your account representative.

Video and Audio Clips and Monitoring Services

You can also monitor the success of your publicity campaigns that target broadcast media outlets. It's easy to set your VCR or audiotape recorder to capture local TV and radio interviews or news segments; you can record

How to Select a Broadcast Monitoring Service

Brent Bamberger, vice president of marketing at multivision, inc. in Walnut Creek, California, suggests that companies selecting a broadcast monitoring service look for wide coverage areas. "Do you need to know if your company or product is mentioned in New York City, Oklahoma City, Jersey City, or everywhere in between?" he asks. Consider whether you need next-day delivery of videotape, or digital copies in a matter of hours. Make sure your source can provide the delivery service you need. Finally, he says, if you need a service on an ongoing basis, look for hands-on account management. You want one person assigned to your company so there's more accountability—and fewer missed video clips.

national TV interviews, as well. When doing radio interviews in other markets over the phone, you can often ask the station to send you a cassette of the interview. But campaigns targeting a broader area often require a monitoring service that will provide videotapes, audiotapes, and interview transcripts for a fee. If you plan to use your TV interviews as part of your tradeshow display continuous loop footage, it's worth it to secure a copy of that spokesperson interview or product mention.

Broadcast monitoring service fees vary. Look for a service that doesn't require a monthly monitoring fee and will charge you on a "per show" or "per clip" basis instead. While many of the print clipping services monitor broadcast programming too, there also are services that specialize in broadcast monitoring, including Video Monitoring Services of America (*www. vidmon.com*), multivision, inc., (*www.multivisioninc.com*), and Metro Monitor (*www.metromonitor.com*).

Updating Your Media Database

Once you start receiving clippings, either through a service or otherwise, update your media database with the names of the reporters whose bylines appeared on the articles referring to your company or product. These are the people who will be most receptive to your news the next time you mail a press release or pitch an article idea, too. Update your list every six months, too, by sending an e-mail or making a phone call to the media outlet to verify that the names on your list are still current.

Measuring the Impact

Was your publicity campaign worth the money and effort? Did it meet your expectations? Was the publicity meaningful, carrying your key messages, or did the media coverage simply get your name out there—and is that acceptable? Measuring the impact of your campaign allows you to justify the expenditure to management in a way that helps ensure that future efforts will be funded. In addition, proper evaluation gives you the opportunity to better understand your successes while learning from mistakes, both of which contribute to better subsequent campaigns.

Evaluation Methods

As with most everything else, whether or how you evaluate the effectiveness of your publicity campaign depends on what kind of information you need and how much time and money you have for evaluation. Classic public relations evaluation often involves pre-campaign research to provide a benchmark that defines the level of awareness, attitudes, or opinions about your company, product, service, or issue. This is followed by post-campaign research designed to reveal how much attitudes or awareness have changed after you've performed that public relations magic. But research is expensive and often unaffordable for a small company unless it serves another marketing purpose as well, essentially killing two birds with one stone.

Compare Results

The most meaningful way for a small business to evaluate the impact of its publicity is to compare the results with the publicity plan goals and objectives. Perhaps your goal was to make your company more appealing to a particular type of potential employee. Did you see an increase in job applications from these individuals? A company that used publicity to help

> Measuring the impact of your campaign allows you to justify the expenditure to management in a way that helps ensure that future efforts will be funded.

expand distribution can determine its success by comparing the scope and depth of distribution before the campaign and after it. But when the goal is to sell products, it is difficult to separate the effect of news coverage from that of advertising, direct mail, and telemarketing. While asking customers to tell you how they heard about your product is one way to pinpoint the source of a sale or inquiry, most people will refer to a publicity item about your product as "your ad," which steals credit away from your publicity results by attributing it to advertising.

To determine if your sales are generated by publicity, remove other marketing methods from the mix while your publicity campaign is in play. It also makes good business sense to do this—when AT&T evaluated the relationship between news media coverage of the company and its advertising in the late 1990s, it discovered that publicity brought in as many new customers as advertising did. In addition, AT&T's research showed that during periods of heavy positive news coverage, less advertising was needed to generate customer loyalty.

Analyze Content and Extent of Coverage

In addition to comparing results with goals, many businesses also analyze the content and extent of the media coverage. Because managers often understand advertising dollars better than they do the implied editorial endorsement of publicity, many publicists calculate the cost of their placements as if they had been purchased as advertising. They measure an article's column inches and calculate what those inches would have cost them as ads, or they calculate the amount they would have had to pay for their broadcast exposure. The cost to generate this publicity is usually less than the equivalent advertising cost, even without factoring in the value of the implied editorial endorsement, so this is a "feel good" approach. (This method doesn't translate well to placements on Web sites or in e-zines that don't include advertising, though.)

Comparing news coverage to advertising costs works well for those who relate to numbers but falls flat with people who are more interested in the content and context of the coverage. They want to know if the clippings contained the right messages and if news items appeared in media read or viewed by your target audiences. For them, you need a clipping content analysis that ranks the clippings as positive, negative, or neutral, indicates geography of the publication if that's relevant, categorizes the media outlet, comments on whether the clips contain key message points, and so on.

Content analysis also is useful when your goal is to communicate that your company cares about its community. If you can't afford to measure your impact with pre- and post-campaign focus groups or telephone survey research, you can compare how your company is described in pre-campaign clippings with how it is described in clippings after the campaign. Look for whether the references are more positive, and whether there are more clippings related to your community relations activities. Regardless of your needs, you can produce a clipping report internally, or work with your clipping service to do it for you.

Content analysis can be very useful when shaping your next publicity campaign, too. If you've introduced a product in an entirely new category and your clippings indicate that the press consistently describes the category inaccurately, you can work to change that. Similarly, if your coverage is based on interviews with the company spokesperson and the clippings show that those messages are rarely used, then it's time to either media train your spokesperson or to alter the language of the messages to make them more memorable and usable.

Maximizing the Impact of Your Publicity

It's not enough to secure great publicity and just leave it hanging out there for the world to notice. Make sure as many of your target customers as possible see it. Take the extra steps to maximize the impact of the free media exposure by merchandising your results both externally, with customers and prospects, and internally, with management and others in your organization. The first step toward maximizing the impact of your company's publicity successes is to set up a system for showcasing the results.

Reprinting Clippings

News items and articles are usually the most visible rewards of a publicity campaign. Turn them into marketing tools by preserving and reproducing them. Begin by determining if you need to get permission to reproduce the clipping for marketing purposes. Then, neatly clip the article or news item from the publication. Using a glue stick or spray-on adhesive, mount the clipping on the center of a plain piece of paper. If the news item is small and dwarfed by white space, enlarge it on the copier for a more impressive appearance. Print the publication's name, date, and circulation on another piece of paper, cut it out, and glue it to the top of the mounted or enlarged clipping. (Do not handwrite the publication information.) Underline all references to you or your company on the mounted clipping so that you draw the reader's eye to the most important part of the news—you.

Many magazines offer article reprint services as well, producing color or black-and-white articles on glossy paper with your logo, address, phone number, and Web site URL. These top quality reprints look like they were snipped from the original magazine and make a much better impression than a photocopy. For around $1 per copy, it's money well-spent, especially for articles you've written or that position your company in an ideal way.

Other Ways to Leverage Clippings

Don't limit your clipping distribution to your sales kits—here are more ideas for getting the most mileage:

- Good news about the company is a morale booster, so route clippings internally within the company.
- Give copies to telemarketers and salespeople so they can refer to them appropriately, or are knowledgeable about the publicity if a customer or prospect mentions it.
- Mount and frame clippings to hang on a store or office wall.
- Distribute copies of service-oriented clippings to customers through a "take one" service counter or checkout display.

Use Reprints in Direct Mail, Sales Kits

Always assume that nobody with whom you have (or want to have) a business connection has seen the articles about your company . . . and also assume that they will want to. Merchandise the articles by incorporating them into all of your marketing communications efforts. (Remember: Most people have no idea how easy it is to get your name in the news, so they will be impressed with your media coverage.) Show clients and prospects that the media respects your organization as a source of reliable information by sticking a preprinted "Thought you'd be interested in this" sticky note to the top of each reprint and mailing a copy to everyone on your marketing-mailing list. Add copies to your next direct-mail package, too.

If you make sales calls with leave-behind literature or folders, make sure the folder always includes copies of your most recent clippings.

- When the publicity placement is particularly noteworthy, add a banner that says "as seen in Publication XYZ" to your print ads to impress people.
- Post the articles on your Web site to read online or to download; make sure the page is identified appropriately so it can be found by a search engine.
- Link your Web site to the article on the publication's Web site.
- Incorporate a clipping into the design of your direct-mail piece.
- Build a brochure around a montage of clippings.
- Write a short news item about noteworthy publicity successes—or a longer article about the entire campaign—for your company's marketing or employee newsletter.
- Borrow an idea from the entertainment industry and add quotes from favorable clippings, articles, and broadcast news reports to your ads, flyers, brochures, sales materials, and Web site.
- Considering that some people consider their campaign a success when the CEO says it is, make certain she sees the clipping and has an opportunity to be impressed, too.

Using Clippings to Generate More Publicity

Publicity truly does beget publicity. When one media outlet runs a story about your company or quotes you as an expert, it tells other media outlets that you're a good source of information—so you get more calls. Sometimes that happens without any help from you because your article shows up in a topic search and the reporter tracks you down. But a savvy business owner makes it happen by including those clippings in press kits and with media pitches. It's how you prove that your company or topic is newsworthy while communicating that you are a proven source of good information. Clippings provide you with almost instant credibility with reporters or producers, so use them as "credentials" when pitching the press.

Extend the impact of a magazine interview or article with newspapers in small- to medium-sized cities by sending a copy to the business section editor. Highlight your byline or the article text that refers to the company and attach a short note telling the editor what your company does. He'll be able to write a short news item for the business page that showcases your national media exposure ("Acme Explosives, which produces dynamite sticks from a plant in Waukegan, was recently featured in an article about safe manufacturing procedures in *Explosives Monthly*.").

But don't stop there. Do you or your company belong to local organizations that publish newsletters with "member news" sections? Send a copy of the clipping to the newsletter editor. Do the same with college alumni organizations—they can't produce those long "alumni news" sections without material like this, so feed it to them!

Using Local TV Interviews for Something Bigger

Interviews with local TV stations are a necessary stepping stone for company spokespeople or leaders who aspire to be interviewed on national cable or network television programs. Producers of national TV talk shows need to be assured that you're a great guest—and the best way for them to do this is by viewing a tape of your previous TV interviews. Getting a national TV interview takes more than a good interview videotape, of course—you have to be able to say something worth hearing on an interesting topic and have the credentials that position you as a better resource than someone else. But if everything else is in place and your interview tape showcases you as lively, dynamic, and engaging, then you have an advantage over other potential experts when that producer says, "Can you Fed Ex a videotape to me?"

Getting a national TV interview takes more than a good interview videotape.

If you've done several interviews, hire a professional to produce a single demo tape that showcases your best work. Shorten long interviews by pulling out your best segments; use the same approach to minimize the damage of uneven interviews. Eliminate completely anything that lacks energy. Introduce each interview with the segment set-up—typically, the host or newscaster reading a script that introduces you and your topic. String these together into a tape that's three to five minutes long, make duplicates, and add labels with your name, topic expertise, and phone number. Update the master videotape as you do more and better interviews; when you've done a few national segments, create a new tape that showcases them and eliminates the local footage unless it is exceptional.

TV publicity also can be used as a product marketing tool when news

Use TV Clips for Speaker Demo Tape

TV interviews can be incorporated into a demo tape that promotes your public speaking. A demo videotape is essential for conscientious meeting planners who need to see how you present before a group—and how a group reacts to your presentation—before they book you for a large meeting. It must include excerpts from your speeches, but it can also feature your best TV interviews, especially if those interviews help highlight your communication skills and your content expertise. If you are captivating on a local TV talk show, you will probably hold the attention of a live audience, too. A speaker's demo videotape is essentially an electronic brochure—let it reflect the same creative approach you apply to other marketing materials by recycling your broadcast interviews.

segments and interviews are spliced together on a continuous loop. Play it at your trade show display, in your office lobby, in sales presentations, and anywhere else you have an opportunity to use a VCR to capture attention.

The implied editorial endorsement of the media gives your company, product, or service much more credibility than you can generate on your own. Maximizing the impact of your publicity success is all about capitalizing on that good will by reusing existing material so that as many people as possible see it—and see it more than one time. Never just let a clipping or an interview sit there. Always use and reuse it so that you get the most from your publicity investment.

> **Chapter 25**

Putting What You've Read into Practice

Getting a Refresher Course

If you've read most of this book, you can create a publicity plan that meets your company's unique needs. You understand the importance of goals and objectives to achieving publicity success, you have a grasp of the various publicity tools and how to create and manipulate them, you know how to target the media and give them information in the form they want to receive it in, and you can pull all of this information together into a plan that will open new doors for your business while giving you additional marketing tools. Let this chapter serve as the "refresher course" later, when you develop additional publicity plans and want to review the highlights to jog your memory.

What Publicity Can Do for You

Savvy entrepreneurs understand that publicity, with its credibility-building implied editorial endorsement, has a far greater impact on customers, prospects, and other key audiences than advertising, direct mail, or most other marketing tactics. It costs less, too, making it popular with small businesses looking for big impact with little money. Publicity can find customers. It can sell products or services. It can create experts. It can shape corporate images. It can recruit employees. It can uncover untapped marketing niches. But it's not magical—publicity can't create something out of nothing. In order for a company to generate good, rather than bad, publicity, there must be a solid basis to build from.

Publicity that moves a brand or company forward is built on a publicity plan that begins with an understanding of target audiences and what they read, watch, and listen to; the publicity campaign's goals; and well-defined objectives. A goal tells you what you want to achieve with publicity—sell more products, increase awareness, change opinions—while an objective tells you how you're going to get there. To support the campaign and generate maximum results, objectives must be specific and measurable. Objectives outline *who* is going to do *what* to make sure you reach your goal.

Publicity Plan Tactics

You can't have publicity without news, so one of your first challenges is figuring out what's going on in your company that is newsworthy. Keep in mind that "newsworthy" doesn't mean what you or your colleagues find interesting; what is "newsworthy" is actually defined by media gatekeepers—reporters, editors, and producers. They are the people who decide whether their readers and viewers will be interested in the information you have to share.

What if you understand the concept of "newsworthy" so well that you realize your company isn't doing anything that will get it that free media exposure? It's not uncommon for a company to simply send out new personnel press releases and nothing more because it has decided that it has no news to share. *There is always news to share—especially if you create it!* When you have no obvious announcements to make, keep your name in front of the press by generating newsworthy information through tip sheets that offer advice, by conducting an interesting survey, or sponsoring a clever contest, by making yourself available to the press to provide expert local commentary on a breaking national news story, and by connecting your business to a popular holiday that always gets press.

Most newsworthy information is carried to the media through specific kinds of publicity tools. The press release is the most versatile and the most common, while it is also the most overused and abused tool. A press

Who's on Your Mailing List?

Who should you send your press releases to? The best publicity campaigns target very specific media outlets with customized materials. Once you know what your audience watches, reads, and listens to, you can study those media outlets to uncover publicity opportunities for your business. It's okay to send press releases to a large list of media outlets, but it's not wise to mass mail a letter pitching an article idea. That's because while nearly all media outlets have space or time allocated to news, their "feature" content varies widely. An article idea that suits one magazine will not be right for most others.

Release Writing Tips

Beginners often make the mistake of writing press releases with language similar to that of advertisements. Press releases should use neutral, news-style language without the hyperbole or superlatives found in ad copy. Study the news sections of magazines and newspapers to absorb the clean, facts-oriented approach favored by journalists. Writing in this style will make it easier for an editor to review and edit your news, which makes it more likely that your news will be used. When your own press release gets used, compare what you submitted with what appeared in print, and use what you learn when you write the next release. Worry less about grammar and more about communicating just the facts clearly and cleanly.

release needs to contain news, and that news needs to be at the top of the release so a reporter sees it immediately. Reporters fill their recycling bins every day with press releases that are self-promotional but contain no news, or that contain information that is not interesting to the readers or viewers of that media outlet. Press releases are useful for all types of media.

A key step in the publicity process is identifying the media outlets that are most important to your publicity goals. Then you must determine who at each outlet should receive your information. There are a number of resources available to help publicists compile media lists for press release mailings. There are also a variety of organizations that help companies get their press releases to the media. While these services are quite useful, they are not a substitute for knowing the content and editorial needs and direction of the key media targets in your publicity plan.

Press Releases

Most comprehensive publicity plans will include at least one press release; many contain far more. Because it is such a basic and essential publicity tool, the savvy entrepreneur will take the time to learn how to craft one that gets read before it's recycled. A compelling press release begins with a snappy headline that announces the news in the release with active, exciting language. The headline is followed by an attention-getting first—or lead—paragraph that summarizes the news or announcement without getting into too much detail. Specifics—who, what, when, where, why, and how—then follow in a way that supports the lead paragraph.

Tip Sheet

A tip sheet is a specific type of press release that offers advice in the form of bulleted tips or points. Print publication editors love tip sheets because good ones provide great space fillers for short news brief sections; talk show producers like them because they offer a quick synopsis of a company or expert's content expertise. Just about any type of business can produce tip sheets that help others learn from its knowledge or experience.

Pitch Letter

The sales language common in advertising is more appropriate in a pitch letter used to sell an article to print publications or a guest or segment idea to broadcast outlets. But even then, the language should focus on convincing the editor or producer that readers and viewers will want to have the information you're presenting through this idea. What makes your idea so compelling? Prove it. A pitch letter is essentially a one-page sales tool that makes a case for your idea. Provide additional background information as attachments.

Pitch letters are written to secure placements for articles and case histories. Articles can cover a wide range of topics while case histories always address a problem and a solution. Bylined articles are, for publicity purposes, those written by you that offer information and advice in a format used by a specific publication. Writing articles and case histories is like writing a school report: You outline your article, gather the appropriate information, organize your material, and piece together the information in a way that flows easily. Editors don't expect perfection from content experts, so don't worry about writing Pulitzer Prize–winning prose. Your goal is to share useful information in a way that is interesting and not self-serving. If it needs polishing, the editor will assist with that.

Columns, Op-Eds, and PSAs

Columns, op-eds, and public service announcements (PSAs) are shorter than bylined articles and case histories, making them less intimidating writing assignments. They are less commonly used tools, however. Both columns and op-eds are essays that express opinions, but op-eds also work to change the views or opinions of others. Both require less research than other types of articles because the content comes from your heart and your head, not from interviews with others. PSAs are broadcast publicity tools that promote the causes or events of nonprofit organizations. Because they are very short, they require the writer to be extremely focused on a single message that needs to be communicated in a way that interests and engages the listener or viewer.

Press Kit

A press kit is to publicity what chicken broth is to a cook—it's a staple. The press kit provides the media with both news and background information that is used immediately or filed for later reference. Press kits contain a mix of press releases, fact sheets, backgrounders, and photos, all designed to address a specific aspect of a larger topic. You'll need a press kit when you're making a big or complicated announcement or when you want a media outlet to have background information about you or your company on file for future reference when an interview source with your content expertise is required. If you send a press kit solely for "file" or "background" purposes, make that clear to the recipient so it isn't thrown away because it doesn't have a hard news connection.

More Sophisticated Tactics

While some small businesses build their publicity plan around press releases and kits, others need to include more sophisticated elements to secure media placements.

Press Conferences

Many companies believe they need to host a press conference to get publicity, but, more often than not, a press conference is not the solution. Press conferences should be staged only for very big announcements that are of interest to a widespread audience. When a press conference is the solution, be sensitive to key media deadlines when scheduling the event. Distribute press kits with the announcement to attendees, deliver the materials to non-attendees, and be certain to allow time for individual interviews.

Publicity Interviews

Many of the written publicity tactics—press releases, pitch letters, articles, press kits, and so on—are used to secure publicity interviews. While the telephone call or the pitch letter outline why the interview is a good idea, the other pieces provide the supporting material that can prove to a reporter or producer that your idea is solid and that you have the credentials for the interview. But that interview is wasted if you haven't prepared for it properly by developing key messages that you repeat in interviews and by becoming comfortable with the interview situation through role-playing. Knowing what you want to communicate in an interview—and practicing how you will do it—will put you on a path to success, not disappointment.

> Knowing what you want to communicate in an interview will put you on a path to success, not disappointment.

Special Events

Carefully thought-out and executed special events can stimulate awareness and visibility while they generate publicity. Special events hosted by a small business are usually either celebratory occasions marking an anniversary or similar achievement or they are created solely to attract media exposure. Those designed to draw the press must incorporate unusual, highly visual elements—the ingredients for the community's biggest-ever pizza-making party, big chef's hats for a chili-making contest, or fun costumes for a Halloween 10K race. Regardless of the reason for the event, those that are most successful at securing media interest often have a charity tie-in, involve media celebrities, are very visual, and are newsworthy. On-site signage in the form of apparel and banners helps make sure that the sponsor organization gets on-screen credit in media coverage on those occasions when the reporter avoids mentioning the company name on the air.

Sponsorship

Sponsorship of special events hosted by other organizations helps many small businesses secure visibility with specific target audiences. It's important for companies to seek out appropriate sponsorship possibilities rather than just accepting the opportunities that walk in the door. Before committing to a sponsorship, be certain that it's a good fit for your company, that it will reach your target audience, that it helps you reach your goals, and that it's affordable. Sponsorships don't always come with large price tags—you can often link your name to an event by providing "in-kind" services or by waiting until the sponsorship deadline to negotiate a better package for a lower fee. Certain sponsorships often have publicity value. Make sure the organizers include your company name in the press releases and other publicity materials, but do your own publicity as well. You want to maintain more control and better communicate your company's messages.

Public Speaking

It's also possible to secure publicity through public speaking engagements. This is a more sophisticated tactic for those seeking the credibility needed for "expert" status because it involves both speaking *and* marketing skills. You must be comfortable speaking before large groups while, at the same time, you must be marketing your speaking topic (and yourself) to organizations whose meetings are attended by your target audience. Sharp business owners who see the potential of public speaking also understand how to use publicity to maximize that exposure. They send press releases announcing their speaking engagements, they invite reporters to attend the events, and they distribute press releases summarizing their remarks after they've spoken. All help to build awareness with potential customers as well as with the media gatekeepers.

Being Opportunistic

Becoming more opportunistic means being as proactive as possible with your publicity efforts. It involves making certain that every relevant reporter has background information on you and your business, monitoring the news and offering yourself as a local expert on a breaking national story, trend spotting, and tapping into the media relations activity of your national trade associations. Those who are opportunistic don't wait for reporters to find them—they contact reporters first.

Media Relations Tools

There are several tools available if you're interested in being more aggressive with your media relations activities; most involve spending money but are usually well worth the cost if you use the tools wisely to secure media exposure. The tools range from free editorial calendars published by trade magazines to subscription media opportunity newsletters, advertising in publications that are distributed to reporters and producers, and paying to be included in Web sites that market topic experts. Many of the subscription media newsletters offer free trial subscriptions that allow you to determine which one has the greatest potential for your company.

Creating and Carrying Out Your Publicity Plan

Creating a publicity plan requires taking everything you've learned in this book and applying it to your business situation. When you have goals and objectives in place, you can outline the strategies and tactics needed to secure publicity in appropriate media outlets. Many times, the tactics applied will be influenced by the company's budget. Publicity becomes a higher financial priority, however, among businesses that realize that it is far more powerful than other promotional means, including advertising and direct mail.

While many small businesses execute their own publicity plans, others are not staffed appropriately and hire outside resources. When selecting a public relations firm, ask for recommendations from other business owners and from editors and reporters. Look for a successful track record, an acknowledgement of the importance of accountability, and good chemistry between your organization and the individual or individuals who will be working on your account. Get your agreement in writing, making certain to outline responsibilities and deadlines for both your organization and the agency.

"In Cipro We Trust"

On October 15, 2002, a little more than a month after the East Coast terrorist attacks and shortly after anthrax-laden envelopes began arriving at major media outlets, NBC *Nightly News* anchor Tom Brokaw held up a bottle of his antibiotic, smiled at the TV camera, and concluded the evening newscast saying, "In Cipro we trust!" The potent anthrax medicine was well on its way to becoming a household name, gaining fame and notoriety as quickly as Tylenol in the midst of its 1980s tampering incidents. While Bayer AG, the maker of Cipro, later struggled with issues ranging from product availability to pricing, and then with reports that other antibiotics were just as effective, the fact remains that one of the most trusted faces in broadcasting—one you would probably love to have endorse your product or service—put his trust in Cipro.

Killing a Rumor

Imagine that your company's sales or image are being hurt by rumors that aren't true. Stopping those rumors isn't easy, but it can be done. First, share the facts—in person and in writing—with employees. Tell them about the rumor, and tell them about the truth. If the rumor has spread outside the company, employ your media relations tools. (Sean Connery appeared on David Letterman's show to dispel rumors he had cancer; an ill but healthy looking Ryan O'Neal did an interview with *Entertainment Tonight* to prove he was not on his deathbed, as was rumored.) Issue a press release with a statement from the CEO or president that denies the rumor and states the facts along with any supporting evidence. Set aside a specific page on your Web site to dispel the rumor. If that's not enough, buy an ad to communicate your message through the appropriate medium. Be consistent and persistent.

Evaluating and Leveraging Your Publicity Success

It's important to track, monitor, and evaluate your publicity program so that you can learn from mistakes and successes, and adjust the plan accordingly. It's easy to monitor the local press and a small number of trade publications, but larger publicity campaigns also need help from clipping services and video and audio monitoring services. For a fee, these companies will identify all print, Web, or broadcast mentions of your company, brand, or individual. Reviewing these clippings lets you determine if you're getting your messages out while you use the information in the reports to update your media database.

Monitoring your publicity success also gives you tools that will allow you to leverage your success—and isn't that what this is about, after all? There's no point in securing great publicity if you don't share the results with as large an audience as possible. Use reprints of newspaper, Web, and magazine clippings in your marketing efforts; use video and audio clips in sales presentations or as tools you use to generate more interviews. People are impressed when they see your name in the news—take advantage of that by making sure that those who didn't see your interview when it aired or appeared get a chance to see it when you mail it to them or show it at your trade show booth.

Publicity power is awesome. Tap into this power by identifying the media gatekeepers at outlets read, watched, or listened to by your target audiences, getting newsworthy information about or connected to your company to those gatekeepers, and giving it to them in a format that they will expect. Do this on an ongoing basis and it won't be long before you discover that you've capitalized on an inexpensive way to be even *more* visible than your competitors.

Worksheets

■ Press Release Writing Worksheet

Use this worksheet to guide you through the press-release writing process (see Chapter 7). Fill in the blanks, and then use the completed worksheet to create your press release.

FOR IMMEDIATE RELEASE (or Release Date)

If you need the release held until a certain date, that is the "release date." If you want it used as soon as possible, use FOR IMMEDIATE RELEASE.

Contact Name and Phone Number

Who should take the calls from reporters?

Attention-Getting Headline

Use active verbs, colorful words to announce your news.

Lead Paragraph

Write one sentence that summarizes your announcement. Don't get too detailed. Just summarize your news. That is your lead. Then look at it again. Can you make it sound more interesting?

Five Ws and One H

Who, what, when, where, why, and how. Answer these questions in the next one or two paragraphs.

Paragraph about Your Company

Conclude with a standard paragraph that summarizes what you do. Do not use your mission or vision statement.

■ Questions to Ask When Writing a Press Release

These questions are designed to get you thinking about what you need to ask someone when interviewing them for a press release (see Chapter 7). You might not use all of them . . . and you might need to ask others. Use this worksheet as your starting point.

Who

What is the complete legal name of the company or organization making the announcement?

Who is/are the individual(s) to be quoted?

What are their titles?

Which categories of media outlets are you targeting with the release?

What

What is the name of the person to be listed as the media contact?

What organization is he/she with?

What are the contact person's phone number and e-mail address?

What does the company/organization do?

What is the announcement?

What is the impact of this announcement on your company, the community, your customers, etc.?

What do you want the person you're quoting to say about this news? (Use this thought to shape the question you ask the person you'll be quoting.)

Where

In what city is the announcement originating (your headquarters or at a trade show)?

In what city is the company or organization headquartered?

What is the company's complete address?

If the announcement is about an event, where is it taking place (facility name, city, state)?

When

What announcement date should appear on the press release?

Is the release being held until a specific future date? If so, when?

When did the news occur (such as the date of a new product introduction)?

If an event, when will it take place (day, date, time)?

Why

Why is this particular announcement/news significant?

Why did it occur?

How

Describe how the good news came about (through an award nomination, promotion, good work of a team, etc.).

How much does the item/event cost?

How can people purchase the item, buy an event ticket, etc.?

■ New Employee Press Release Template

Use this release to let media outlets know about your newest hires.

FOR IMMEDIATE RELEASE   CONTACT: (your name)
                                                          (your phone)

(Name of your company) hires new (job title)

(CITY, State) – (Date) – (Name of your company) announces it has hired (name of new hire) as (job title).

(Last name of new hire) joins (name of your company) from (previous employer), where (he/she) was (previous job title). In (his/her) new position, (last name of new hire) will (insert brief summary of job description, no more than two sentences).

(Last name of new hire)'s previous experience also includes employment with (list one or two previous employer names). He/She is a graduate of (college name) with a degree in (field of study). He/She is a member of (list any professional affiliations) and has been honored by (list any awards).

(FOR LOCAL PUBLICATIONS ONLY) (Last name of new hire) resides in (city).

# # #

■ Article Writing Worksheet

This worksheet can help you start working on your ideas for articles (see Chapter 10).

Publication _____

Deadline _____

Number of words _____

Working title of article _____

Special instructions/guidance/notes from the editor

_____

_____

_____

What do you want to accomplish for your business with this article? (Why are you writing it?)

_____

_____

_____

What is the single concept you want people to understand after they read it?

_____

_____

Write a one-paragraph summary of the article.

_____

_____

_____

_____

_____

Outline

Lead/opening thought

_____

_____

_____

Support that expands your lead and states or suggests the article's purpose

_____

_____

_____

Body of the article—list your main points in order of appearance

_____

_____

_____

_____

_____

_____

_____

_____

Conclusion

_____

_____

_____

_____

_____

Keeping the magazine's style in mind, consider what additional information you need to write this article. (Statistics? Anecdotes from your sales force? Interviews with others in your field, including customers? Topic research?) List the additional information you need and where it will come from.

_____

_____

_____

_____

_____

_____

_____

_____

_____

_____

■ Press Conference Checklist

Before your press conference (see Chapter 13), double-check the following.

Pre-Conference

Invitations

- ❏ Date and start time with brief agenda indicating timing of events
- ❏ Street location of venue and directions if necessary
- ❏ Brief description of press conference purpose
- ❏ Names, titles of speakers
- ❏ RSVP name, phone number/e-mail, and deadline
- ❏ If meal will be served before or after the press conference, say so
- ❏ Event planning
- ❏ Select appropriate date, time, place
- ❏ Reserve appropriate location (in terms of size, budget, and event personality)
- ❏ Select speakers
- ❏ Develop invitation list
- ❏ Create, mail invitations
- ❏ Arrange for food and beverage
- ❏ Write script
- ❏ Hire photographer
- ❏ Assign on-site responsibilities to staff
- ❏ Rehearse speakers
- ❏ Follow up on phone to invitees who have not responded
- ❏ Send reminder memo to press
- ❏ Create event timetable
- ❏ Create staff list that outlines responsibilities
- ❏ Arrange for on-site AV equipment, telephones, specific technical capabilities if needed
- ❏ Discuss room set-up with facility

- ❏ Create press materials
- ❏ Create checklist of RSVP'd guests for use on-site

On-Site

Room Set-Up

- ❏ Chairs
- ❏ Electricity power points—are they where you need them to be?
- ❏ Telephones (in case reporters need them)
- ❏ Food and beverage set-up
- ❏ Registration desk
- ❏ Nametags
- ❏ Light switches
- ❏ Signage
- ❏ Coat check
- ❏ Name cards for speakers
- ❏ Display materials, including products
- ❏ AV equipment (Projection? Computer? Other?)
- ❏ Raised platform for speakers
- ❏ Press materials
- ❏ Test the AV
- ❏ RSVP checklist at registration table
- ❏ Pens, pads of paper at registration table

Speaker Set-Up

- ❏ Table
- ❏ Chairs
- ❏ Podium
- ❏ Props
- ❏ Script
- ❏ Microphone
- ❏ AV materials (Slides? Overheads? PowerPoint presentation on disc or hard drive? Flip chart? Poster board?)

■ Special Event Checklist

This checklist for staging special events (see Chapter 14) was created by FridaysGirl.com.

Event: _____ Location: _____ Date: ___ / ___ / ___ Time: _____

Planning of Event	Due Date	Vendor Name	Phone	Status
Staff				
Request for volunteers	/ /		( ) -	
Orientation meeting	/ /		( ) -	
Staff/volunteer assignments	/ /		( ) -	
Facility				
Reservation of facility	/ /		( ) -	
Set-up/layout map	/ /		( ) -	
Decorations	/ /		( ) -	
Safety check	/ /		( ) -	
Parking	/ /		( ) -	
Equipment				
Complete equipment list	/ /		( ) -	
Reserve special equipment	/ /		( ) -	
Purchase orders	/ /		( ) -	
Publicity				
Flier completed	/ /		( ) -	
Flier distributed	/ /		( ) -	
Media fact sheet	/ /		( ) -	
Invitations	/ /		( ) -	
Photographer	/ /		( ) -	
Posters	/ /		( ) -	
Radio/TV announcements	/ /		( ) -	
Awards	/ /		( ) -	
Miscellaneous				
Special permits	/ /		( ) -	
Insurance	/ /		( ) -	
Maintenance/clean-up crew	/ /		( ) -	
Follow Up				
Thank-you letters	/ /		( ) -	
Media releases	/ /		( ) -	
Evaluations	/ /		( ) -	
Awards for staff	/ /		( ) -	

■ Editorial Calendar Grid

Use this calendar (see Chapter 17) to note when your target publications publish specialty articles.

Month	Publication	Article	Contact Name/ Phone	Deadline
January				
February				
March				
April				
May				
June				
July				
August				
September				
October				
November				
December				

■ Publicity Plan Worksheet

When developing your publicity plan (see Chapter 21), use this worksheet to brainstorm ideas.

Situation/Overview

_____

_____

_____

_____

Objectives

_____

_____

_____

Audiences

_____

_____

_____

Strategy

_____

_____

_____

Goals

_____

_____

_____

Tactics

_____

_____

_____

Budget

Itemize estimated expenses; include staff time if appropriate.

_____   _____

_____   _____

_____   _____

Timeline

Week/Month for Activity	*Activity*

Sample Publicity Documents

Appendix A

Appendix B

■ Press Release for a Book

The following is an example of a press release. While this is written specifically for a book, you can use a press release for nearly any type of information. See Chapter 7 for the lowdown on when and how you can use press releases; see Chapter 8 for more samples.

Proper nutrition can guide you through menopause

COLUMBUS, Ohio—According to *The American Dietetic Association Guide to Women's Nutrition for Healthy Living*, more than 40 million American women are over age 50, the point when menopause typically occurs. "This is greater than a third of the female population," notes the book's author, Susan Calvert Finn, Ph.D., R.D., F.A.D.A., who says that proper nutrition during menopausal years can minimize subsequent health risks.

"Among the hidden effects of menopause are its long-term impact on bone, heart, and breast health," Dr. Finn explains.

Dr. Finn recommends the following nutritional strategy for the long-term health of menopausal women:

- Reduce the risk of osteoporosis by adding more calcium and Vitamin D to your diet.
- Calcium contributes to bone formation and strength, and Vitamin D helps your body absorb calcium. Avoid excess protein and sodium in the diet, because both contribute to calcium loss.
- To reduce the risk of heart and breast disease, enjoy a low-fat diet.

For short-term relief to minimize menopausal symptoms, Dr. Finn recommends:

- Ask your doctor about taking Vitamin E (30 to 300 milligrams) to ease hot flashes.
- Boost low serotonin levels caused by a lack of estrogen by eating nutrient-rich complex carbohydrates such as grains, rather than by eating sugary foods.
- Eat fewer calories because your metabolism slows down, and exercise more to build muscle and keep your weight stable.

"Menopause is not a disease, but a normal life passage that signals a significant change in a woman's body," explains Dr. Finn. "Some of these changes put us at risk for certain diseases. Paying attention to nutrition during this time can make a big difference in your overall health.

###

■ Pitch Letter for a Nonprofit Organization

This pitch letter for the president of the Squirrel Lovers Club, who sent it to several national television talk show hosts, secured an appearance on Rosie. *See Chapter 9 for more on writing pitch letters.*

Date
Name
Show
Address
City, state, zip

Dear:

Squirrels. You either love 'em or hate 'em. While your neighbors complain that squirrels are giant rodents who eat too much birdseed or squirm into the eaves, *you* might think they're cuter than kittens.

I discovered how many people truly adore squirrels a year ago when I founded the Squirrel Lovers Club and people climbed out of the bushes to sign up. Today, with nearly 400 members through word-of-mouth only, I've tapped into a passion for these bushy-tailed busybodies.

I'd like to be a guest on your show so your viewers will learn they aren't the only ones who are nuts about squirrels. I can share many stories about how clever these little critters are. For example, I modified a cat-feeding machine from my pet supply business for my squirrel friends. While it usually takes cats days to figure out the device, the squirrels mastered it in minutes. You might be surprised at how people-friendly squirrels can be, too. I have a videotape showing one running up my body to take a peanut from my mouth. The video also shows squirrels tapping on my window to tell me they want a treat . . . and entering my house for a snack.

I've enclosed a press release announcing our nationwide membership drive; one of our club newsletters, *In a Nutshell*; press clippings and a photo of a squirrel taking a peanut from my lips. I hope you'll consider me as a guest on your show to discuss why people are so fond of these creatures, demonstrate through video the friendliness and intelligence of squirrels, and tell viewers how they can share their affection for these animals through a nationwide organization, the Squirrel Lovers Club.

Please don't hesitate to call me toll free at XXX-XXX-XXXX to request a preview videotape or to get more information. I look forward to hearing from you soon.

Sincerely,

■ Pitch Letter for a Documentary

This pitch letter (see Chapter 9) was sent to the health reporters at newspapers in cities where the PBS documentary was scheduled to air. It was customized with the date and time of the show's scheduled airing in each of the cities.

Date
Name
Title
Pub
Address

Dear:

While most women believe breast cancer is their biggest medical threat, the fact is that heart disease kills more women than all forms of cancer combined. Recognizing the importance of communicating this health risk to women, PBS is broadcasting nationwide *Women's Hearts at Risk*. The show is scheduled to air on (insert PBS affiliate) on (insert date and time).

The attached news release explains the program and its content. I am writing to offer one of the expert panelists featured in the program for telephone interviews should you decide to write a feature before it airs in (city). Former heart patient Charlotte Libov is a journalist and medical writer who coauthored *The Woman's Heart Book* (Plume, 1994) and *50 Essential Things To Do When the Doctor Says It's Heart Disease* (Plume, 1995). She served as the program's consultant.

Libov, who in 1991 underwent open-heart surgery for a potentially life-threatening heart problem, is a nationally recognized expert well-qualified to discuss why heart disease is overlooked in women, how to recognize the warning signs—which differ from those experienced by men—and what women can do now to prevent heart disease. She is articulate and knowledgeable.

Please call me at 555-555-5555 to schedule an interview with Charlotte Libov at your convenience. I hope to hear from you soon.

Cordially,

P.S. I can provide a preview videotape of the program as well as a black and white photo of Libov shot on the set of *Women's Hearts at Risk* to illustrate your article.

■ Pitch Letter for an Interview

This pitch letter (discussed in Chapter 9) was used successfully to secure an interview for a nationally known expert on women's nutrition who is based in Ohio but speaking before a group in Indianapolis.

March 17, 20XX

Ms. Jane Smith
Food Editor
Indianapolis Star News
PO Box 145
Indianapolis, IN 46206-0145

Dear Ms. Smith:

Dr. Susan Finn, author of *The American Dietetic Association Guide to Women's Nutrition for Healthy Living,* will be in Indianapolis April 15 to speak at the Indiana Dietetic Association's annual meeting. Her keynote is titled, "Nutrition: The Best Opportunity to Improve the Health of Women."

Dr. Finn is a nationally known expert on the vital role nutrition plays in the lives of women so we hope you'll consider interviewing her while she's in Indianapolis. Possible article topics relevant to the food page include:

- What women can do nutritionally for their children now so they become healthier adults later
- Good fat, bad fat: What's a woman to do?
- "Functional Foods": making choices for your family
- Why women's health is about more than the health of women
- A nutrition expert offers her top ten tips for a healthier year

I've enclosed additional background information to help you make a decision about interviewing Dr. Finn the morning of April 15. If you decide to meet with her, I will send a copy of her book immediately. (It does not contain recipes.)

I will call soon to determine your interest.

Cordially,

■ Case History for a Communications Company

This case history was written by marketing communications and public relations consultant Bob DeRosa. See Chapter 10 for more on writing case histories and articles.

Want to Become More Competitive?
Take a Look at Your OSS.

By Sam McLamb, Network Services Manager, CT Communications,
Concord, North Carolina

Until recently, being a local telephone company was fairly easy. Most of us were monopolies and as long as we met federal and state service guidelines, we were free to run our operations pretty much as we wanted to.

With the Telecommunications Act of 1996, that picture changed dramatically. By opening local and long-distance markets to competition from other telcos, resellers, cable companies, and others, the act significantly changed the way we need to think about our business, our customers, and our operations.

About two years ago, anticipating both the regulatory change and new competition, we at CT Communications took a hard look at our operations. We found that even though we had always taken pains to provide excellent service, some of our operations were pitifully slow and more labor-intensive than they needed to be. In the new competitive age, this kind of service would never do.

Our service-order system, for example, required both a customer-service representative and an assignment clerk to make even the smallest change. Each had to log into a different system and enter five or ten commands. Changes took anywhere from one to three hours from order placement to installation. Since we were processing approximately 300 service orders a day, this operation was much too slow.

Our problems stemmed from the inability of our systems and switches to communicate with each other. Like many other telcos, we use dedicated legacy systems, each of which does its own job and requires its own baby-sitting. But because these systems aren't integrated, the "right hand" often doesn't know what the "left hand" is doing. Fixing this problem would be simple if budget weren't an issue—simply scrap all the systems and start again, or buy additional specialized hardware. These solutions, however, are outrageously expensive and impractical, and neither of them could demonstrate payback in any less than five years.

A Software Solution

A telecommunications software and consulting firm, the Hutton Company of Spencerport, New York, claimed they could speed up our operations and solve other problems as well. They recommended a software solution that would integrate our systems and switches—essentially, making them operate as if they were one system. This software would run on an existing PC and would be completely self-maintainable because it is table-driven rather than source-code-driven.

As a result of taking them up on their offer, we are now a faster, lighter, more efficient company with much tighter control over our operations support systems and labor costs. Service orders now take ten minutes rather than three hours. We also discovered and fixed some problems that we never knew we had. Best of all, the solution paid for itself in a single calendar year.

Increased Voice-Mail Business

Our increased efficiency has also enabled us to double our number of voice-mail users—from 5,000 in March of 1996 to 10,000 a year later. This growth of our user base would not have been possible with standalone systems. Previously, two clerks were required for data entry; now, the software automatically dials into the voice-mail system to perform moves and changes. In addition, the database is always current because an audit process tracks the operation of both physical and logical mailboxes, looking at both the bill and the switch.

Efficient Disconnects

The new system has also been able to improve our efficiency in dealing with disconnect-for-non-payment situations. Previously, our procedures for processing disconnects were completely manual. We would address each switch and enter three commands for a temporary disconnect, track the account manually, then enter another three commands when it became permanent. Now, the system performs temporary disconnects automatically. If payment is not made, the account is permanently disconnected in 30 days. If the account is rectified, service is automatically restored in 10 minutes rather than the half day that was previously required.

The Trouble with Trouble

The integrated system also increased the efficiency of our trouble-testing procedures. Previously, our test board was manned by six testers, each of whom would look at trouble tickets and decide which of three procedures to follow—send for dispatch, send to central office, or send to outside plant for repair. Furthermore, each tester had his or her own procedures for making these decisions.

With our new system, these decisions are made automatically in less than a minute. Much of the dialogue—and with it, much of the cost—has been removed from the operation. Our previous six-person staff has now been reduced to one tester/administrator.

Savings to Date

In the year that we've been using our new, integrated system, we have been able to eliminate eight workstations at $5,000 to $6,000 each. In addition, we have been able to reassign at least nine staffers, reducing payroll and reassigning some to more desirable roles, increasing their job satisfaction.

Because our systems are now one, we can audit our operations almost automatically. In the first month, we discovered 237 accounts where services were being provided but not billed. At $6 to $9 per account per month, this savings proved to be substantial.

Enhanced Customer Service

What's more, because our systems are now integrated, we have been able to dramatically improve our customer service, leading to the increased satisfaction that's essential as a competitive differentiator. Simply being able to process customer requests faster enhances satisfaction. But in addition, we are able to provided new services faster and more efficiently than ever before.

One of our greatest challenges has been setting up the entire communications infrastructure for one of our favorite customers—the Charlotte Motor Speedway. Six times a year, we would have to dedicate three weeks to providing a temporary dial tone for major auto races. With our new system, we can accomplish this and more in less than a week.

In the Future—More with Less

Although we are very pleased with the numerous advantages of our integrated systems today, we are even more excited about the vision of tomorrow that's now possible.

We are able to envision a day in the very near future when both customers and our own repair people will be able to access our integrated system directly. For customers, this will mean being able to select new services, experiment with them on a trial basis, initiate them, and guarantee that they are accurately billed—all without any CSR (customer service representative) intervention.

■ Case History for a Photo Imaging Supply Company

Marcia Layton Turner of Layton & Co. wrote this case history—see Chapter 10 for more information.

Police Put Color Image
Management to Work

*Image management tech makes the
Rochester police's system much
more than a booking terminal*

In the last few years there has been a revolution in color-image management. Traditional processes for retrieval of photographs are cumbersome and time-consuming. These methods require the user to leave the work area, search manually through photographic documentation for the desired file, respond to the inquiry, and perhaps make photocopies. Today there exist digital imaging systems that replace this manual, multistep process with a single, fast automated operation. Most importantly, this advantage can be realized anywhere large numbers of photo images are retained.

An impressive example of this type of system at work was designed for the City of Rochester, New York, Police Department by Edicon, an Eastman Kodak Company. The Edicon Photoimage Management System is designed to provide solutions for previously unsolved problems of managing photographic images. But the forte of the Edicon Photoimage Management System is its ability to display images simultaneously with text and graphics on a single screen. Utilizing a photo image relational database, the system allows information and pictures to be rapidly updated, recorded, and transmitted to any location.

The Rochester Police Department (RPD) was searching for a photo image management system to replace the manual process of storing and sorting through mug shots. Some people in the department were sure an electronic system existed that could handle their massive mug books. Their existing mug books were used for manual photo identification; Edicon looked at their needs and customized a system to be used as an investigative tool.

System Components

An Edicon system workstation contains four major components: A video camera, an Edicon system unit, a color monitor, and a printer. A standard video camera, or any other NTSC source (VCR, videodisc player, etc.) is used as the input device. The Edicon System unit holds a 386 processor (16 MHz) with 32-bit high-speed memory.

To display the text and the digitized image, a flat-screen, non-interlaced color monitor is employed. For hard-copy reproductions of the images there are a variety of choices. These range from traditional and instant photography to color thermal printers or black-and-white laser printers. (Edicon recommends the Kodak SV6500 Color Thermal Video Printer.)

One unique feature is the flexibility in the use of images; possible because the color images are all captured, stored, and displayed in digital form. With analog or part-analog technology, images cannot be transmitted over local area networks (LAN) and telecommunications until they have been converted to a digital format. And this system not only stores the images digitally, it uses data compression techniques that allow greater storage capacity and faster transmission. The storage media range from magnetic disks to digital optical disks. The 1.3 GB 12" Digital Optical Disk has the ability to store nearly 400,000 images. Even more can be stored with the use of a juke box.

In rapid data retrieval and user-friendliness, the Edicon Photoimage Management System is breaking developmental ground. For example, the user can search even huge databases and see an image on-screen in three seconds or less. The search can be accomplished using any number of parameters or descriptors.

The Rochester Application

The potential applications for this technology are limitless. The Edicon Photoimage Management System is valuable to anyone managing large photographic libraries. This includes police departments, government agencies, museums, and *Fortune* 1,000 companies—to name a few. The law enforcement and security sectors have been some of the first to implement digital storage of color images.

The system developed specifically for use by law enforcement agencies is called the Edicon Suspect Identification System. With this system, the RPD officers use a video camera to take an electronic color photograph of the arrested individual upon entry to the jail. The image is then stored digitally in the computer database, along with detailed information on physical description, age, moniker, *modus operandi*, past record, and recent address.

With approximately 25,000 misdemeanor and felony arrests per year, the RPD mug books were becoming overwhelming. Working with RPD, Edicon determined that they needed four workstations and two video cameras. These workstations are linked to a file server by an IBM Token Ring to form a LAN.

There are two types of video cameras employed in the RPD application: a high performance video camera and a dual-purpose camera. The first installed was a Panasonic Color Digital Video Camera, used to enter existing mug shots into the system.

Approximately 12,000 pictures have been entered into the database since the system was first installed in August 1989.

The booking sight uses a dual-purpose camera, the Kodak Prism Camera, to take traditional color negative film photographs and digital images at the same time. Both photos are taken simultaneously. Hard-copy photographs of arrested individuals are still kept in individual criminal history files in the department's Identification and Records section, while the digital images are stored in the Edicon System. The camera is stationed on a motored mechanism that can raise or lower the camera according to the subject's height at a touch of the keyboard.

During the taking of a mug shot, there are often times when the picture is not what was wanted. For example, if the subject blinks or moves during the shot, the officer simply blanks the screen and takes another. The photos and the text are not saved in the database until the user gives the final command. This way, no unwanted images are saved.

The Image Database

Along with the system's database parameters, such as aliases and ID numbers, comes a large array of user-defined fields. Generally, suggestions are given as to the type of fields that would be most appropriate. Edicon worked closely with the RPD to learn the department's specific needs. Investigator Joe Murphy notes, "Edicon sat down with us and designed a system to meet all our needs, which is virtually unheard of in business these days."

The RPD formed a user committee that helped to define and recommend descriptive parameters to be used, based on the expertise of the law enforcement personnel. In addition to common descriptors, such as age, race, sex, and hair, the user committee recommended such parameters as tattoo and body oddity, location, crime type, weapon used, and gang/group affiliation.

When all of this information is entered, the police can do a search on any one of those parameters to locate possible offenders. If a good description from a witness is obtained, the search can often be narrowed to a handful of suspects for a line-up. Even when a poor description is given, the speed of the Edicon System retrieves hundreds of images in seconds for the witness to view.

To view records, investigators simply key in descriptors. The system retrieves only those suspects who match the description given. Then witnesses can view each suspect's photo and press a key to "keep," "reject," or "positive" (positively identify) the subject.

A line-up of six suspect images can be assembled on the screen for comparative purposes. A full-color printout of the line-up is then made on an electronic color printer as a record of the session. A black-and-white print of a suspect record and image can also be printed on a laser printer. These prints are often used with warrants or as departmental bulletins.

Although the process may sound complicated, using the system turns out to be quite easy. All of the officers in the RPD booking area were taught to use the system, on the job, in about twenty minutes. Training the other employees to handle the data entry and suspect identification took about four hours.

Recent Example

Recently, the Edicon System was used to verify the identity of a suspected criminal. In 1989, the City of Rochester was besieged by alleged serial killer Arthur Shawcross, who murdered local prostitutes and left few clues at the crime scenes. The Edicon System helped to keep track of as many as 17 victims, most of whom had prostitution-related arrest records already in the system, and was ultimately used to confirm the identity of Shawcross.

During the course of the investigation, many victims were reported as missing. Another function that the system provided was the ability to disseminate information on the missing women. A laser printer was used to print missing persons reports rapidly, and were distributed among the department and community.

The Edicon System was used to compile an on-screen line-up of suspects for witnesses to view. With the traditional method of gathering and sorting mug books by hand, it might have been necessary to examine every possible photograph before locating a likeness.

Before the Edicon System was implemented, it could take a witness up to eight hours to locate a suspect in the mug files. The Edicon System reduced the time needed for this task to an average of only ½ hour. In this particular case, says Investigator Murphy, "one witness who had contact with Shawcross identified him in 12 minutes through the database search!"

Other Features

In addition to suspect images, fingerprints are often used in identification. The Edicon System has the ability to save fingerprints on disk in digital format as part of the same suspect record. A problem with the traditional mug books was that of sealing files for those whose cases had been disposed of in favor of the defendant, i.e. not guilty, acquitted, failed to prosecute. When the case is disposed of, the file must be "sealed." Formerly, when a record was sealed, the police department had to check all mug books for photos and destroy them. Now the Edicon computer can monitor who has the files and seal them electronically. When a record is sealed, a large yellow sign appears on the individual's file reading "SEALED," and no one has access to the record, except on court order.

"With the system's database, mug shots, and fingerprints," Murphy views the system as a "comprehensive investigative tool."

The RPD application was an important step in furthering the practical use of such innovative imaging technology in law enforcement agencies. There is little doubt that this technology will continue to be implemented where large numbers of images or photographs are currently being used.

Other Applications

The range of potential users of this technology is reflected in the growing list of Edicon clients. From *Fortune* 500 companies such as Merrill Lynch, the Boeing Company, and Eastman Kodak, to U.S. and international airports, organizations are finding the system invaluable for managing employee identification and security. Airports especially are being required to improve security measures, and many are turning to Edicon for help. Los Angeles International Airport, Hartsfield/Atlanta International, Kansas City International, and several airports in the United Kingdom (Heathrow, Gatwick, Stansded, to name a few) have installed the system.

In addition to security and personnel management, Edicon provides an Access Control and Alarm Monitoring System to link ID badges with card readers. Firms requiring high-level security, such as research laboratories, defense contractors, and government agencies, are implementing Edicon systems.

Organizations with photo library and cataloging needs are also using the system. Museums, libraries, real estate firms, and corporate inventory control departments are a few of the potential users.

Growing interest in digital imaging technology indicates that uses for these products will continue to be developed. For those investigating the implementation of such a system, the benefits include tremendous improvements in efficiency, cost savings, and increased organizational effectiveness. Over the next few years, Edicon expects the popularity and usage of these tools to expand to the level of the personal computer today.

# # #

■ Op-Ed Piece

This op-ed was written by the U.S. Chamber of Commerce for the <u>Washington Times</u>. See Chapter 11 for more on op-eds and columns.

Ergonomics Edict Out of Joint

Thomas J. Donohue
Wednesday, March 7, 2001

Pardoning fugitive billionaire Marc Rich wasn't the only controversial last-minute action of the Clinton Administration in its final days of power—it also issued one of the most ill-conceived, unscientific, far-reaching, and costly regulations in American history, the so-called ergonomics standard. Unlike the Rich pardon, Congress can undo this action by voting to repeal the rule under the 1996 Congressional Review Act (CRA).

The CRA allows Congress to repeal any government regulation within 60 session days of its official publication. Congress has yet to exercise this authority, but the fatally flawed ergonomics standard demands it.

What's wrong with the ergonomics standard? It is overreaching and prohibitively costly. The standard, which OSHA claims will alleviate musculoskeletal disorders (MSDs) caused by workplace activity, consumes more than 600 pages of fine print in the Federal Register, covers 102 million employees, 18 million jobs, and 6.1 million businesses of all types and sizes, and will cost businesses nearly $100 billion a year, resulting in higher consumer prices for products and services. It is, in no sense, limited to jobs involving repetitive motion.

A regulation of this breadth might be justifiable if it was based on sound science and common sense, but the ergonomics standard clearly is not. In its rush to please labor union bosses, the Clinton Administration issued the rule despite agreement by leading scientists and medical practitioners that not enough is known about ergonomics injuries—what causes them and how to prevent them—to warrant a regulation of this size and scope. Even the American College of Occupational and Environmental Medicine (ACOEM) does not support OSHA's standard, noting that "the final standard appears to require neither a medical diagnosis nor a causal assessment."

OSHA's ergonomics standard could require businesses to modify any job that requires only occasional bending, reaching, pulling, pushing, and gripping. Such jobs could have to be adjusted to match employees' various physical conditions—height, weight, and gender—as well as "psychosocial" factors that include depression, job satisfaction, stress, and interpersonal relations in the workplace, all factors that a recent study by the National Academy of Sciences found to cause MSDs. The regulation might also require businesses to hire additional workers to do the same amount of work and dramatically increase the number of work break periods to slow the rate and number of repetitive motions.

In addition, the regulation requires businesses to foot the medical bill for injuries caused primarily by nonworkplace activities. Every employee ache or general pain allegedly caused, or potentially worsened, by workplace activities could require up to three company-paid medical exams, and the examining medical professional is prohibited from informing the employer of nonwork-related explanations for an employee's alleged on-the-job ergonomic injury.

The regulation completely undermines state workers' compensation laws. It overrides well-established state standards in determining whether a condition is work-related. It even supersedes state standards establishing levels of compensation for injured workers. If a condition is determined to be work-related within the meaning of the OSHA standard, the employer must provide full benefits and 100 percent of the employee's pay for up to three months while he or she is in a light-duty job, or 90 percent of pay and full benefits while not working.

Finally, one must question the need for such a sweeping, one-size-fits-all regulation. Evidence shows that business is voluntarily and effectively dealing with real ergonomic issues. MSDs in the workplace are declining. According to the federal government, repeated trauma injuries such as carpal tunnel syndrome have declined 24 percent since 1994. Many businesses have successfully implemented common sense ergonomics programs that address real, identifiable workplace problems and achieve measurable results. OSHA's ergonomics rule will undermine these highly successful, custom-designed programs.

The business community is willing and prepared to work with OSHA on reasonably and effectively addressing the ergonomics issue, but this regulation is unacceptable. Congress should exercise its authority to repeal this egregious standard. If they don't, we'll see OSHA in court.

# # #

■ PSA Scripts

Here are two sample radio PSA scripts (see Chapter11) from Cancer Pain Relief of Utah and the Partnership to Improve End-of-Life Care in Utah:

Announcement #1

Female actress: On an average day we see maybe fifty patients in this clinic, many of them with life-threatening diseases that cause pain. But here's the sad part: Many of them won't tell us that they're hurting. I guess they must be afraid that we'll think they're complaining. And sometimes they're afraid of what the pain might mean. It's really too bad, because pain can be controlled.

Announcer: When facing life-threatening illness or death, having support and the right information can make all the difference. Visit our Web site at *carefordying.org*.

Female actress: If you're in pain, speak up. We don't mind. Really. That's what we're here for. And it's the only way we know you need help.

Announcer: To learn more about local resources visit *carefordying.org*. Living and dying: Let's talk about it.

# # #

Announcement #2

Female: Mom is really something else. Seventy-two years old and still walks almost a mile every day. To look at her, you'd never know she has cancer. The pain used to be almost unbearable at times, and she absolutely refused to ask her doctor for additional medication. She was afraid of becoming an addict.

Announcer: When facing life-threatening illness or death, having support and the right information can make all the difference. Visit our Web site at *carefordying.org*.

Female: Mom finally told her doctor about the pain. She learned that if you take the right dose of the right medicine, the pain can be controlled, and there's no need to fear addiction. Now she can go on doing what she wants. What a relief.

Announcer: To learn more about local resources visit *carefordying.org*. Living and dying: Let's talk about it.

# # #

■ Media Alerts

These two media alerts, discussed in Chapter 6, use the five Ws and one H.

Who: Shared Results, Inc.'s new Computer and Communications Training Center.

(Shared Results is a communications firm that helps people use technology and communicate better. The company provides training and consulting services and publishes *TECH TALK*, a newsletter that helps beginning and intermediate computer users understand the world of technology.)

What: An open house to showcase the new training center, which will be used primarily to train Rochester's underprivileged youth and adults through contracts with various social service agencies. In particular, on April 23, young mothers (ages 16 to 18) who are receiving computer and communications training at the center through the YWCA/SPCC (Society for the Protection and Care of Children) "Successful Futures for Youth" program will speak at 2 p.m. about the impact this training is having on their lives. Students from other groups speak at 4:30 p.m. and 6:30 p.m.

When: Monday, April 23, 2001, 2 p.m. to 7 p.m., with remarks from student program participants at 2 p.m., 4:30 p.m., and 6:30 p.m.

Where: Shared Results' new Computer and Communications Training Center, 162 Andrews Street, down the hill from the corner of St. Paul.

Why: Because of its affiliation with a number of local social service agencies, the training center serves as an example of the community's efforts to assist youth in becoming lifelong learners with the necessary skills to support long-term success in the job market. This is a "good news" story with great visuals. You will be able to interview students.

In addition, you will be able to speak to Nydia Benitez, the new receptionist and bookkeeper at the training center, who was hired as a result of her participation in training provided by Shared Results under contract with Rochester Rehabilitation Center's Welfare to Work program.

Please call Sandy Beckwith, Beckwith Communications, 222-222-2222, with questions and to RSVP.

# # #

Media Alert—Save the Date!

Who: Learn it Live, Inc. and Goal Oriented Training & Consulting, both of Rochester.

What: A half-day preview for "Motivation LIVE!," a unique and highly visual theater-based training workshop using professional actors.

When: Wednesday, November 3, 1999
9 a.m. to 1 p.m. (continental breakfast and lunch included)

Where: Mario's Via Abruzzi, 2740 Monroe Ave., Brighton

Why: Motivation LIVE! is a new product of Goal Oriented Training & Consulting collaborating with Learn it Live, Inc. These Rochester-based trainers are introducing the program to training executives and sales management professionals through a special half-day preview on November 3.

We are inviting media representatives to the local preview so you can experience firsthand how this novel technique—theater-based training—makes a positive impact on the skills of local employees. We believe the story of this collaboration of two local training professionals, their memorable delivery technique, and the highly effective content of their program will be of interest to your readers. *The visual, action-oriented nature of the workshop makes it worth considering for TV news.*

Motivation LIVE! uses the power of live demonstrations presented by a team of professional actors to train sales managers on how to create a motivating environment. The demonstrations are high-impact, reality-based learning experiences that communicate how to coach *creatively* through existing conversations and interactions. The program's content brings a new approach to sales management coaching while the delivery technique—using live actors—ensures the information will be learned, retained, and implemented.

We will send you more detailed information soon. In the meantime, please *save the morning of November 3* and call Sandy Beckwith, Beckwith Communications, 222-2222, with any questions.

# # #

■ Product or Service Backgrounder

This backgrounder (see Chapter 6) is an example of what Learn it Live, Inc., a firm specializing in theater-based training, can send to media outlets.

What is theater-based training?

Theater-based training engages and entertains by using professional actors to present live demonstrations that show participants how to use—and how not to use—the skills and concepts being taught.

It is an effective method—97 percent of 900 people surveyed by Learn it Live, Inc., a Rochester, N.Y., firm specializing in theater-based training, said that live actor demonstrations were more effective for learning than training videos. In addition, 85 percent of those surveyed said that practicing skills through role-playing with trained actors was better than the more common method—practicing with other workshop participants.

Theater-based demonstrations are similar to theatrical plays. They are scripted, reality-based, live performances with a small cast of characters led by a professional trainer. Performances range from one to 20 minutes and are customized to fit the learners' work environment. Use of professional actors creates a realistic and risk-free learning environment for participants.

Theater-based training is effective because it:

- Provides realistic examples of correct and incorrect behaviors and their positive and negative job-related consequences. In fact, according to a U.S. Department of Education study of 20 teaching methods, learners can't be expected to change behaviors if they don't recognize what is inappropriate or don't understand the consequences.
- Uses actors, rather than colleagues, to provide realistic and risk-free learning experiences. Participants must be able to practice new behaviors without fear of reprisals or embarrassment, while seasoned individuals may need to be challenged according to their experience levels.
- Supports current research on adult learning principles. In order to provide significant, sustainable learning, training programs should be designed so learning is active, personally relevant, experienced in a group, happening in a challenging and supportive environment, and taking place as a transformation over time. Good theater-based training does all of this.
- Captures the attention of participants. Live actors with a script that is customized to a particular organization tend to increase the participants' attention span, which is particularly important with participants accustomed to visual entertainment.

- Provides both behavioral and cognitive examples. Research shows that either behavioral or cognitive modeling performed *with* lecture or discussion provides better learning than lecture or discussion alone.
- Supports the principle of "identical elements" that are important to learning. Research indicates that the more similar the training experience (through surroundings, tasks, equipment, etc.) is to the work environment, the more participants learn what is taught, retain that knowledge, and transfer it to their work. Reputable theater-based training companies customize their programs to include "identical elements" for each client organization.

This popular training format succeeds because it is live and entertaining, according to Tina Smagala, owner of Learn it Live. "It is critical to capture the participant's attention, which isn't always easy. We do this with live demonstrations because they are more captivating than videotaped role-playing," she explains.

There are approximately eight organizations nationwide offering theater-based training. Learn it Live, Rochester's only corporate theater-based training provider, presents workshops and training programs on topics ranging from a new coaching program for sales managers called Motivation LIVE!, to diversity, customer service, conflict resolution, and sexual harassment prevention.

# # #

■ Biographical Backgrounder

This biographical backgrounder (see Chapter 6) from a press kit promoting the appearance of poet Maya Angelou at a nonprofit fundraising dinner was condensed from a great deal of research so it wouldn't overwhelm reporters looking for career highlights.

Backgrounder: Maya Angelou

Maya Angelou was born Marguerite Johnson in 1928 in St. Louis, Mo. After her parents divorced when she was three years old, Angelou and her brother were sent to live with their paternal grandmother, "Momma" Henderson, in Stamps, Ark. Momma was a significant influence on Angelou, teaching her the value of hard work and courage in a segregated South where the depression made life even tougher for Black Americans.

On several occasions during her youth, Angelou and her brother returned for brief periods to live with their mother. At seven years old, Angelou was raped by her mother's boyfriend. One summer she stayed with her father, but that visit also ended in disaster after Angelou and her father's girlfriend fought continuously. Angelou eventually ran away and lived in an abandoned van with other homeless children.

She became a single parent at age 16, working at various jobs from Creole cook to nightclub waitress to barroom dancer. A marriage at 22 lasted less than three years. At 26, Angelou eventually landed a role in *Porgy and Bess* and toured with the production in 1954–1955. It was about this time that she adopted her present name from her brother's nickname for her (Maya) and a variation of her first husband's surname, Angelos.

Almost six years later, Angelou went to Cairo with her son and freedom fighter Yusumzi Make. Although Angelou and Make never married, they lived together for several years. While in Africa, Angelou worked as the editor of the *Arab Observer*. After her relationship with Make failed, she moved to Ghana. She continued her writing career including a position as a feature editor of *The African Review* in Accra. She also taught at the University of Ghana.

Angelou returned to the United States in the mid-'60s, landing a role in Jean Anouilh's *Medea*. She wrote songs and television scripts and was the first black woman to have a screenplay, *Georgia, Georgia*, produced.

In 1981, Angelou was appointed to a lifetime position as the first Reynolds Professor of American Studies at Wake Forest University in Winston-Salem, N.C. She has received honorary degrees from Smith College, Mills College, and Sarah Lawrence University.

■ Fact Sheet for an Insurance Company

Here's a sample fact sheet (see Chapter 6) that you can use as a model for your product or service.

Fact Sheet: Omega Insurance Services, Inc.

- Omega Insurance Services is a sophisticated, high-tech investigations firm specializing in workers' compensation insurance fraud in the southeastern United States and expanding nationally. Omega's professional investigators are experts in the identification, surveillance, and reporting of individuals who attempt to defraud America's insurance companies of billions annually. The firm combines modern investigation techniques with state-of-the-art video and communications technology to conduct efficient investigations and quickly report results to clients, which include many of the nation's best-known insurance companies.

- According to a report published in 2000 by industry consultant Conning & Company, "industry experts have estimated the cost of workers' compensation fraud to be between $1 billion and $20 billion annually."

- In 2000, Omega became the first private-investigation firm in the country to provide completely Internet-based customer service for its clients. Omega's customer-service technology, called PowerFacts, allows claims representatives and risk managers to request a surveillance, monitor its progress, and receive interim and final case reports—complete with still photos and streaming video—from Omega's Web site *(www.omegais.com)*. All records are password-protected and the site is secure.

- Founded in 1996 in a spare bedroom with a credit card to cover expenses, Omega has expanded to 12,000 square feet of space in one of St. Petersburg's newest commercial buildings.

- Omega is one of the top five private investigation firms in the country. Year 2000 sales are $6.7 million, up from $4.1 million in 1999 and $23,000 in its first year.

- The company's cofounders, Tim Fargo and Rich Taffet, share management responsibilities. With exceptional marketing instincts and a degree in financing, Fargo is president. Taffet, a highly skilled investigator, is vice president/director of investigations.

- Contact Omega Insurance Services, Inc. at 144 First Ave. So., Suite 530, St. Petersburg, FL 33701, phone, 555-555-5555, fax 555-555-5555, *www.omegais.com*.

# # #

■ Fact Sheet for a Nonprofit Company

This fact sheet, which is nothing more than a bullet list of facts (see Chapter 6), was part of a press kit promoting a PBS series on women's heart health for one of the show's consultants and on-camera experts, the author of a book on women and heart disease.

Statistics on Heart Disease in Women

- Heart disease is the number one killer of American women.
- Every year, an estimated 485,000 women die of cardiovascular disease (heart disease and stroke), more than twice the number who die of all forms of cancer combined.
- An estimated 240,000 women die annually of heart disease, *five* times the number who die of breast cancer.
- Women suffer nearly half (49 percent) of the 480,000 heart disease deaths that occur each year.
- More women than men die of heart attacks within the first year of their first heart attack (44 percent versus 27 percent).
- More women than men will suffer a second heart attack within four years after their first heart attack (20 percent versus 16 percent).
- Heart attacks kill nearly 21,000 women under the age of 65; more than 29 percent of them are under the age of 55.
- One in eight women age 45 and over has had a heart attack.
- Black women have a 33 percent higher death rate from coronary heart disease than white women, and a 77 percent higher death rate from stroke.
- Coronary heart disease is a major risk factor for stroke, which kills more than 87,000 women each year.
- It is estimated that nearly 1 million Americans are currently living with heart defects. Some defects occur more commonly in women and can remain undetected until well into adulthood, putting their lives at risk.

#

■ Cover Sheet for a Press Kit

Here's an example of a cover sheet that accompanies a press kit—see Chapter 12 for more.

Mr. John Smith
Editor
Sales & Marketing Executive Report
360 Hiatt Dr.
Palm Beach Gardens, FL 33418

Dear Mr. Smith:

Technology-based learning is a hot topic in corporate America today. But one expert says that if you want sales managers to remember what they've learned, you need the help of professional actors.

That's right. Professional actors. Not remote instructors sending information electronically. Not demonstrations on videotape or CD-ROM. Actors. In person. It's called theater-based training.

The enclosed press kit announcing a new training program for sales managers also explains how and why theater-based training is one of the most effective delivery techniques available. We hope you'll consider using some of the press kit material for:

A "Sales & Marketing Briefs" item announcing Motivation LIVE!, a unique sales workshop using actors and trainers to show how to effectively coach individuals through brief, opportunistic conversations—without increasing the time spent with employees.

A "tips" item on how sales managers can coach effectively during day-to-day brief conversations or encounters.

Information contributing to an article on what's working in sales training today.

Please don't hesitate to call me at 222-222-2222 with any questions. If you would like me to e-send you any of the enclosed text via e-mail, send me a note at SandraBeckwith@compuserve.com.

Thank you for your time and interest.

Sincerely,

Sandra Beckwith

\# \# \#

■ Cover Letter for a Press Kit

Here's a cover letter sent with a press kit (see Chapter 12) to targeted U.S. daily newspapers. It was customized for each publication through a mail merge.

Name
Medical & Health Editor
Newspaper
Address
City, State Zip

Dear:

We've enclosed information about a groundbreaking new book, *The American Dietetic Association Guide to Women's Nutrition for Healthy Living* (Perigee Books) by Susan Calvert Finn, Ph.D., R.D., F.A.D.A. Designed to provide women of all ages with the knowledge they need to eat healthy and maintain their energy and well-being, Dr. Finn's book provides useful information and tips women can use now to improve their health today and in the future. Reading this book could be a turning point in the nutritional health of many women.

Please consider the enclosed information for articles on these and other topics:

- The most important New Year's resolution you can make
- Easy, painless tips for making the new year healthier
- Holiday gifts that say, "I care"
- Women's nutrition needs depend on their life stage
- What we can do nutritionally for our children today so they're healthier adults
- How disease prevention and nutrition correlate in women

It is our understanding that you've already received a review copy of the book from the publisher. If not, or if you need another copy, please call me at 222-222-2222, e-mail me at *SandraBeckwith@compuserve.com,* or return the enclosed blue postcard, and I'll send a copy immediately. I hope we can work together to give women in your area a chance to learn more about the role of nutrition in their long-term health.

Cordially,
Sandra L. Beckwith

# # #

Index

OTHER TITLES IN THE STREETWISE® SERIES:

Streetwise® Achieving Wealth Through Franchising

Streetwise® Business Letters

Streetwise® Business Valuation

Streetwise® Complete Business Plan

Streetwise® Complete Business Plan with Software

Streetwise® Complete Publicity Plans

Streetwise® Crash Course MBA

Streetwise® Customer-Focused Selling

Streetwise® Do-It-Yourself Advertising

Streetwise® Finance & Accounting

Streetwise® Financing the Small Business

Streetwise® Human Resources Management

Streetwise® Independent Consulting

Streetwise® Landlording & Property Management

Streetwise® Low-Cost Marketing

Streetwise® Low-Cost Web Site Promotion

Streetwise® Managing a Nonprofit

Streetwise® Managing People

Streetwise® Marketing Plan

Streetwise® Maximize Web Site Traffic

Streetwise® Motivating and Rewarding Employees

Streetwise® Project Management

Streetwise® Restaurant Management

Streetwise® Retirement Planning

Streetwise® Sales Letters with CD-ROM

Streetwise® Selling Your Business

Streetwise® Small Business Start-Up

Streetwise® Start Your Own Business Workbook

Streetwise® Structuring Your Business

Streetwise® Time Management